Shtetl Jews under Soviet Rule

JEWISH SOCIETY AND CULTURE

General Editor DAVID SORKIN

Edited by David Cesarani *The Making of Modern Anglo-Jewry*
Ben-Cion Pinchuk *Shtetl Jews under Soviet Rule*

FORTHCOMING

Tony Kushner *The Jews in Post-War Britain*
Frances Malino *Zalkind Hourwitz: A Jew in the French Revolution*
Peter Pulzer *Jews and the German State 1848–1939*

Jewish Communities of the Modern World

Todd Endelman *The Jews of England*
Paula Hyman *The Jews of France*
Aron Rodrigue & Esther Benbassa *The Jews of Turkey*
David Sorkin *The Jews of Germany*
Norman Stillman *The Jews of North Africa*
Steven J. Zipperstein *The Jews of Russia*

Shtetl Jews under Soviet Rule

Eastern Poland on the Eve of the Holocaust

Ben-Cion Pinchuk

Basil Blackwell

First published 1990
First published in USA 1991

Basil Blackwell Ltd
108 Cowley Road, Oxford, OX4 1JF, UK

Basil Blackwell, Inc.
3 Cambridge Center
Cambridge, Massachusetts 02142, USA

British Library Cataloguing in Publication Data

A CIP catalogue record for this book is available from the British Library.

Library of Congress Cataloging in Publication Data

Pinchuk, Ben-Cion.
Shtetl Jews under Soviet rule: Eastern Poland on the Eve of the Holocaust
Ben-Cion Pinchuk.
p. cm. — (Jewish society and culture)
Includes bibliographical references (p.).
ISBN 0–631–17469–9
1. Jews — Poland — History — 20th century. 2. Poland — History — Occupation. 1939–1945. 3. Jews — Byelorussian S.S.R. — History — 20th century. 4. Byelorussian S.S.R. — Ethnic relations. I. Title.
II. Title: Shtetl Jews under Soviet rule 1939–1941. III. Series.
DS135.P6P49 1990
943.8′004924 — dc20 90–126
CIP

Typeset in 10 on 12 pt Ehrhardt
by Setrite Typesetters Limited
Printed in Great Britain by T.J. Press Ltd, Padstow, Cornwall

Contents

Foreword

Shtetl Jews under Soviet Rule: Eastern Poland on the Eve of the Holocaust is an attempt to describe the history of the Jewish community in the Polish provinces annexed by the USSR in the autumn of 1939. The territories that became part of the Soviet Union did not possess any inherent unity, whether geographical, political or ethnic. They were regions with different historical backgrounds and economic structures and ties. So too were their Jewish communities. However, all inhabitants of the regions that made up the new Soviet lands shared the experience of being transformed during the 21 months of Soviet rule into citizens of the socialist state. Local historical differences as well as minor regional policy variations fade into insignificance when compared to the magnitude of the transformation, thus justifying the treatment of the entire annexed area as one.

About 95 per cent of this study is derived from piecing together thousands of pieces of primary evidence (the introductory chapter, which provides background, being the only (partial) exception). Most of the evidence came from hundreds of small towns (*shtetlach* in Yiddish), scattered throughout the area. While the shtetl was not the only form of settlement in which Jews lived, it was certainly the predominant and typical one in what was basically an economically backward agrarian region. Hence the title *Shtetl Jews*. Where necessary, differences between the shtetl and other types of settlement will be made clear, but the changes which took place in the economy, education, culture, religion etc. affected all Jewish settlements in the area and they can therefore be treated together. Variations warranted by the sources have been duly dealt with.

Acknowledgements

Libraries, archives and their staff are the obvious object of gratitude of the historian. The *Yad-Vastem* files in Israel, Sikozski Institution in London and *Yivo* collections in New York provided the bulk of the material on which this book is based. Many thanks are due to their staff and administrators. A Sherman fellowship granted by the Israeli Ministry of Science facilitated my research in London. Thanks are due above all to the many hundreds of people whose personal stories, biographies, autobiographies, memoirs, interviews, etc. served to piece together the history of the period and the region. To them this book is dedicated.

For transliteration the author has used the Library of Congress system with only slight phonetical departures, mainly when names of places were transliterated in the original source. Hence the occasional inconsistencies in the spelling of places and names. However, the reader is always in a position to identify correctly the origin.

Source: Jan Tomas Gross, *Revolution from Abroad*, Princeton University Press.

Introduction

Between 17 September 1939 and 21 June 1941 the USSR ruled over what were formerly the eastern provinces of the Polish Republic. Approximately one and a half million Jews lived in that area at the time. It was one of the largest pre-Holocaust Jewish communities in Europe. The present study is an attempt to write the history of that community during the last stage of its existence. Continuity and change under the impact of the new regime are the subject matter of this book. It describes and analyses the mutual relations between an ethnic minority and the Soviet regime in the multi-ethnic environment of former Eastern Poland. It is a study in recent history and not in political science or sociology and as such is supposed to illuminate one of the less researched periods in the history of the Jewish communities of Poland and the USSR. At the same time the investigation undertaken here is an integral part of East European history and deals with a period and subject which are of vital importance even to the present day. The Sovietization of the Eastern Polish provinces between 1939 and 1941 should be regarded as a forerunner of the Sovietization of Eastern Europe in the wake of World War II.

The territories annexed by the Soviet Union included most of the eastern Kresy and eastern Galicia. They had an established population of over 13 million people and an area of over 200,000 square kilometers. The region was a transition area – it did not constitute a distinct geographic or ethnic unit. For generations it had been contested by Poland and Russia, while the majority of its inhabitants were neither Poles nor Russians, but Ukrainians and Belorussians. In Tsarist Russia it was the heartland of the Pale of Settlement, the classic shtetl country. It is on the whole flat land, favouring human movement from east to west, facilitating invasions from both directions.

Most of the territory, except its southern fringes, consists of flat-lands containing few natural resources and poor soils. In general it was a backward agricultural area with meagre transportation and little contact with the outside world. Crop production for local consumption was the predominant form of agriculture and much of the trading was by barter. Many peasants lived close to subsistence level. The towns for the most part were small and of a strictly local character; this was the pattern of the typical shtetl. The economic function of the town was to satisfy the needs of a surrounding rural area. Lvov and Bialystok were the two major modern urban centers. In north Belorussia the peasants were mainly Belorussians with smaller numbers of Poles and some Lithuanians and in the south the Ukrainians were the predominant element in the countryside. The landowners were almost always Poles, with Jews and Poles constituting the majority among city dwellers. Blocked from engaging directly in agriculture, the vast majority of the Jews of the annexed provinces lived in the numerous small towns, or shtetlach. Thus the history of the Jews in the area is the history of shtetl Jewry and most of the references in this book relate to the shtetl and its inhabitants.

The period of the late thirties in the history of the USSR has not been adequately researched. This situation is mainly the result of the repressive Stalinist regime and its monopoly on information. Soviet archives of the period remain inaccessible to Western research. The particular subject of this study did not receive more than very general treatment in Jewish historical literature[1] and there were very few secondary sources that could be used in preparing this book. Soviet secrecy, monopoly by the government of all sources of information and use of the media for propaganda and indoctrination were among the methodological problems which had to be overcome. Available non-Soviet sources at least partially compensated for the problems inherent in research on the USSR.

A broad variety of primary sources was used in preparing this study. Quite often Jewish, Polish and Soviet materials were used to illuminate the same problem. The archive of the Polish Government in Exile, deposited at the Sikorski Institute, London, contains many detailed reports on developments in the Soviet occupied territories. The Central Zionist Archive and foreign sections of the British Public Record Office were consulted for relevant material. Other archival collections were checked, but produced very limited results. Contemporary newspapers, Western and Soviet, served as an important source of information. The two most valuable sources of material for the book were the testimonies accumulated in the *Yad Vashem* archive and the so-called *Memorial Books* of the shtetlach.

Yad Vashem is the Israeli authority established to document and investigate subjects related to the Holocaust. Its archive, assembled since 1945, contains large collections of documentary material on various aspects of Jewish history between 1933 and 1945. The authority also conducted a thorough interview programme that encompassed thousands of witnesses. Many testimonies contain sections relating to Soviet rule in Eastern Poland, 1939–41 and they were used extensively in this book. Their quantity, geographical spread (coming from dozens of shtetlach from all over the territories), and the different backgrounds of the witnesses, provide a valuable source for assessing developments in the area. Memorial books are collections published after 1945 to memorialize the Jewish communities annihilated during the Holocaust. They contain Hebrew and Yiddish sections, occasionally even an English translation, and provide extensive information on different aspects of the history of the Jewish communities. Over 70 memorial books that included memoirs or descriptive surveys of the Soviet period were used for this study. The *Yad Vashem* testimonies and the memorial books were most valuable as a supplement to printed memoirs and official reports of Jewish leaders and institutions. Quite often the testimonies and memorial books came from people of a more humble economic and social status than the authors of the more artistic memoirs and official reports. They enable us to get a more balanced picture of everyday life and developments under Soviet rule, particularly in the shtetl.

Given the paucity of non-Jewish sources on the period, one is left largely with the testimonies in memoirs, interviews, questionnaires, etc. of the survivors. It is clear that the presence of the narrator on the spot at the time does not in itself guarantee authenticity. Given the strong tendency to reconstruct the past from the vantage point of the present, and the very high possibility of forgetting many details, one has to be very careful in using the evidence. However, it should be noted that the same basic problems of authenticity and reliability exist for the historian in the use of primary sources of any kind. The methods used to verify the data contained in the *Yad Vashem* files or the memorial books are not different from those employed to check other historical sources. In our case, the large volume of testimonies and their geographical spread ensure a high degree of reliability regarding the verification.

In some respects the opportunity to draw on unrelated Polish, Soviet and Jewish sources to shed light on the same problem, is the realization of a historian's dream and no doubt the study benefitted from the availability of sources coming from different, independent backgrounds. Yet all the sources used were singularly defective in one respect: the absence of reliable statistics. These were simply not available. Whether one might find them hidden in some Soviet archive, or, as appears quite likely, they do not exist at all because of war and destruction, Western researchers do not have them at present. Hence while it was possible from the extant sources to gain an overview, a general picture, and to distinguish trends, etc., it has been impossible to provide precise figures and numerical data. It should be noted, however, that despite this deficiency the volume of evidence used enables us to draw a fairly clear picture of our subject.

Soviet–Jewish relations, from the very beginning of the Communist regime in Russia, were a sensitive subject. The regime pretended to solve the Jewish problem and cut off all contacts between Soviet Jewry and the rest of the world's Jewish communities. After the annexations of 1939–40 the USSR had the second largest Jewish community in the world. Its policy therefore had a tremendous impact on the fate of the entire Jewish people. The present study is an attempt to describe the unfolding relations of the USSR and the Jewish people on the eve of the Holocaust. It tries to analyse the impact of Sovietization on an entire Jewish community living in the shadow of impending destruction. Yet it is also the final chapter in the history of one of the oldest Jewish communities in Europe – the Jews of the small town, the shtetl Jews.

1

Joining the Soviet Family of Nations

In the early morning of 17 September 1939 Soviet troops crossed the Polish border. It was the seventeenth day of the German invasion and the Polish republic was falling apart. For many the Red Army appeared as a saviour from Nazi occupation and even among Poles there were those who greeted Soviet tanks with relief. They did not know that the USSR was just implementing the secret clauses of the non-aggression pact signed with Germany on 23 August.[1] The Soviet government could not remain indifferent to the plight of its kindred peoples the Ukrainians and Belorussians, Molotov the Soviet Prime Minister announced in his speech in the Supreme Soviet. The disintegration of Poland left the 'kindred nations' defenceless and posed a great danger to the Soviet Union itself, stressed the Premier.[2] The final boundaries between the USSR and Germany were agreed upon in September 1939,[3] the new borders coinciding roughly with the so-called Curzon Line, which loosely followed ethnic divisions.

The local population, particularly the Belorussians and Jews, and to a lesser extent the Ukrainians and Poles, greeted the Red Army warmly. The cheers were genuine, and the decorations and reception parties of bread and salt were mostly spontaneous. 'Except for the relatively small groups of citizens who knew that there would be no room for them in the Soviet realm, people seemed to have no fear of communism', N. Vakar claimed in his book on Belorussia.[4]

While the 'liberated' might have been divided in their feelings, the 'liberators' were single-minded in their actions. The Soviet authorities proceeded with the formal and complete integration of the newly-acquired territories into the USSR, and with the transformation of their inhabitants into full-fledged Soviet citizens. Less than a month after the occupation People's Assemblies, elected in the best tradition of Soviet democracy, were convened in Lvov and Bialystok. Under the supervision of Nikita Khrushchev and his loyal assistant, an NKVD (security police) general, I. Serov, the assemblies voted unanimously for the incorporation of western Ukraine and western Belorussia into the USSR. These areas would become integral parts of the Soviet Republics of the Ukraine and Belorussia. Khrushchev, who followed the deliberations of the assemblies, did not hear 'even a single speech expressing even the slightest doubt that Soviet power should be established in the western Ukraine.'[5] The Sovietization machine was working without fault. On 1 and 2 November 1939 the Supreme Soviet of the USSR agreed to incorporate the new territories into Soviet Ukraine and Belorussia.

Soviet citizenship was bestowed upon the inhabitants of the annexed territories on 29 November. According to the law all Polish citizens residing in the territories on the day of their formal integration into the USSR (1 and 2 November 1939) automatically became Soviet citizens. Those who were transferred to Soviet territory following the exchange agreement with Germany on 16 November 1939 were also entitled to Soviet citizenship. People not included in the former categories could become Soviet citizens by required naturalization procedures.[6] The rules concerning citizenship and naturalization were of the utmost importance for thousands of refugees who fled from the Nazi-occupied territories.

The headlines of the Soviet newspapers were full of slogans welcoming the newcomers to the 'Soviet family of nations'. Military occupation and the formalities of incorporation were just first steps in the absorption and integration of the territories into the USSR. To assure the permanence of the annexation, the Soviet authorities sought to bring about a general transformation of the political, economic, social and cultural life of the area. Sovietization in this context meant an attempt at total transformation of the various spheres of social activity in order to achieve conformity with the regime existing at the time in the USSR. In constant danger from the new-found friends in the West, the Sovietization was conducted with particular urgency and brutality. The monolithic machine of coercion and terror developed since the revolution, and refined during Stalin's regime, acting under cover of a massive propaganda campaign, tried to create the new Soviet citizen in Eastern Poland.

The Soviet government justified its annexation in historical and national terms. The Red Army had come to liberate its Ukrainian and Belorussian 'brothers', this being the pretext for a policy designed to promote the two nationalities and achieve a new national balance in the area. In fact, the Belorussians and Ukrainians barely constituted a majority in the former

Polish provinces and were a definite minority among the urban population.[7] De-Polonization in the area was accompanied by an increase in Ukrainian and Belorussian influence. The large Jewish minority played a particularly sensitive role in this 'balancing' policy, as they could tip the balance in the way the Soviet government wanted.

Ukrainians and Belorussians were preferred in appointments to government jobs, in the elections at all levels of representation, etc. Ukrainian and Belorussian became the official languages of the territories, also frequently becoming the languages of instruction in schools where Poles and Jews constituted the majority. The authorities showed special sensitivity in the Ukrainian territories, because of the intensity of Ukrainian nationalism. Even when the number of qualified Ukrainians was insufficient for the jobs needing to be filled, they held the job-title while Jews or Poles performed the actual work.[8] The new regime was particularly afraid of being accused of favouritism towards the Jews and was careful to avoid such 'accusations'. In Belorussian territory a vigorous campaign was conducted to form a Belorussian majority in Bialystok by promoting an influx of Belorussian peasants from the countryside and deporting many of the resident Poles and Jews.[9]

The most effective tool used to strengthen the Ukrainian and Belorussian elements was the physical removal of several hundred thousand Poles who constituted the former ruling elite of the provinces. Their deportation changed the demographic balance of the region.

The policy *vis-à-vis* the Polish population went through several phases during the 21 months of Soviet rule. It was obvious from the beginning that the new rulers were trying systematically to destroy Polish hegemony in the provinces. The attack on the Polish language, traditions and culture included the physical removal of Poles and was conducted with the help of local Ukrainians and Jews. It is thus no wonder that to many Poles it appeared an attempt at what they called genocide, designed to wipe out Polish presence in the area altogether.[10] Reports reaching the Polish Government in Exile in London towards the end of 1940, however, indicated that a change was taking place in Soviet attitudes. The mass deportations ceased and the authorities tried to gain the favour of the Polish population, by allowing access to new jobs,[11] the teaching of more hours of the Polish language and the use of Polish in public places.[12] In the months preceding the German attack the softening of the Soviet attitude towards the Poles became increasingly obvious: a 'tremendous change took place in the attitude towards the Poles by the Soviet authorities. They are now favoured openly.'[13] There was a general improvement in food supplies; Polish patriotic sermons in churches were allowed; Polish military units were established.[14] The nearer the war, the more obvious it became that the Soviet authorities were less and less confident as to the future reaction of the Ukrainians. There was a mutual disillusionment between the Soviet authorities and Ukrainian nationalists who expressed open sympathy towards Germany.[15] In this context the Poles appeared to be a more reliable element, despite the fact that they had paid a high price during the Sovietization process.

Sovietization, which involved the destruction of the old order and the building up of new Soviet institutions, was a complex process, varying in speed and intensity. The reaction of the local population, availability of material and human resources, and external developments – particularly the fear of Nazi Germany – were among the major determinants of the speed of the process. One can distinguish roughly two major phases in the transformation. The first lasted from the time of the occupation through the incorporation of the area until January 1940. There followed a transition of a few months to the second phase that started in the summer of 1940 and lasted till the end of Soviet rule in June 1941.

The first phase was characterized by relative leniency (except towards the Poles) and an attempt to gain the favour of the local population. This stage coincided with the beginning of the occupation, elections to the assemblies and the first stages of forming the new administration. Paradoxically, perhaps, it was concomitant with the destruction of much of the old order. While having a good idea of what they wanted to achieve and how to achieve it, the occupying authorities nevertheless were not always consistent or unequivocal. There was a gap between planning and execution, particularly in view of the chaos that reigned in the territories and the size of the area and complexity of its problems. The former political structure and administration disappeared during the first few weeks after the occupation. Many of its functionaries were arrested, or attempted to avoid public attention. The new institutions sprang forth almost spontaneously; temporary committees created by local sympathizers and Communists took over for a while.[16] Workers' committees were organized to supervise production and voluntary red guards patrolled the streets. Soon a more permanent administration was established: Soviets were formed in the villages and towns and local Communists were relegated to secondary positions. All key roles were occupied by the so-called *Vostochniki* (Easterners) who presided over the Sovietization of the new lands. The Communist Party replaced the old political and national organizations.[17] Radical changes took place in all spheres of social life. All the institutions and organizations of the former regime ceased to exist or were adapted to the Soviet model. The entire educational system was reorganized to conform to the structure and content of that of the USSR. Newspapers, literature, the arts, etc. were shaped in accordance with Soviet ideas.

The economic policy of the first few months reminded contemporary observers of the NEP period in Soviet history. The new regime nationalized the banks, factories, wholesale trade and national resources; large estates were confiscated and allotted to poor and small-holding peasants.[18] Small enterprises and shops remained for the time being in private hands and artisans remained independent. It appears that the new authorities were careful not to interrupt production too suddenly before a Soviet administration had been established to cope with it. There was a certain amount of gradualism in introducing the Soviet economic system. There is no official explanation for this pseudo-NEP. Was it the result of a deliberate attempt not to antagonize large sections of the lower middle class while the new regime was still in the process of organization? Or was it the result of the shortcomings of the still embryonic Soviet supply system which was not able to cope with the basic needs of the population?[19] The small tradesman was able to get supplies from the villages more easily than were the government stores. Whatever the reasons, private small-scale business was allowed to continue to function, temporarily.

January 1940 brought with it the end of the pseudo-NEP. On 1 January, the Polish zloty ceased to be legal currency in the annexed territories. People were not allowed to convert more than 300 zlotys into Soviet roubles, but salaries were paid up to the last day in zlotys.[20] This political and economic act signified the end of the pseudo-NEP and was designed to accelerate the Sovietization of the most difficult section of the private economy. The middle-class owners of small enterprises found their property expropriated and were left with useless piles of paper money.

Thus the short lived 'breathing space' of the pseudo-NEP fast came to an end during the first week of 1940. There was no need for harsh legislation; most businesses closed down by themselves.[21] High taxes, lack of new supplies and massive purchasing by Soviet soldiers and civilians literally emptied the stores. The owners were forced to put on sale their entire stock which had been registered in advance. 'Never before was the selling so great as in the first weeks after the entry of the Red Army', relates an eyewitness, 'the streets were lined with merchandise, and the soldiers were buying everything.'[22] With the annulment of the zloty, the shopkeepers and artisans were left with a useless currency and empty shops. Everybody had to look for work. The lower middle class was thus forced to join cooperatives or look for salaried government employment. However, while some of the artisans found employment in cooperatives, shopkeepers, like other property owners, found it difficult to get a job. The Soviet regime defined them as 'class enemies' – a potential threat to state security.[23]

The second, more accelerated phase of Sovietization was characterized by harsher measures in every field. The Soviet administration, particularly the secret police, had a firm grip on developments in the annexed territories by the end of winter 1939–40. There was no incentive to perpetuate a different regime in Eastern Poland, since it might be considered dangerous to the order of the USSR. The danger of a German attack was ever present and it was necessary to safeguard and ensure the reliability of the border areas. German advances in Western Europe in April to June 1940 convinced the Soviet leaders to tighten their controls over their border territories. Confiscation of remaining properties, the eviction from the larger towns and border areas of 'unreliable elements', mass arrests and deportations to the interior of the Soviet Union were common features of the second phase of Sovietization. During the summer of 1940 collectivization and industrialization, considered under Stalinism to be the prerequisites of a stable Soviet regime, received added impetus.[24]

The harshest and in the short run probably the most effective method to achieve control of the new Soviet territories was the systematic elimination of any overt or potential opposition in the area. The Soviet purge machine with its long history and experience in the elimination of entire social strata was used relentlessly in the new territories. Intimidation, detention, transfer, imprisonment and deportation were among the various methods used to destroy and eliminate the former elites and those elements in the territories deemed by the regime to be undesirable or unadaptable.

The elimination of individuals and entire social groups started with the entry of the Soviet troops and did not stop until the last days of Soviet rule. The purge, however was not uniform in its intensity and varied with policy decisions taken outside the annexed provinces. The arrests and deportations at the beginning of Soviet rule were aimed at ensuring a 'smooth' execution of the formalities connected with the integration of the provinces into the USSR.[25] The deportations at this stage involved mainly Polish officials and settlers, to achieve what the Soviets considered to be the 'correct' ethnic composition of the provinces. Included also was the local leadership that might have opposed the formal annexation. These arrests were to a large extent directed against individuals, and were selective in nature.[26] Deportations on a mass scale started in February 1940. It is possible to distinguish four major waves of mass deportations – the first three took place in February, April and June–July 1940, and the last coincided with the outbreak of the war in June 1941.[27] Each wave lasted several days or weeks and concentrated on a particular section of the population. The Polish Government in Exile estimated the total number of deportees to be about 800,000 – 52 per cent Poles, 30 per cent Jews and 18 per cent Ukrainians and Belorussians.[28] What might have appeared a haphazard operation was in fact a well-designed scheme to remove and destroy all the elements that could have provided leadership at any level to oppose the regime and its goals. The dynamics of the purge machine were responsible for the 'overkill' nature of the operation and the large numbers involved.[29]

'Joining the Soviet family of nations' was a painful process for the 13 million or more inhabitants of Poland's eastern provinces. They had to travel in 21 months a road traversed by the Soviets in over 20 years. By the time of the German invasion former Eastern Poland had gone a long way towards becoming an integral part of the USSR. Its political institutions, administrative structure, educational system and economy were almost completely identical to those of the annexing country. With few exceptions, the local population, willingly or out of fear and coercion, accepted its fate. The large Jewish community was involved in the same process, yet was affected by it in a particular way.

2
Shtetl Jews

The Jews living in the eastern provinces of independent Poland, like their brothers in other parts of the country, constituted a distinctive nationality. Religion, language and separate cultural, educational and civic-public institutions united the Jewish community and gave it exclusive characteristics. Independent Poland recognized the Jews' distinctness and promised to safeguard their minority national rights.[1] The predominant human-geographic structure of the Jewish community in those regions of Poland was the small town, the so-called shtetl, while only a minority lived either in villages or in larger urban centers.

Approximately 1.2 million Jews lived in the eastern provinces of Poland when this area was annexed by the Soviet Union.[2] They constituted about 9.9 per cent of the total population.[3] Between 300,000 and 350,000 Jewish refugees from the Polish provinces occupied by Germany must be added to the local Jewish population,[4] thus making the Jewish community of Eastern Poland among the largest in Europe.

The fundamental features of the community and its relationship to the non-Jewish world were generations old. They conformed to the basic structure of Jewish life in the Diaspora, which had been shaped long before. The Jewish community of Eastern Poland had lived in the region at least from the fourteenth century. Nevertheless, it was considered as an alien entity by the non-Jewish population, and also by most of its own members. They were at best tolerated, yet always remained dependent aliens and were frequently discriminated against and persecuted. The vast majority of the Jewish population spoke Yiddish, a distinct language that had no affinity at all with the languages of their gentile neighbours. Lacking territorial concentration, the Jewish community organized its life within an elaborate network of autonomous institutions, voluntary and those that had the sanction of the Polish government. The *kehilla*, the Jewish autonomous communal organization, was given an official status in 1927, yet it followed the centuries-old practice of Jewish autonomy.[5] The *kehilla* was governed by an elected body which had the right to levy taxes and was in charge of the religious affairs of the community. The synagogues, the maintenance of the Rabbinate, the ritual bath, cemeteries and religious education as well as philanthropic institutions and general welfare were included within the jurisdiction of the *kehilla*. It also subsidized various cultural and social programmes, thus making it a vital institution in Jewish autonomous life.

An elaborate educational and cultural establishment had constituted part of the distinct national existence of the Jewish community throughout the ages. The community of Eastern Poland possessed an extensive network of schools, Jewish publications, including several dailies (in Lvov, Grodno, Bialystok, Rowno) and cultural and political associations. The intense struggle between Polish, Ukrainian and Belorussian nationalisms for cultural and political supremacy had its effect on Jewish behaviour. National consciousness among the Jews of the region was more acute than in other parts of Poland, as were Jewish separateness and exclusiveness.[6] To avoid entanglement in the struggle between Poles, Ukrainians and Belorussians, the Jews established their own educational system to include as many of its pupils as possible. The local Jewish community maintained most of the Hebrew and Yiddish schools in Poland.[7] Many of the more famous *yeshivot* (institutes of higher learning) of Poland, such as Mir, Grodno, Slonim, as well as numerous smaller *yeshivot* were to be found in this region. *Kheders*, the most elementary schools for children, as well as more advanced primary schools and community Talmud Torahs, were found in every shtetl.[8]

The basic traits of the Jewish society and economy, as well as geographic distribution, had been formed many years previously and had changed very little with time. The Jews were primarily an urban population in a country whose majority was rural.[9] The Jews were city-dwellers from the early Middle Ages on, not only in Poland but throughout Europe and unlike other minorities, they were distributed widely throughout Poland. What was to a large extent unique was the very high concentration of the Jews in the many shtetlach, many of these having a Jewish majority, and many being almost entirely Jewish.

The socio-economic structure of the Jewish population on the eve of the Soviet occupation had not changed radically since the area became part of the Pale of Settlement or even of pre-partition Poland. The basic occupational distribution of the Jewish community was similar to that of

Diaspora Jewries: a very high percentage working in commerce, handicrafts and services and a minority engaged directly in agriculture and industry.[10] This fundamental distribution had remained for centuries. Eastern Poland was mostly an agricultural area, with only small pockets of modern industrial development, hence the preservation almost intact of the traditional Jewish occupational structure. The Jews were engaged chiefly in supplying the rural population with consumer goods, through peddling, retail commerce and handicraft production, and as workers in small enterprises processing the agricultural products and national resources of the region.[11] In Eastern Poland, to a higher degree than in other parts of the country, Jews were over-represented in business, crafts and the free professions. Seventy-six per cent of the businesses, 52 per cent of crafts and industry and correspondingly high proportions of the free professions were in Jewish hands.[12]

One may be misled by the terminology and statistics of the Jewish occupational structure. It is true that the majority of Jews were concentrated in the lower middle class, yet they were by and large far from economic well-being. The two decades of independent Poland saw a general decline and impoverishment of the Jewish community. There were many paupers, hard hit by the economic policies of the regime. Many suffered from oppressive poverty, the result of discrimination and the frequent crises of the times.

The Jewish community in the inter-war years was neither static nor homogeneous. The Jews comprised different levels of economic well-being and political persuasion, and held different attitudes towards religion and the outside world. The period was characterized by increasing internal differentiation. Changes took place in intensity of attachment to traditional Jewish cultural and religious values. Acculturation – the adoption of the culture of the surrounding nation – and secularization – the desertion of the traditional way of life with its religious observance and values – were two dominant characteristics of the inter-war period. Polish Jewry in general ranged between two polar types: orthodox traditionalists and assimilationists.[13] There was a significant correlation between age, occupation and place of dwelling, and acculturation. The older generation, petty tradesmen and craftsmen living in the shtetlach, tended to be more traditionalist and orthodox. The richer workers, younger generation and dwellers in larger cities tended to move away from tradition and religious observance. Frequently the differentiation was accompanied by a generational conflict. The traditional orthodox supporters were still prevalent in the East Polish shtetl, yet the younger generation was even here moving away from the old ways. On the whole there was a marked and accelerated diminution in religious observance, traditional dress, and use of Yiddish.

Acculturation in independent Poland virtually meant Polonization. The use of the Polish language and the adoption of Polish surnames and dress were among the more conspicuous characteristics. Public schools and gymnasiums were most effective agents of acculturation.[14] Polonization of the Jewish community was much weaker in the eastern regions. Because of the provinces' ethnic composition, with a predominance of non-Polish elements and strong Russian past influences, the Jews tended to adopt more of a neutral stance with regard to the contending groups. Here Yiddish remained the language of a large majority, especially in the shtetl.[15]

Secularization was more pronounced than Polonized acculturation in the eastern provinces. Here one found that while moving away from religious observance and traditional attire and appearance the Jews tended to adhere to the folk elements of Jewish culture, Yiddish literature and language.

Nevertheless, a large proportion of the shtetl Jews in the East were still traditional orthodox.[16] The external features of the traditional male shtetl Jew were highly visible, with his special dress, side-locks and beard and with Yiddish as his spoken language. These Jews lived a traditional Jewish life, observing the Law (Torah), *Shabat* and holidays and customs.[17] They segregated themselves from the non-Jewish world, thus hoping to preserve their distinct identity. Having no feeling of inferiority *vis-à-vis* the gentiles, their main concern was physical and economic survival, which became ever harder in independent Poland.

The younger generation of the shtetlach of Eastern Poland was moving away from religious observance and becoming increasingly secularized. The movement of young people from the shtetl to larger urban centers and abroad was among the important factors in weakening the traditional way of life and the younger and the less affluent were less immune to alien influences. The majority of Jews who departed from the traditional way of life were looking for equality without the need to sacrifice their Jewish identity.

However, secularization created strains and conflicts within the Jewish community and within individual families. The wide range of attitudes towards the traditional way of life and towards religious observance in the community at the time were reflected in competing political organizations, movements, parties, sects, etc. The Jewish family was frequently torn apart by inter-generational disagreement, conflicting values and ways of behaviour. Change accompanied by strains and conflicts characterized the Jewish community on the eve of the Soviet invasion.

Even the economically stagnant shtetls of the eastern provinces felt the winds of change that swept the Jewish community of Poland. Nevertheless, the shtetl on the eve of the Soviet invasion preserved many of its basic characteristics as they were formed long ago. The region at large remained agrarian and backward and its small urban settlements, usually away from modern roads or railways, maintained the traditional role they had performed for generations and with it their basic structure.[18]

The shtetl reflected the civilization of its inhabitants as well as the economic and cultural levels of the surrounding countryside. The major features of the shtetl and its community were determined by the demographic preponderance of the Jews, and the rather poor agricultural countryside the shtetl served. Frequently the shtetlach in the eastern provinces and Galicia had an absolute Jewish majority, or at least Jews constituted the largest single ethnic group. Jewish dominance of commerce and the crafts in the small towns made them the major urban element, while many of the non-Jewish inhabitants engaged in agricultural pursuits. As a result much of the character of the small towns was determined by the Jewish community. With little exaggeration they could be described as Jewish islands in a non-Jewish ocean.[19]

Externally the shtetl carried the imprint of its Jewish inhabitants.[20] That image of the Jewishness of the shtetl emerged very clearly in the classic Yiddish literature as well as in the visual arts. Mendele, Sholem-Aleichem, and Shagal, to mention a few, by depicting the shtetl as a Jewish world (even though of a previous period), were not describing an imaginary world. Their shtetl was based on the demographic and physical realities of the small town of the region. Many shtetlach had a large Jewish majority. No wonder then that by their sheer numerical presence and their dominance of the urban occupations the Jews bestowed Jewish characteristics on the external appearance of the small town.

The many Jewish public buildings were prominent marks in the shtetl. The central synagogue, frequently a large and impressive building, stood at the center of a large court (*shulhoif*) where many more public institutions were concentrated. Smaller prayer houses that went under different names (*beit-midrash*, *kloiz*, *shtibl*) and served different sections of the community, were spread throughout the town. *Khadarim* (rooms that served for elementary teaching), the *mikveh* (ritual bath), slaughterhouse, etc., all typical Jewish buildings, were prominent landmarks in the small towns. Moreover, the entire built landscape, the houses and their surroundings, reflected the attitude of its Jewish residents. Frequently poverty combined with a general attitude towards life in exile as a temporary experience to produce a 'Jewish appearance' in shtetl houses. Very little attention was paid to external decoration, painting or gardening – these were more characteristic of their non-Jewish neighbours. The market-place with the shops and workshops surrounding it and lined along the streets leading to it was dominated by Jews. Here they made most of their livelihood. Thus for Jew and gentile alike the shtetl looked very Jewish.

On the usually unpaved and inadequately drained streets, most of the people either hurrying on their daily chores or just strolling along, were Jewish. In spite of a certain degree of external acculturation among shtetl Jews by 1939, they were still easily distinguishable from the non-Jewish population. Many of the men still wore the traditional Jewish attire and had beards and *peyes* (side-locks), that set them apart from the non-Jews. Even those who did not manifest their Jewishness by clothing or appearance were usually still easily distinguishable from their Slavic neighbours by their complexion.

Not only people and buildings gave the small towns of Eastern Poland a Jewish quality. The structure of everyday life, too, reflected the life of the Jewish community and its civilization. Being the dominant urban element in the small towns, Jews to a large extent determined many aspects of the rhythm of economic life. Daily prayers and the *Shabat* affected opening hours of businesses and workshops. Preparations for *Shabat*, with the Friday ritual bath, change of attire, going and returning from synagogue, were all prominent Jewish sights in the shtetlach. The Jewish holidays were also important occasions. *Yom Kippur* or *Rosh Hashana* (Day of Atonement or New Year), Passover or *Simkhat Torah* (the Torah holiday), were occasions for stopping almost all economic activity in many of the small towns of the eastern provinces of Poland. Preparations for the holidays were tangibly felt in every corner of the shtetl; the lights of the *Khanukah* candles did as much as the joyful feasts of *Purim* to give the town a Jewish imprint.[21]

Intensity of community life, intimacy of family and friends, as well as a very high social cohesiveness, were among the characteristics of shtetl life as they have been reported by people who lived there.[22] For good or bad, the individual Jew who lived in the small town had been surrounded by a sense of intimacy and relative security. In part it was the consequence of the relatively small size of the shtetl and its population. However, it can mainly be attributed to the intricate and dense network of institutions and organizations that were conducive to intensive social interaction within the Jewish shtetl community. Of course, the numbers, size and scope of the activities varied with the dimensions of the town. Yet the basic institutions and organizations could be found in almost any shtetl.

In the shtetl, the officially recognized *kehilla* and its dependent affiliated institutions existed side by side with voluntary and *ad hoc* organizations formed to carry out specific tasks. They were no different from those mentioned above in the description of the entire Jewish community of the region as a whole. Small size, close acquaintance, relative remoteness and isolation from larger centers, bestowed upon the shtetl community a strong sense of Jewish solidarity and identity which was expressed in and fostered by its autonomous institutions.[23] From cradle to grave the individual in the shtetl was catered for by the organized community. He received an elementary education in one of the many *kheders* of the shtetl. Some went on to a *yeshiva*, a more advanced educational institution, but these did not exist in every shtetl.[24] The *kehilla* and the many voluntary organizations covered every conceivable aspect of life. This elaborate autonomous structure, together with other characteristics of the Jewish shtetl community, set it apart from the surrounding non-Jewish environment. There were very limited contacts, certainly on a social level, between the shtetl Jew and his gentile neighbour. There were no enterprises where Jews and non-Jews worked together. Enveloped by the autonomous organizations of the community and strengthened by his beliefs and customs, the individual shtetl Jew lived an intense and separate national and religious Jewish life.

There was not only intimacy and social cohesiveness in the Jewish shtetl community. It had also, in the thirties, its strong internal tensions and political struggles. These were the result of the dire economic situation, government policy and the process of secularization that took place in the numerous small towns of the region. The ensuing debates as to the course to be followed brought about the creation of a multitude of political movements: orthodox and secularist, Zionist and Bund, socialist and liberal. Each movement in its turn was split internally into many factions and each had its own youth movement.[25] Politics thus enhanced even further the intensity of public life in the shtetl. Towering above the Jewish shtetl community were the economic realities of over-concentration in petty commerce and small crafts. There were far too many Jews trying to sell their meagre merchandise or handicrafts to the poor peasants of the countryside. Many faced a hopeless future, particularly the younger shtetl generation.[26]

The inter-war period in independent Poland witnessed the growing deterioration of the economic, social and also personal or emotional well-being of the Jewish community. This reached its nadir in the years 1936–9. Poland, particularly its eastern provinces, suffered from general economic backwardness. The Polish government followed a systematic policy designed to curtail Jewish economic activity. Anti-Semitism in inter-war Poland was a respectable ideology and culminated in an official policy of ridding Poland of its Jews. Poland's leaders after 1935 used anti-Semitism to direct public attention away from the country's real problems.[27] Overt discrimination in all government institutions and enterprises, limitation of the number of Jewish university students, as well as physical harassment and bloody pogroms were among the manifestations of Polish pre-war anti-Semitism.

In the last years before the German invasion, the feeling in the Jewish community was one of closing horizons. While the cultural and educational activities of the Jews had reached heights unsurpassed by other Jewish centres, the economic and social prospects became ever blacker.[28] The number of Jews needing social relief reached unprecedented heights, as did the numbers of unemployed.[29] Opportunities to find a way out, whether in new fields of economic endeavour or by emigration were almost non-existent, as the Polish government and the immigration policies of overseas countries blocked every opening and escape route.

The Jewish community of Eastern Poland in 1939 still preserved the basic structure of Polish Jewry as it had been formed hundreds of years previously. Yet it became evident that it was coming under increasing external pressure as well as experiencing internal divisions and conflicts. This would affect the reaction of the community to future events.

3
The Shtetl Meets the Red Army

What might be called a 'transition crisis' occurred during the period lasting from the disintegration of Polish rule until the firm establishment of the Soviet regime. This crisis exposed some of the characteristic features of the Jewish community. During the tense weeks of drama and disappointment were revealed many of the fears and hopes, sympathies and animosities, attachments and deep divisions within the community. The interval between the destruction of the old order and the institution of the new saw the dissolution of long-established barriers and restraints. As Nazi occupation seemed a very real possibility and people were looking with apprehension towards the future, there was a unique opportunity for the outside observer to delve into some of the deeper emotions of the community, to examine its peculiar position between the different ethnic groups and its inner relations and external attitudes.

The dominant sentiment was a deep-seated anxiety concerning physical survival. This preoccupation with physical survival was no new phenomenon in Jewish life, but its strength and pervasiveness were dramatically revealed. The German invasion of Poland and collapse of the Polish army presented the community with a desperate situation. Nobody could have imagined what was really in store, however, and even what was anticipated sufficed to fill hearts with terror.[1] That fear was the most important single factor that determined Jewish attitudes towards the Red Army.

The days between the collapse of Polish rule and the establishment of Soviet control saw the danger and in many cases the eruption of anti-Jewish riots. It took the Red Army about two weeks to occupy the area. Meanwhile the countryside teemed with disorganized Polish units and roaming bands of peasants who tried to exploit the situation for looting and rioting against the Jewish population in the neighbouring shtetlach.[2] The threat to the Jewish population came mainly from the Ukrainian peasants. Their bands tried to penetrate the defenceless towns, posing a threat to the entire population which was mostly Polish and Jewish. Thus the Polish population frequently faced the same dangers. Catholic churches and monasteries as well as government officials were victims of Ukrainian mobs.[3] The disorganized Polish units, many still possessing their weapons, presented another danger to the Jewish population. The Polish soldiers tried to settle accounts at the last minute before their final destruction and on such occasions the Jews had the Ukrainians as their fellow victims.[4] Numerous rumours about impending pogroms reached the Jewish communities. The organization of self-defence units and the earlier than expected arrival of the Soviet army prevented their occurrence.[5]

The Jewish communities of the territories occupied by German troops and later ceded to the USSR when the final boundaries were determined gained a foretaste of the fate awaiting them from the Nazis. Even Polish reports, critical of the favourable reception of the Red Army by the Jews, had to admit that 'After the horrible occurrences of the few days of German occupation the entrance of the Soviet troops was understandably greeted with relief, particularly by the Jews'.[6] During the short period of their rule, the Germans used every opportunity to rob, beat up and execute Jews without excuse.[7] There were mass executions of hundreds of Jews when the German troops started their retreat.

An outburst of joy and relief was the overwhelming reaction of the Jews in the many shtetlach of Eastern Poland to the entry of the Soviet army. It is true that there were those who followed with apprehension and misgivings the advancing columns of the Red Army, and for good reasons. Yet at the moment of first encounter the dominant sentiment in 'the Jewish street' was that they were rescued. Numerous reports, testimonies, memoirs, and newspapers tell us about 'deliverance', 'rescue', 'liberation from the German nightmare', 'the relievers'.[8] Z. Segalowicz, the poet, in describing the prevailing atmosphere, remembered that 'Even the rumour that the Soviet army might enter the city brought life again to the frightened Jews. People became talkative, smiled, ate with renewed appetite.'[9] When the Red Army entered the city 'There was a holiday atmosphere. Things changed overnight. The world had changed: the Germans would not enter, and that was most important of all.'[10] In Slonim thousands lined the streets to greet the approach of the 'rescuers'. They were not Communists, nor fellow-travellers. 'Who cared about Communism at the moment? Who could be concerned with theoretical problems of national economy while life itself was at stake? A good or rotten regime? Who could pay attention to such "respectable" yet worthless problems?', relates one of the bystanders.[11] Rich and poor, young and old sighed with relief. The unanimity of Jewish reaction, in spite of differences in tone and enthusiasm, was noticed by many and was particularly resented by the Polish population. Yet occasionally the Polish populace itself and even some elected officials greeted the advancing Soviet army with flowers. The rapid collapse of the Polish army contributed to the confusion in the area. The secrecy of the Soviet–German agreement and the flow of misleading propaganda presenting the Red Army as liberators created the false impression that they had come to help the Poles.[12] Still, the confused were a minority. If there were Jews who had their reservations about the jubilation, Polish eyes did not record them. Endless reports testified to Jewish demonstrations of enthusiasm and jubilation with the entrance of the Red Army. 'Everywhere the Jews receive with enthusiasm the Russians', repeat the reports. Jewish readiness to co-operate with the new rulers was interpreted as ingratitude bordering on treason.[13] The Poles disregarded the discriminations, harassments and pogroms of the very recent past. Pogroms and Nazi terror, not enthusiasm for Communism, were the dominant forces that drove the Jews towards the Soviets.

This time Soviet reports were supported by Polish sources and confirmed by the Jews themselves. The press coverage of the reception reflected fairly accurately what was happening in reality, representing genuine events. Occasionally Soviet reporting even used terminology borrowed from some of the local Jews.[14] The Soviet press in Yiddish emphasized two subjects: the enthusiastic reactions of the local population, and the miserable life that the Ukrainian and Belorussian local populations had under Polish rule. Peasants and workers lining up along the roads of towns and villages of western Ukraine and Belorussia, cheering, covering the marching soldiers of the Red Army with flowers; offerings of bread and salt (the traditional greeting ceremony) – these were the standard descriptions.[15] Allegations of national discrimination and the social oppression of the Ukrainian and Belorussian populations were presented as the main explanation for Soviet 'liberation'.

'Rescued', 'liberated' and facing a 'new life' also were the Jewish masses. 'Not less oppressed than the Belorussian and Ukrainian masses, were the Jewish workers. Oppressed, like the others, by the Polish *Shliachta*, they had to face also Polish anti-Semitism. The Jewish masses met with the greatest of joys the Red Army. They are convinced that for them the hour of redemption – true redemption from social and national oppression – has arrived.'[16] Referring to Polish plans to get rid of one million 'redundant' Jews, an editorial in the *Oktiaber* proclaimed that 'there are no more redundant Jews . . . There is one country in the world where the Jews are not superfluous and that is the great and mighty Soviet Union.'[17] Only in the USSR was the Jewish problem resolved and had the Jews become productive people, maintained the Soviet publicist. Those were the high days of Stalin's personality cult. Among its characteristics as reflected in the press were bombastic language, exaggerated metaphors and descriptions of joy, enthusiasm, expressions of affection and gratitude.

While Polish and independent Jewish sources stress the large-scale Jewish expressions of enthusiasm towards the Red Army, Soviet sources tend to underplay the Jewish reaction. Very little space was devoted to specific Jewish reactions, even in the Soviet Yiddish press. The reason was quite obvious: the fear of being depicted as 'Jew-lovers' was strongly present in Soviet minds. That trend could be detected in the Soviet Union prior to 1939; in Eastern Poland, however, it was strengthened further by the desire to counteract Nazi propaganda, and strong local anti-Semitism.

It is interesting to note that by identical phrases, quite often Soviet and local Jews meant different things. Uppermost in the minds of the Jews of the eastern Polish provinces was the danger of Nazi Germany. The Soviet press, however, was referring only to Polish anti-Semitism. For the rescued Jews there could be no doubt that Polish discrimination and pogroms appeared secondary when compared to Nazi atrocities. Nevertheless it was still true that the exaggerated and inflated descriptions of gratitude and love towards the Soviet soldiers in the Soviet press reflected genuine relief and sympathy.

The behaviour of the Soviet army and individual soldiers contributed to the sense of security and relief. The Jews of the eastern provinces still remembered the Russian soldier of pre-revolutionary times. For the Jew the Tsarist soldier represented violence and pogroms, particularly the fierce Cossacks. Now their behaviour was blameless,[18] and the first impressions overwhelmingly favourable. 'He does not get drunk, curse or rob', noted an astute observer M. Kleinboim (Sne).[19] The transformation was such that it was impossible to identify the Russian soldier with the new Soviet man. 'He even eats differently', remarked an eyewitness from eastern Galicia.[20] The Red Army did not behave, as could have been expected, like a conquering force. Its soldiers were civilized, polite and friendly, projecting a most positive image of the new Soviet man.[21] There is no doubt that the soldiers were briefed and instructed in advance on how to treat the local population. Cigarettes, confetti and matches were thrown by passing soldiers to the cheering crowds.[22] Most impressive for a population used to pogroms and unpunished plundering was the absence of any looting by the Red Army soldiers. Not that they were immune to the charms of the goods stacked in the shops; on the contrary. It appeared that everything that could be bought, at any price, was irresistible. Almost all the memoirs of the time report the insatiable thirst of Soviet soldiers for consumer goods.[23] They had plenty of Polish money and the volume of their purchases brought about almost daily rises in prices. Yet they paid for all the merchandise, remaining disciplined and friendly. No wonder that one finds shtetl Jews who were truly enthusiastic. 'Who could have imagined such a Russian soldier? You can talk with him as if he is one of us. Our children have awakened to new life. They walk to school and cross the street without any fear,' related an old shtetl Jew.[24] 'I am going from place to place, from one shtetl to another, and find true enthusiasm for the Soviet regime,' recorded F. Zerubavel in her impressions of the first weeks of Soviet rule.[25]

The presence of Jewish soldiers and officers in the ranks of the Red Army contributed to the feeling of relief and solidarity that many shtetl Jews felt. In rudimentary Yiddish the soldiers explained that they came 'to liberate the working people from Polish exploitation,' thus serving the Soviet propaganda machine.[26] Some felt a sense of belonging and pride when they found Jewish commanders among the mighty army that had come to rescue them from the Polish yoke. 'That night no Jew closed his eyes in Lipniszki,' recalled one of its Jews. 'In the market square rested an army unit and for the first time in our lives we saw officers speaking Yiddish. We could not believe our eyes ... We had bright hopes for a great future.'[27]

The feeling of relief from an impending threat was widespread, but enthusiasm was not universal. There were also reservations and deep apprehensions in the Jewish community. Different sentiments reflected the internal differences, and divisions according to wealth, attachment to tradition, and political orientation. While the shtetl Jews were generally happy and expressed enthusiasm towards the new regime, Jews in the larger urban centres were more reserved.[28] The basic division was between those who stood to gain and those who thought that they might lose from the expected social and economic transformations. An eyewitness from Czortkow related:

> Whole families of tailors, cobblers, carpenters and other poor people were streaming from the back streets to the shtetl's high street to greet the Red Army. ... They felt proud and happy – their sons and daughters had become important people now. While another part of the population, including the wealthier families as well as people active in the Zionist movement and other nationalistic organizations did not take part in the celebrations.[29]

The younger generation was usually more receptive, as was the working intelligentsia. New opportunities for study and employment were to be opened up before them.[30] The youth was 'drawn by the declarations, and slogans of equality and justice, the simple manners of the Soviet men, the charm of the Russian songs . . . Those songs and even more the movies conquered many hearts.'[31] No wonder that in the God-forsaken shtetlach of Eastern Poland, without electricity, running water or decent roads, the impact of the Soviet promises on the young was tremendous. Many had lost interest in and attachment to tradition long before the advance of the Red Army. For the younger generation, who knew little and hoped for much, the Soviets represented new horizons and they reacted enthusiastically. Yet the older generation and the well-to-do had their doubts and qualms. They rejoiced in having been rescued, but had their misgivings about the future.[32]

Indicative of the human resources and potential in the Jewish community was the important role played by Jews during the transition period and the first phase of organizing the new regime. There were many places, usually those removed from the major routes of the advancing Red Army, where the interregnum lasted for some days. The power vacuum created was filled quite often by local temporary executive committees. Jews played a prominent role in those committees, which lasted in many places until they were replaced by officials who came from the Soviet Union.

The creation of the temporary committees was a local initiative in response to special circumstances before the entrance of the Red Army. In some places the committees started as self-defence organizations to prevent pogroms, usually by Ukrainian peasants from the countryside.[33] These self-defence organizations used weapons taken from the retreating Polish units. They took upon themselves, usually under the leadership of local Jewish Communists, the responsibility for maintaining order until the arrival of the Red Army. There were places where committees were created to organize the reception for the Soviet units and provide what they considered a new Soviet-like authority as a temporary replacement for the disintegrating Polish administration. 'Revolutionary committees', as some of the committees were called, according to numerous Polish reports consisted almost entirely of Jews, with a few Ukrainians.[34] A citizens' militia served as the executive tool of the committees. In the two organizations Jews played a dominant role, according to Polish sources.[35] Jewish communists tried in some places to establish what they considered a Soviet administration.[36] The committees behaved as if they were the government until the entrance of the Red Army. They initiated 'socialist' reforms, occasionally coming into conflict with the local population.

Expression of suppressed grudges and hatreds against the haughty Polish officials could be detected during the transition. For the downtrodden it was a time for settling scores, a time of retribution. Detectives and policemen were disarmed and arrested.[37] Polish officials reported that they were told by local Jews 'Your time has passed, a new epoch begins.'[38] The

Polish population felt itself alienated and threatened and tried to avoid public attention, while the Jews moved around 'with a new sense of security and equality,' related M. Grosman.[39] There were many instances of arbitrariness and of settling accounts with all those who were well-to-do or in authority in the old regime, Jews and Poles alike. Those who were Communists before were 'engaged now on their own in "nationalizing" stores, houses, merchandise, and settling old grudges. Arbitrarily they make arrests and investigations,' related a survivor.[40] Harassment of the more affluent, expropriation and distribution of goods among the poor without authorization from the incoming regime, were typical of the transition time.[41] The persecution, expropriations and occasional imprisonment were indicative of the social changes that would take place. A new class of leadership and authority was coming into being and the old one felt uneasy.

Jews participated in disproportionate numbers in the Soviet-established institutions during the first few weeks of the new regime.[42] The Soviet authorities were eager to return to a semblance of normality in the shortest possible time. They intended, with the arrival of cadres from the Soviet interior, to transfer to them the controlling positions. Meanwhile, any local cooperation was encouraged, particularly of Ukrainians and Belorussians.[43] However, the local Ukrainians and to a lesser degree Belorussians exhibited strong nationalistic and anti-Russian feelings. The preference of Ukrainians in appointments, even when they lacked the proper ideological background, created awkward situations that the Soviets would have to deal with later by massive dismissals and arrests. Local Communists, when employed, were closely watched, being suspected of Trotskyite deviations.[44] The Polish population could not serve as a source of manpower for the new institutions; at this stage they were reluctant to cooperate with the invader, to avoid the stigma of treason. The Jewish community particularly in the shtetlach constituted a large reservoir of manpower, relatively well-educated, reliable as far as its outside relations were concerned and, what was equally important, available and eager to cooperate.

Jewish youth formed special organizations whose role was to facilitate the establishment of the new regime. In many places the first Soviet-appointed institutions contained a very high proportion of Jews.[45] Governmental and economic institutions, the militia in particular – organized by the authorities as a local police force – employed many Jews.[46] The shtetl Jews, with a very high unemployment rate, were willing to fill every available opening, thus playing an important role in the initial stages of building the Soviet system in former Eastern Poland. However, after consolidating their position the new rulers relegated the local Jews to inferior positions or got rid of them altogether.

The reaction of the Jewish community to the changes that took place in Eastern Poland during the transition from Polish to Soviet rule were indicative of its situation. The Red Army was greeted with relief and in the shtetlach even with enthusiasm. Even though there were many who had hidden fears for their personal well-being, the immediate sentiment was a positive one. During the transition many suppressed emotions, energies and talents surfaced within the Jewish community. Particularly the younger generation was eager to grab any hitherto denied opportunity and make the most of it. The new authorities needed help to build the Soviet system and they were able to tap the large reservoirs of energy, talent and goodwill, which had been frustrated and alienated by the former regime. This was particularly so in the shtetl. Hence the prominent role played by Jews in the initial stages of Soviet rule. The generally favourable predisposition of the Jewish community should have augured well for the future integration of the Jews into the Soviet system, but no ideological conviction, only the former oppressive anti-Semitic regime and above all the looming threat of Hitler, were responsible for positive Jewish attitudes.

4

The Dissolution of the Old Order and Emergence of the Lonely Jew

The Soviet system was built on the ruins of the former order. The old structures, institutions and organizations in the different spheres of political, social, economic and cultural activity were dissolved by the new rulers. The policy towards the Jewish community in Eastern Poland was, with minor deviations, the Stalinist policy towards the Jewish minority in the USSR itself.[1] Accordingly, the Polish Jews were treated without any regard for their unique situation. The goal of the Soviet Jewish policy was to assimilate the Jewish community completely and to eliminate as many of its distinctive features as possible.

What were the major elements of Stalinist policy concerning the Jewish community? The components of the Stalinist 'Jewish policy' were yet another facet of the totalitarian regime in the USSR. Centralism, and a violent attempt to achieve uniformity in all spheres of social activity were among the striking characteristics of the regime. Any expression of ethnic or cultural pluralism was regarded as deviation from accepted norms and a danger to the regime. The entire Soviet social structure, its institutions, organizations, activities, was totally mobilized to serve the goals of the regime. Within that context Soviet culture had to become as homogeneous as possible. Its aim was to follow norms and criteria centrally decided, with the sole purpose of serving the socialist state.[2]

For the Soviet Jewish community the application of Stalinism meant a further deterioration in the different expressions of Jewish distinctness. The Jews had to conform to Soviet society and participate actively in the transformation that was taking place. Most organizational and institutional tools that served to maintain Jewish autonomous existence had already been eliminated in earlier periods of Soviet history. In the thirties there was a reduction in Yiddish publications and schools and the teaching of Jewish history and cultural traditions was almost completely eliminated. At the same time an increase in the number of mixed marriages and accelerated pace of assimilation appeared to indicate that the regime was succeeding in achieving its basic goal – the gradual disappearance of a distinct Jewish community in the USSR.

Soviet policy concerning the Jewish community underwent several shifts from the time the Bolshevik leaders formulated their views on the subject. Lenin and Stalin were responsible for the basic ideas of the regime concerning Jewish nationhood and the desired policy of a future socialist state. According to Lenin, the Jews were a caste which owed its continued existence to external persecution and discrimination.[3] Hence when the Jews were given equal rights and the external pressures disappeared, he argued, so would the Jews as a distinct social entity. Lenin regarded as reactionary and reproachable all claims to recognize a separate Jewish nationality and culture. The absence of a common territory and language excluded any possibility of Jewish nationhood. The solution to the so-called Jewish problem consisted, according to Lenin, in the abolition of all discrimination. It would bring about a gradual assimilation of the Jews into the surrounding society. For Lenin, assimilation did not have negative connotations. On the contrary, when it is not imposed by force, assimilation may be considered a progressive social-historical process and it was certainly viewed by the founder of the Soviet State as a favourable development where the Jews were concerned. In the USSR Lenin's doctrine on the Jewish problem was never challenged or questioned. It remained the basic theoretical assumption behind policy-making.

Stalin added his share to his mentor's assumptions. Early in his career Stalin became the Bolshevik expert on the nationalities problem. In his 1912 essay, *Marxism and the National Question*, Stalin maintained that the Jews lacked some of the basic elements that constitute a nation. Thus out of four necessary conditions for a nation – namely common language, territory, economy and character expressed in culture – the Jews lacked the first three. The Jews had a common religious descent and character, yet the absence of a common economy proscribed the evolution of a Jewish nation, according to Stalin. Their economic situation, he claimed, created conditions for integration of the Jews into the surrounding society, and furthered their assimilation; this was not only desirable, but also the only way to resolve the Jewish problem.

With the establishment of the Soviet State, its leaders had to find solutions to problems that party doctrine was not sufficient to resolve.

Assimilation still remained the desired goal; theory was maintained. Yet in real life the Soviets had to deal with several million Jews who did not show any signs of disappearing by way of assimilating into Soviet society at large. Until the end of the twenties we find in Soviet society a certain tolerance towards local differences and ethnic pecularities and cultures. The authorities tried to integrate the Jews into Soviet society by reconstructing their socio-economic composition. The Jews were allowed a certain degree of cultural autonomy in the form of the continued existence and encouragement of Yiddish culture and education. The Jewish sections of the Communist Party (the *Evsektsiia*) were designed to promote that line.[4] The *Evsektsiia* had to contribute to the integration of the Jews into the Soviet family of nations, and the Jew as an individual into Soviet society. However, the *Evsektsiia* activists had never considered their role as being the destruction of Jewish distinctness. This attempt at integration while preserving some of the singularity of the Jews failed eventually. The Communist Party paid little attention to the peculiar conditions and development of the Jewish community and the preservation of the special characteristics of the Jewish population was not the goal or the desire of the authorities. At the same time the Jews themselves in increasing numbers were deserting their traditional identity in response to pressures from above and the temptation to succeed in Soviet society. Thus the twenties prepared the ground for Stalinism by destroying the traditional order in the Jewish community without creating a new synthesis.

On the eve of extending its borders in the West, the USSR was conducting a policy that disregarded the special character of the Jewish community. The avowed goal was complete integration of that community into Soviet society and loss of its separate identity. Yet actual conditions prevented the complete disappearance of the Jew with his distinct identity. Great Russian nationalism and intensified anti-Semitism in Europe in general contributed to the Soviet government's disregard of the Jewish problem of the time. This policy meant also a refusal to acknowledge openly that there existed any specific Jewish problem, or danger from Nazi Germany.

When preparing the ground for building the Soviet system in the annexed provinces, the authorities treated the Jewish community by using, more or less, the same criteria which applied to the rest of the population. They did not deem it necessary to pay special attention to the unique position of the Jewish population in this multi-ethnic area. The economic marginality and unique autonomous institutions and cultural traditions of the Jewish community were of no interest to the authorities. As we shall see later, this 'equal treatment' had disastrous effects on the Jewish community as an entity and was painful for the Jew as an individual.

The destruction of the old order in the Jewish shtetl community, particularly its institutional and organizational forms, was an easy task to accomplish. Soviet law was instituted as part of the annexation. The destructive phase was relatively mild in the use of open violence and coercion and coincided much of the time with the period of maximum goodwill on the part of the local population and with Soviet endeavours to gain its sympathy. The elimination of the institutions and organizations of the old regime was achieved after the first few months. It was different for the new rulers when they came to root out the various elites that were responsible for running and leading those organizations and institutions. Their removal, with varying intensity, lasted throughout the Soviet rule of the area. The situation was even more complicated with the attempt to destroy some of the basic cultural-religious values and attachments (see chapter 6).

The dissolution of the established order in the Jewish community started with the entry of the Red Army, as if it were a spontaneous decision by all concerned. 'Communal and cultural life ceased by themselves', recalled a survivor from the shtetl Byten.

> All the local institutions ceased to function without outside order or interference. The libraries closed down: the charitable loan society disappeared as did the different mutual aid organizations. The ardent political strife stopped as if the small shtetl did not contain over half a dozen competing 'ideologies'. As if all party differences died all of a sudden. All the Jewish platforms that served as centres for the youth, were eliminated. Everything vanished as if by itself.[5]

From Luck another eyewitness reported in almost identical terms: 'Community and social life of the local Jewish organizations stopped entirely. With the entry of the Red Army nobody dared to call a meeting of an organization or institution. All community or national contacts from that day on went underground.'[6] Even before the new authorities had published a single decree, 'the entire social structure collapsed of its own' maintained a witness from Pinsk.[7] Thus the same story of almost voluntary dissolution of organized Jewish life was repeated in shtetl after shtetl.[8]

The *kehilla*, the Jewish communal organization, ceased to function even before the Polish legal code was abolished officially. The Soviet authorities did not have to decree the dissolution of the *kehilla*. With the new regime it could no longer levy taxes, as it had been entitled to do during the old regime. But what probably counted even more, as with most Jewish organizations, the management and major contributors were people who had every reason to fear the new order. In Grodno, 'the board of the *kehilla* dissolved itself, when the Bolsheviks entered the town. The leaders remained hidden, each in his corner, thanking God for remaining alive, for anonymity', recalled A. Zak in his memoirs of the period.[9] The Jewish elite had few illusions as to the attitude of the new rulers – they knew what had happened to Jewish institutions in the USSR proper and there was no reason to expect anything different in the new Soviet lands. The well-to-do of the Jewish community, who traditionally provided leadership and funds for community activities, were destined to disappear as a class, thus striking a mortal blow to all the Jewish institutions.

The structure of Jewish community autonomy and institutions was such that the dissolution of the *kehilla* precluded the continued normal functioning of the rest. Thus funds for the maintenance of many religious functions and societies such as the synagogues, cemeteries, the rabbinate, social welfare, education, etc. were to a large extent financed through the *kehilla*. Its dissolution meant that other Jewish institutions would shortly cease to function. There were variations from place to place as to when the various organizations stopped functioning. Some of the social welfare societies continued their existence for several months until they ran out of funds.[10] Others were closed down and their funds expropriated immediately with the entry of the Red Army. There were instances when former Jewish organizations were 'coopted' by the new authorities, as was the case with Jewish labour trade unions, which were merged with their Ukrainian and Polish counterparts.[11] Whatever the reason for existing inconsistencies in Soviet policy, by the beginning of 1940 the generations-old autonomous communal structure of the Jewish population in the provinces of Eastern Poland had disappeared for ever.

In the annexed territories, as in the other parts of Poland, existed a broad spectrum of Jewish political movements. Their fate was no different from that of Jewish communal autonomy. As related by one of the Zionist leaders of western Ukraine, all 'political activities of the Jewish parties ceased by themselves. No official prohibition of their activities was pronounced. The activists thought that it would be wise on their part to stop all activities. This act of voluntary dissolution was common to all political parties, Polish, Ukrainian and Jewish alike.'[12] Without any official ban on Jewish political organizations, in all of Eastern Poland the same phenomenon repeated itself: 'voluntary' dismemberment of any existing organized Jewish political entity. A few weeks after the territory was invaded, all Jewish political organizations disappeared. By 1939 it was common knowledge that the USSR did not tolerate any form of independent Jewish political activity. That was sufficient to terminate all open public activities.[13]

During the first few months, one could discern local differences in the attitude of the authorities towards the various Jewish political movements. There were places where, with the cooperation of local Jewish Communists, all political activists were immediately apprehended.[14] The extreme orthodox religious movement, the *Agudat Israel*, was hardly noticed by the authorities, who considered the movement harmless, for a while.[15] The socialist Bund was destined for special treatment by the new regime. It appeared that, because of ideological affinity, thc assumption among Soviet policy-makers was that after removing the Bund's leadership, the rank and file would be easy prey for communist takeover. Hence Bund leaders were the first to be arrested. 'When they entered a shtetl and found there a local Bund society they used to arrest the secretary, call for a meeting and elect a new board. The society remained the same and only the secretary, occasionally a few other leading members, were apprehended. Everything remained as before. Frequently even the pictures on the walls were not replaced', recalled M. Kleinboim (Sne).[16] The two prominent Bund leaders W. Alter and H. Erlich were arrested in the first month of the occupation.[17]

The Zionist parties were destined for the same fate as the other Jewish political organizations. The long years of anti-Zionist propaganda and persecution left no doubts as to the future attitude of the new rulers. The many and varied Zionist parties, associations, unions, clubs, etc. deemed it wise to cease all official public functions. Some stopped their activities altogether, others tried to continue by developing an underground structure.[18] The activities of the youth movement continued underground for some time, trying to maintain contacts between the isolated local Jewry and the outside world.[19]

The communes of the Zionist movement, where pioneers were training in agriculture for their future life in Palestine, were of special interest to the Soviet authorities. Those Zionist organizations were occasionally the target of local authorities who attempted to coopt them and use the communes for Soviet collectivization plans. Whether the result of central policy decision, local initiative, or ineptness, quite a few communes continued a precarious existence for some time in the annexed provinces.[20]

The dissolution of the Jewish public organizations and institutions was an easy and bloodless task. The autonomous structure in its various forms, one of the more lasting features of Jewish ex-territorial life, disappeared almost overnight. The elimination of individuals who gave substance to the institutions and organizations was a much longer process. The people, unlike the organizations, did not fade away by themselves. Some went into hiding, but the majority, who did not flee from the country, were slowly hunted down. This lasted throughout Soviet rule of the territory and involved much human hardship and suffering. This was the 'permanent purge', whose goal went beyond eliminating Jewish leadership, it turned into an attempt to uproot from the midst of the community the leadership infrastructure, and anybody with authority – any person who could provide leadership and thus potentially become a nucleus for opposition or threaten the re-education of the new Soviet citizens. Eventually the Soviet authorities 'purged' the territories of all the 'undesirable' elements, those who could not or would not for whatever reason be integrated and fully trusted.

The destruction of the various elites of the old order in the community was a continuous process with several peaks. It started with the very entrance of the Red Army and did not stop until the last day of Soviet presence. A broad variety of methods was used to root out the undesirables: detention for longer or shorter periods; imprisonment in local penitentiaries; being sent to the USSR proper; removal from one locality to another, particularly from the border areas and larger urban centers; mass-scale deportations to different categories of labour- and prison-camps in Siberia and the Northern parts of the Soviet State. From the evidence available it appears that the Soviets used basically the same criteria for the Jews as for other ethnic groups in the area. The Jews were, however, over-represented in the more suspicious sections of the population. The towns where the Jews lived were more affected than the countryside by the ongoing purge. Large sections of the Jewish community were made up of what was called in Soviet terminology 'non-productive' elements. Jews were disproportionately represented among those that the new regime and communist ideology considered 'class enemies' who had to be eliminated. The relatively large proportion of Jewish refugees, a group which the authorities did not know how to assimilate into Soviet society, contributed its share to the high percentage of Jewish victims. It should be noted, however, that from the evidence available, anti-Semitism played no manifest role in the imprisonments and deportations.

The Soviet governing apparatus entered the provinces of Eastern Poland well prepared in its experience of rooting out enemies of the regime. The most active and sophisticated arm of the administration that came from the East was the security police, the NKVD. Within three or four weeks the NKVD had spread its net over the entire territory.[21] It was a relatively easy task to locate and eliminate the first-line political leaders, those of them who did not escape into non-Soviet territories were apprehended in the first few weeks. But, in order to achieve the much broader aim of destroying the existing leadership infrastructure and undesirable elements of all kinds, the authorities had developed a refined search and control method. State, city and police archives were among the first institutions to be occupied and guarded by the new rulers.[22] They were curious to discover the secrets guarded in the archives. Local collaborators translated from Polish and prepared detailed lists of suspects, to be used in the future. A fine net of informers was spread throughout the territories, in every institution, factory, enterprise and tenement.[23] Local former Communists and new recruits were included among the informers. It should be pointed out that having belonged to the local Communist Party in the past was not a sufficient alibi. The local Communists were frequently suspected of Trotskyite deviations and were therefore targets of suspicion and persecution.[24] Nevertheless, local Jewish Communists played an important role in locating former political activists and compiling the lists of 'undesirables' and 'class enemies'. The NKVD tried, often with success, to recruit people who had previously been active in Jewish institutions and political organizations and thus created an atmosphere of mutual suspicion and fear among former friends and colleagues.[25]

Repeated registrations and passportization were yet other means to control the population and locate and apprehend the undesirables. Registration with the police for various purposes was one of the characteristics of the new regime. By comparing different sources, the NKVD was able to track down people who for one reason or another wished to hide their past. Granting Soviet passports after March 1940 was one of the most important means of control and identification.[26] The Soviet passport was not given to all the inhabitants of the annexed territories: there were those who were simply arrested on the spot;[27] others received passports for shorter than the maximum of five years. Only 'spotless' local inhabitants received regular passports. Many of the indigenous Jews and almost all the refugees received passports valid for shorter periods and with attached 'paragraphs'. This meant the inclusion on the identity card of a section number from the criminal code that specified a specific 'crime' of the owner. Usually it related to social or economic origin or to past political activities. Each paragraph carried with it certain liabilities and limitations.[28] The paragraph most frequently included in passports granted to the Jews was number 11. It was applied to former businessmen, owners of shops or landed property, and bankers as well as to quite a few who did not know exactly what their 'crime' was. The major limitation of paragraph 11 was the restriction to live within one hundred kilometers of the border and in the central cities of the territories. Many were thus forced to move from their homes to smaller shtetlach and villages.

For many Jews living in former Eastern Poland, receiving a Soviet passport involved at least some inconvenience or worse. For the Jewish refugees it meant a clear break with their former homes and families (see pp. 102–16). The passportization, as the registration and granting of Soviet identity cards was called, heightened the suspicions and fears of the population. As with other actions of the new regime, passportization was accompanied by an information-gathering and propaganda campaign: special theatre performances were dedicated to the 'Soviet Passport'.[29] While lines of frightened Jews were waiting for Soviet passports, the Minsk *Oktiaber* was reporting in Yiddish from Bialystok about 'the pride, excitement, joy and the great happiness' awaiting them at the end of the queue.[30] I.

Fefer, the famous Soviet Yiddish author, on a trip in the 'liberated territories' described in yet another Yiddish newspaper, *Der Shtern* of Kiev, the pride of 'being a Soviet citizen, being in possession of a Soviet passport . . . A holiday atmosphere prevailed among the travellers on the train.'[31] Fefer was travelling in company with Jewish refugees, the majority of whom refused to accept Soviet passports.

Registration, the granting of a passport, or any other encounter with the authorities might have served as the preliminary to detention and deportation.

> There were dozens of ways in which one was asked to come to the NKVD. There were some who were simply asked to come over to the nearest police station. Yet that was a rare exception. People were mostly asked to present themselves to the bank, or recruiting center, municipality, education office, etc. The NKVD man was waiting in civilian dress and would utter only three fateful words 'please follow me'. Frequently that was the beginning of a long journey,

related a survivor from Pinsk.[32]

Interrogation, imprisonment and deportation became an integral part of daily life in the cities, shtetlach and villages of the annexed territories. The first arrests were selective and individual in character. Not surprisingly, those arrested were connected with the defunct Polish administration and prominent political and community leaders. Families of officers and soldiers who had become prisoners of war were deported during the first weeks of Soviet rule.[33] The arrested were few, yet their detention followed the warm reception of the Red Army and created an uneasy feeling in the Jewish community as to the future.

Jewish leaders in the different fields of public activity, regardless of ideology or occupation, were from the very beginning prime targets for the NKVD. At the time of the occupation the larger part of the Jewish political and intellectual leadership was to be found in the eastern provinces of Poland. They left Warsaw after 7 September 1939. The Polish government organized special convoys to the East for selected groups.[34] Thus a large section of the Jewish leadership was within easy reach of Soviet police. The arrests, however, were selective and few in number during the first weeks. The goal of the police was to use threatened as well as actual arrest of selected leaders to accelerate the self-dissolution of the Jewish organizations. Their system was also designed to prevent the political movements from going underground, hence what appeared as the haphazard and sporadic nature of the first arrests, although this might also have been the result of the disorder of the Soviet apparatus which was still in the process of getting organized. Systematic arrests were to begin later, as part of a more energetic drive for Sovietization.

The arrests of such prominent leaders as Dr. E. Zomershtein, who was among the more important Jewish delegates to the Sejm;[35] the Bundists Alter and Erlich;[36] the Chief Warsaw Rabbi M. Schorr;[37] and dozens of prominent Zionists,[38] had the desired effect – the dissolution of Jewish institutions and organizations was even further accelerated. Even though almost all of them were later released,[39] at the time 'the arrests during the first weeks horrified the leadership. It started a flight of the entire Jewish leadership. Those who could not escape went into hiding, burning their identity papers . . . many of them fled to Vilnius [Vilno] which became part of Lithuania.'[40] To apprehend those fleeing and hiding, the NKVD used Jewish informers who were positioned in railway stations on the Polish–Lithuanian border, and in streets of the major cities.[41]

Systematic arrests and deportations of the Jewish leadership took place during the first months of 1940. The arrests were still individual in character, but were neither sporadic, random nor limited to small numbers. Now the victims were people at all levels of leadership, from those of national state-wide calibre to those of community and of limited local importance.[42] 'In the spring of 1940 the Soviet authorities had completed the destruction of all the community and political organizations. The leaders of the Bund were arrested and exiled. In April the Zionists were apprehended and deported to labour camps, sentenced to eight years', related an acute observer from Pinsk.[43] 'Systematically and mercilessly all the activists were removed from among the Jewish masses. All those who might or could have expressed opposition to the re-education of the population were eliminated.'

The Jewish community of the former Polish provinces was left leaderless as a result of Soviet policy. The systematic removal of 'any person that carried any authority in the community' was supplemented by the massive flight abroad of Jewish leaders. The migration started even before the arrival of the Soviet troops. In the wake of the Polish government, many Jewish leaders passed over the southern border to Rumania, and then to Palestine and other countries.[44] A new, and what seemed for a while more promising, haven and escape route for Jewish leaders was Vilno, after it was transferred to Lithuania on 27 October 1939. M. Kleinboim (Sne) in his memorandum to N. Goldman on the 'State of East European Jewry at the beginning of World War II', maintained that

> The number of Jewish refugees in Vilnius did not exceed ten thousand. But, they are the spiritual elite of Polish Jewry. To Lithuania fled those Jews who were threatened equally by Nazi and Soviet occupation, i.e. the Jewish intelligentsia of Zionist or Socialist persuasion, Zionist and Bundist leaders, authors, journalists, teachers, scientists, Hassidic and non-Hassidic Rabbis, whole Yeshivot and a large section of the Jewish Plutocracy.[45]

The eastern provinces became a transit area for Jewish leaders and whole organizations on their way to Vilno.[46] The city became the main center for contact with the outside world. The executive boards of most major Jewish organizations found their way to Vilno.[47] Eventually many of the refugees found a way out to the West and Palestine.[48] The net result for the Jewish community in the Soviet-occupied territory was the virtually total loss of its leading elite.

The elimination of leading personalities from the Jewish community was of a selective nature, the arrests of an individual character, and in the final count did not amount to large numbers. However, to consolidate the Soviet hold on the area the former socio-economic structure had to be changed radically. Its ruling classes had to be removed. Thus the majority of those who were arrested and in particular deported were eliminated *en masse*, as entire social groups, and not just as individuals. When individual arrests were carried out, the criteria used were not always obvious to the victims. As far as the mass arrests and deportations were concerned, the criteria were even more vague and loose, following an inner dynamic of ever widening circles of suspects and arrests.

There were several waves of mass deportations of the Jewish community that coincided with those of the population at large.[49] One of the milder methods of removal was the transfer of 'non-productive elements' such as former property owners, merchants, bankers, factory owners, commercial agents, and lawyers together with their families, from towns and shtetlach to smaller or merely other places.[50] The Soviet authorities were following an ancient tradition of dispersing hostile elites, practised already in the fifteenth and sixteenth centuries by the Grand Princes of Muscovy. Thousands of Jews of the more affluent strata of the community were ordered to move to unknown places. There they could hardly find suitable places to live and rarely proper jobs. Even worse for many was the fact that it meant changing overnight from a person with dignity and authority in his community to a homeless refugee in an unknown place.

There were three major deportation waves from the annexed territories in 1940. They started in February and continued in April and June–July. Each wave emphasized a certain section of the population. The first two included many of the community and political leaders. The social and economic undesirables were concentrated in the second and third waves. Jewish refugees constituted a majority in the third wave, of summer 1940.[51] It should be noted, however, that arrests went on throughout the period of Soviet rule and people of all walks of life, social and economic origins, and political persuasions were to be found in all the mass deportations. As the war with Nazi Germany drew closer the authorities in the annexed territories became ever more nervous. The NKVD had little trust in the local population and the result was the beginning of a new wave of deportations on 20–1 June 1941.[52] In some places the NKVD had prepared lists, in other localities it was even less clear this time than on previous occasions why people were deported. 'Jews were kidnapped in the streets, taken from their beds at night', related a deportee from Pinsk.[53] Trains with dozens of wagons moved from different parts of the annexed territory into the USSR proper.[54]

It is difficult to arrive at the precise number of the deported and arrested Jews in the former eastern provinces of Poland. The NKVD files, if they still exist, might have supplied us with more accurate numbers. At present we can arrive at only very rough estimates. There are considerable differences between investigators and specialists in the problem. Thus S. Schwartz maintained that there were about half a million Jews among the deportees from Eastern Poland.[55] B. Weinryb estimated the number to be between 250,000 and 300,000.[56] The Polish Government in Exile estimated the number of Jews among the other deported nationalities as reaching 30 per cent of a total of about 800,000, i.e. approximately 250,000.[57] The latter number, arrived at on the basis of the most reliable sources available on developments in the Soviet-occupied territories, appears the more plausible one.

The destruction of the old order, its institutions, organizations, and leaders brought about the atomization of the Jewish community and the emergence of the lonely Jew. The institutions disappeared completely after a few weeks or months; so did the prominent leaders. The elimination of the lesser leadership took longer, and lasted throughout Soviet rule. The Jewish community of the annexed provinces underwent, more or less the same process of destruction of its long-established order as did other ethnic groups of the region. Yet the effects were somehow different, the consequences harsher. The Soviet authorities destroyed the institutions of the former regime and fought against the nationalistic tendencies of the Poles, Ukrainians and Belorussians in the area. Yet the Kremlin did recognize the Poles, Ukrainians and Belorussians as national entities and acknowledged their national aspirations to be, albeit in a certain guise, legitimate. Not so the Jews. Their national aspirations were condemned and an effort made to force them away from their distinct existence. The special character of Jewish existence made the Soviet policy of destroying the institutions and eliminating the leadership of the former order particularly harmful.

The structure and the very basis of the continued existence of a separate Jewish community were destroyed. Other ethnic groups lost their institutions and leaders, and had to change their life-styles, yet they were reorganized and treated as collective national entities. The Jewish population lost almost all the institutions that expressed its collective existence and were denied any national recognition. Even worse, aspirants of Jewish nationhood were deemed state enemies and as such were persecuted. For hundreds of years the Jews had developed and refined special tools for collective action to defend and preserve their separate identity. Overnight these tools were abolished. Thus came to an end age-old instruments for dealing with the anxieties of the individual and the distress of the collective. The result was the atomization of the Jewish community, the emergence of the lonely Jew. For the first time in the history of the community the individual was left without any collective organization and at the same time the leadership disappeared, whether through arrest, deportation or flight. No attempt was made to provide an alternative Jewish elite, as was the case with other national groups. The ever-present danger of arrest and fear of informers undermined long-established human ties between close friends and relationships in the community. The individual Jew had nowhere to turn to in time of need and distress, except to his closest family. This was to have dire consequences in the near future.

5
Learning to Live with the Soviet Economic System

There was a considerable amount of goodwill towards the new rulers in the Jewish community. A tendency to adapt and integrate into the Soviet economic system characterized large sections of the Jewish population. Yet there were objective factors which made the transition from the former economic and social structure to the emerging Soviet regime difficult and painful. Some of the difficulties were shared by the entire population of the annexed provinces. They were the result of the general poverty of the area, the scarcity of natural resources, the low level of industrialization and the general backward agrarian structure of the economy of the region. The population at large suffered from the dislocations following the war and the breaking up of the Polish supply and marketing system. The Jewish community experienced a scarcity of basic necessities, along with the rest of the population, and also suffered from the dissolution of the former economic order and the attendant miseries, which affected other ethnic groups. They were subject to the same rules, decrees and laws as the Poles, Ukrainians and Belorussians living in Eastern Poland – the introduction of Soviet labour rules and norms affected everybody. However, there were problems that faced the Jewish community in a more acute form than that encountered by other groups.

The incompatibility between the socio-economic structure of the Jewish population and the Soviet economic system and ideology was obvious. The preponderance of Jews in occupations considered negative, class inimical, or non-productive (one of the more benevolent designations in the Soviet vocabulary), required special attention and plans. The presence of many thousands of Jewish refugees complicated the situation even further. Yet there was no special treatment for those who found difficulty in adjusting; no plan or agency was directed to tackle the unique Jewish economic problems. There was no local counter-part to the *Evsektsiia* of the 1920s which might mitigate the transformation that took place in the Jewish community. The Stalinist model, which paid no attention to local differences or ethnic, religious idiosyncracies, was imposed on the annexed territories. The Jews were to be absorbed into the mainstream of Soviet life through industrialization and collectivization. They were left to cope alone, to find their own way and to learn to live in the new economic order. The Jews as a group had, however, the accumulated experience of flexibility and adjustment to changing circumstances which they applied in the new situation.

The entrance of Soviet troops did not mean an immediate end to the suffering that resulted from the dislocations caused by the Polish–German war. Actually, for a while, the situation was even exacerbated. The disruption of the regular supply channels created an acute shortage in basic necessities, mainly food. It took several months for the new rulers to establish their own supply and distribution systems. Until then the authorities ordered the former shop owners and artisans to continue their business. Many of the reports that reached the outside world relate to the first few months of Soviet rule. No wonder that the dominant theme was the hardship and misery of the Jewish community under the new rulers. After the first days of enthusiasm came the great disillusionment: 'Bread, a plain loaf of bread, a herring, several hundred grams of sugar, a piece of meat or butter – their attainment became the main concern of the people in the "liberated territories" of western Ukraine and Belorussia', related M. Kleinboim.[1] The food shortage created a panic situation:

> One cannot receive the food through regular channels of commerce. You have to get up early in the morning to queue for bread. All the members of the family have to stand in line to get, by their common effort, the minimal portion of food. Whole days, until late at night the entire population is standing in lines ... It became the major topic of conversation at home, with friends, in the club.[2]

The shortages did not disappear even at the end of 1939. On the contrary, there were items that completely disappeared from the stores. The great influx of refugees from the German-occupied territory of Poland, the buying of all consumer goods by the Red Army soldiers as well as dislocations in transportation and regular supply patterns combined to create and exacerbate the shortages. There is no doubt that the insufficient supply of food and other basic products affected the mood and attitude of the Jewish community towards the Soviet regime. The most acute shortages disappeared in time after the stabilization of the situation and establishment of the regular Soviet channels of supply and distribution.[3] One has, however, to note that shortages in many basic items and the resulting queues are characteristic of Soviet economic life and did not vanish from the occupied areas altogether as long as they were part of the USSR. A witness from Jezierzany who lived through the entire period, recalled:

> There were lines for the most needed commodities. Yet people bought everything, whether needed or not. It was a disease – this panic of hoarding. After a few weeks all the stock disappeared. With time the flow of supplies improved considerably. But throughout the entire period of Soviet rule the queues did not disappear and people were always lining up before the selling counters.[4]

The destruction of the former economic order in the Jewish community started slowly. The pseudo-NEP, as the transition period might be called, allowed the combined existence of small-scale private enterprise in commerce and production. The small shop-owner and artisan, so characteristic of the shtetl were not only allowed to function by the incoming authorities, but were even encouraged and ordered by decree to continue business as usual.[5] Nationalization, at the beginning of Soviet rule, meant the confiscation of banks, larger factories, larger estates and houses. The criteria for nationalization were ill-defined and depended on interpretation and implementation by local committees. The latter tended frequently to be harsher in the implementation than was actually intended by their mentors from the East. The richer families had played an important role in Jewish communal and public life, but this numerically very small group within the Jewish community was affected by the first wave of nationalization of the larger fortunes in the annexed provinces. Even the people directly concerned were persecuted at this stage beyond the loss of ownership of their property.

It was obvious that the attempt to return to normal economic activity with the functioning of a 'mixed economy' was just a temporary expedient, but people were willing to cooperate. They dreaded the alternative. When asked, by a local businessman, what would happen to them in the future, whether it would be the fate of the Nepman in the USSR, the military governor replied 'There is no place for comparison. Your activities are needed and will be rewarded in the future by the authorities.'[6]

The pseudo-NEP coincided with maximum disruption of ordinary economic life and was destined to disappear. There were also obvious departures from accepted Soviet practice. The owners of the larger fortunes were not yet deported, or arrested, or transferred to other places in the annexed territories. In many enterprises the former owners were asked to remain in a managing or advisory capacity, a practice reminiscent of the first years following the October Revolution.[7] Small shops and artisans' workshops continued to operate, but under conditions that were obviously designed to bring about their final collapse without official closure or confiscation. The monetary and fiscal policies as well as the supply situation were expected to do the job of eliminating small, privately-owned enterprises in the annexed territories. One has to remember that when speaking of shopkeepers and artisans in the new Soviet areas one is actually dealing with a group whose vast majority were Jews. The Polish zloty was made equal to the Soviet rouble and both became legal tender in the area. The influx of a huge army of soldiers and civilian officials starved for consumer goods literally emptied the stores and all available stocks of the workshops. Prices rose daily despite official policy.[8] Yet even the piles of paper money brought in by rising prices could not replenish the stores nor provide raw materials for the workshops. Extremely high taxes made the continued existence of the small enterprise and business impossible and they closed down gradually within the first few months of Soviet rule. Thus large sections of the old economic order were vanishing by themselves. Thousands of Jews were looking for new jobs – the declassed, the newly unemployed joined those who had been jobless before the annexation and swelled the lines at the labour bureaux. They lived by selling their belongings, and while some turned to shady dealings on the black market, others looked for outside help and welfare.[9]

Towards the end of 1939 there were increasing signs that the Soviet authorities had decided to get rid of the vestiges of the former economic order in the annexed territories. There was no reason to perpetuate a different regime within the boundaries of the Soviet State. Relatively little formal enactments were needed by now to dispose of any private enterprise still existing. The small shops and workshops closed down one by one. The massive arrival of technical and administrative personnel from the East and the removal from managerial positions of former owners indicated that an effort was being made towards economic Sovietization.[10]

Yet, the most blatant and harshest sign of the end of the 'special treatment' of the annexed provinces was the sudden abolition of the Polish zloty as legal tender in the area on 1 January 1940. No warning or transition period was given. Only 300 zloty could be exchanged, the rest was lost.[11] For many families it meant the loss of their savings and the entire capital for running their businesses. These developments affected mainly the middle and lower middle classes, in which many of the Jews were concentrated. Another group of Jews who suffered were the tens of thousands of homeless and jobless refugees, who lived on Polish money brought from their former homes. As a result many of the refugees tried to return to German-held territory.[12] The wiping out of many of the financial resources of the local population had an equalizing effect. 'Within an hour, in one stroke everybody became poor: he who owned a million Zloty and he whose entire property did not exceed a few Zloty', recalled M. Grosman, a prominent journalist and an author who lived at the time in Bialystok, of the consequences of the Soviet action.[13] Even people who had hesitated or had been reluctant to look for a job 'were forced now to search and accept any job offered by the only employers – the government. From the beginning of 1940 everybody joined the proletariat. All of us who had no permanent income became Soviet workers gradually adjusting to the labour conditions of the USSR.' related an inhabitant of Pinsk.[14] The end of the pseudo-NEP meant, for practical purposes, one of the final blows to the former economic order of the Jewish community.

To find a job was not that easy in the former Polish provinces, particularly for the large numbers of middle- and lower-middle-class Jews. Finding a job and earning a living, which were not necessarily identical, meant adjusting to the emerging Soviet regime. The integration into the new economic system by the Jewish community was variable and complex. It varied according to socio-economic background, place of domicile and age group.

The Soviet administration, in its efforts to return to normal conditions in the annexed territories, gave special attention to the acute unemployment problem. Labour exchange offices had been opened to take care of the unemployed.[15] Industrialization and collectivization were the Soviet solutions for the economic problems of the annexed territories, but these were processes that took many years to mature. The authorities tried to solve the unemployment problem by reactivating the local industries, by public works and by drawing much manpower into the growing services offered by Soviet institutions.[16] Trained labour found employment relatively easily. Thus we have reports as early as January 1940 of shortages in masons, printers, technicians in the textile industry, etc.[17] 'Unemployment is disappearing gradually' read the title of the *Oktiaber* on 16 January 1940. The report reflected the reality as it began to emerge at the end of the first winter of Soviet rule. During February to April 1940 we can find numerous reports in the Soviet Yiddish press of the decrease and then almost complete elimination of unemployment from the new lands of the USSR.[18] In the spring of 1940, except for particularly difficult cases, like that of the refugees, unemployment as a major problem almost vanished from the annexed provinces. The special labour exchanges, formed to tackle the problem, began to close down.[19] 'After the liquidation of the private enterprises work became available to everyone, whether needed or not. All men and women who wanted and were capable of working received jobs in state enterprises. Whoever had finished even an elementary school received a government post without any difficulties' as an inhabitant of the area summarized the situation.[20] Under the Soviet regime one had to work, not only to maintain oneself but also so as not to be thrown into jail as a loiterer.[21]

The economic backwardness of the annexed territories and their meagre natural resources made it extremely difficult to solve the unemployment problem locally. The authorities tried to deal with the problem on a higher, USSR-wide, level. The unemployed were offered jobs in the USSR itself. In a way, it was one more example of the general Soviet policy of developing the eastern regions. As early as September 1939,[22] the Soviet authorities started registering people for work in different parts of the USSR, mainly in the mines and factories of the Donbas, the Urals, the Caucasus and Central Asia.[23] Some, particularly experts and people with special training, were offered jobs in the pre-annexation Soviet territories of Belorussia and Ukraine.[24] Whether out of a genuine desire to alleviate the lot of the unemployed, or merely to attract much-needed labour to Soviet enterprises, the authorities offered tempting conditions to those willing to move east. Free transport, advance payment and contracts that included attractive living and work conditions were offered to the new Soviet citizens.[25]

It is impossible to ascertain how many Jews actually registered and went east, yet we have enough evidence to conclude that there were thousands who took advantage of the offer.[26] They included newly arrived refugees (see pp. 109–11), and local Jews who were jobless even before the arrival of the Soviets. A large proportion of those registered were young people who were tempted by the promises of representatives of Soviet enterprises who toured the annexed territories to recruit local labour. They were lured by tempting descriptions of the charms of the Caucasus, the sunshine of Central Asia and opportunities to learn new professions and develop their skills in the modern enterprises of the Donbas and Urals.[27]

The Soviet authorities were adept in organizing impressive demonstrations. They used the departure of thousands of people to work in the USSR in a propaganda campaign to emphasize the attractions and advantages of being a citizen of the 'mighty Soviet Union'. High-sounding slogans, patriotic speeches, orchestras and flags accompanied the convoys on departure and arrival. However, those involved in the project of providing work in the USSR for the unemployed of the western provinces of Belorussia and Ukraine underestimated the objective difficulties involved. It became clear to both sides within a few months that it might be a mistake to transfer thousands of unskilled and inexperienced workers to the Soviet interior. For a while the Soviet Yiddish press was full of enthusiastic reports, songs and letters, in the best tradition of the period, about the 'new life in a new fatherland'.[28] The letters published in the press 'thanked comrade Stalin' in the most enthusiastic terms, for the opportunity offered to 'work and contribute to the upbuilding of socialism'.[29] They described the help given by the local population to the newcomers and their fast adjustment to Soviet working conditions. Many were said to have become outstanding workers.[30] The coverage of the subject in the Soviet press became scanty after March 1940, and the subject disappeared from official publications within a few months. It was a reflection of the real situation of the registrants. The true story had already become known in the annexed territories in March and was leaked to the Western press.[31]

The entire enterprise turned out to be a fiasco. Work was difficult for those who were not accustomed to hard physical labour. Contrary to promises, housing and food were inadequate – even compared to the low standards of Eastern Poland. A large number of registrants reacted in a way that proved that they had not yet become true Soviet citizens. Contrary to the behaviour of the ordinary Soviet citizen, the 'westerners' left their work without permission and tried to return to their former homes. Several hundred, finding themselves stuck in Minsk, staged a demonstration, an act almost unheard of in Stalin's USSR.[32] The authorities, shocked by the 'unconventional' reaction, decided that time to let it pass and arranged the transfer of the derelicts to other places. Many appeared in the towns and shtetlach of the annexed provinces only a few months after leaving them.[33] The local authorities were not as lenient as their comrades had been in Minsk. Shortly after arrival, many of the returnees were apprehended and put in jail or deported to labour camps.[34]

Even after the formal incorporation of the territories into the USSR, the new citizens were prevented from moving east without a special permit. Like other Soviet citizens the new ones were restricted in their freedom of movement. The economic problem had to be resolved at the local level. The most promising employers for many Jews appeared to be the emerging Soviet administration and services. We have seen above the crucial role played by Jews during the transition period and the establishment of the first Soviet institutions in the new territories. Yet, the prominent role of the Jews in the temporary administration was a transient phenomenon. Attempting to build a new administrative structure, the Communist authorities had to take into account many, at times contradictory, factors. There was a special urgency to build up a reliable Soviet system, hence, there was no time for thorough training of local personnel. While pretending to be liberators, the Soviet government had few illusions as to the goodwill and gratitude of the local population. Finding itself in a new and unknown environment the Soviet government reacted with suspicion and distrust. The Red Army had come officially to rescue its Ukrainian and Belorussian brethren. Therefore, naturally, the new authorities had to prefer the Ukrainians and Belorussians in administrative appointments. But the local population, particularly the Ukrainians, expressed strong nationalistic and anti-Russian feelings. The

Poles, the former rulers of the lands, resented the conquerors and were justly suspected in return. Those who remained of the local Communists were suspected of Trotskyite deviations. The Jewish population, particularly in the shtetlach, presented a large reservoir of manpower that could be trusted not to cooperate with the Germans beyond the borders. It was also relatively well-educated and available for recruitment because of its high unemployment rate.

How did the Soviets resolve these conflicting factors while building up the administration in their new lands? The solution was not always well-defined or absolutely consistent. Nevertheless, the picture that emerges is sufficiently clear. The Soviet policy was to rely as much as possible on people coming from the east. The easterners (vostochniki) occupied the controlling positions in the local administration from the very beginning.[35] Their number increased all the time. Local Ukrainians and Belorussians occupied subordinate positions, particularly where elections were involved, and the Jews were employed in the lower ranks and in posts requiring special training.

Thus, as a rule, the more important positions in the administration went to the easterners. It was true for small shtetlach as for enterprises in the larger towns. 'All the positions of any weight in the new civil administration, even in a small shtetl like ours were given to officials brought over specially from the other side of the old border. Local officials were appointed only to minor positions mainly of a technical nature. No local people at all could be found in the regional party office.' related an inhabitant of Mlynow, near Rowno.[36] Easterners occupied many of the managerial and professional positions and even those of mere skilled workers in the local enterprises, railways, cooperatives, universities, etc.[37] The great influx of personnel from the east exacerbated the already difficult housing situation in the annexed territories. The families from the USSR, starved of consumer goods, as were the Red Army soldiers, contributed their share to the shortages of food and other basic commodities. Special salaries, housing arrangements, vacations and even restaurants were designated for the easterners. No wonder that, in spite of the official ideology there was distrust mixed with disdain felt towards the locals who occupied only subordinate, minor positions.[38]

The fate of the local communists, mostly Jews in the shtetl was instructive. They had been persecuted in independent Poland, and quite a few spent many years in prison with hard labour. They played an important role in the transition period and in the forming of a temporary administration. As long-time believers, the Communists expected to be rewarded for their past suffering and present expressions of loyalty. Yet no gratitude or reward was forthcoming from the new rulers. There are indications that there were instructions from the central Soviet authorities not to employ local Communists and to treat them with the utmost caution.[39] During the transition period the local Communists were used, nevertheless in helping build up the Soviet system. After the formal annexation local Communists were systematically removed from responsible positions, some were even arrested. Many of them received subordinate administrative appointments, particularly in fields where knowledge of local conditions or direct contact with the population was required. They were employed in factories, schools, the militia, as NKVD informers and later as propagandists in the election campaigns.[40]

Officially there was no discrimination against Jews at any level of the Soviet administration. Yet in reality Jews were hardly to be found in the highest levels, whether elected or appointed. It reflected the situation in the USSR itself in the late thirties. Jews, who occupied a disproportionately high proportion of commanding positions, state and party, during the revolution and the twenties, became scarce in leadership posts in the thirties. In the annexed territories Jews were under-represented in the various national assemblies that decided on joining the USSR.[41] Even before the formal incorporation of the provinces, the principles of 'democratic centralism' were used by the new rulers to ensure the desirable composition of the assemblies. Some Jews were asked not to run for election.[42] Thus in the Ukraine out of 1495 representatives only 20 were Jews, and in Belorussia only 72 out of 926. Not a single Jew was among the representatives to the Supreme Soviet of the USSR in the elections of March 1940. Jews were under-represented in city councils and as mayors. In Lvov, where 30 per cent of the population was Jewish, only 2 out of 160 members of the city Soviet were Jews.[43] In places such as Sarny[44] or Kolomyja,[45] which had absolute Jewish majorities, the mayors elected were Ukrainians. In places where Jews headed the temporary committees during the transition period, they were replaced, almost without exception by Ukrainians or Belorussians.[46]

From the very beginning, Jewish representation in the higher echelons of party and government in the new territories reflected the current situation of Stalin's USSR. Prominent positions in the provinces were usually given to Ukrainians and Belorussians.

Turning to the lower levels, as well as to technical professional personnel in the Soviet administration and institutions, the situation was completely different. Large numbers of Jews were available and willing to enter the service of the new regime. Officially, for the first time in the history of the area, no legal discrimination against Jews existed, and there were almost no reports of unofficial discriminatory practices, excepting at the higher levels of appointments. They availed themselves of the new openings in fields hitherto almost completely closed to them. In the militia, even in commanding positions one could find many Jews acting enthusiastically to strengthen the new regime.[47] 'Offices and institutions that never saw a Jew on their premises abound now with Jewish personnel of all kinds', reported an eye-witness from eastern Galicia, now western Ukraine.[48] Quite frequently 'there were no others available for the job. The Ukrainian intelligentsia was nationalist in its outlook, having only a negligible number of communists. Among the Poles there were no communists at all. So, they [the authorities] had to turn to the Jews', related a report from Lvov.[49] No wonder that foreign witnesses who happened to observe the events taking place in the territories thought that 'Jews received preferential treatment and were given administrative posts', as did the British Consul from Galatj, Rumania.[50] Before the spring of 1940, professionals like doctors and engineers were not scrutinized too closely even about past political loyalties. Moreover, Jews with a middle-class background and past Zionist allegiances were accepted for work at the time.[51]

Being a highly bureaucratic regime the Soviet rulers considerably increased the size and functions of the local administration thus providing many new jobs for the eager-to-serve Jewish unemployed. Places like Baranowicz or Lubcza became centres of new administrative subdivisions with many new jobs. 'The Jews of Lubcza generally, were well-established economically. There was no shortage of work or jobs and anti-Semitism was dormant. The only ones to suffer were those who had been merchants in the past. Yet even some of them received physical or office jobs', recalled a Lubcza Jew.[52] 'The local labour office made every effort to provide people with suitable jobs', reports an inhabitant of Dubno. The report concludes:

> There were many and varied jobs, and it was not too difficult to find appropriate employment. Officials were needed in all the institutions and offices that were reorganized. New schools needed teachers, principals, inspectors. Public works required officials and personnel in offices, warehouses, food facilities ... All those who wanted to work or to study could do so.[53]

And in the same tone, in Slonim

> life became, externally at least, normal in the second half of 1940. The new regime needed many officials, clerks, helpers of all kinds. The administrative staff with its offices, warehouses, stores, absorbed many many workers. This large and intricate apparatus found it difficult to absorb only the group of the more affluent and the elderly ... But the young generation found its way easily. Before Jewish youth were opened fields of economic and administrative activity they could only dream of during the Polish dominance.[54]

Similar reports, relating to the absorbtion of a large number of Jews in the growing Soviet administration, are available from many other shtetlach of the annexed provinces.[55]

There were two groups that found it relatively easy to integrate into the Soviet economic system: the professional technical intelligentsia and the youth. T. Fuks, travelling through the region in 1940 found that 'the youth and the working intelligentsia were really happy, as if awakened to new life. New and unheard of opportunities for work were opened up before them.'[56] B. Weinryb's assertion that 'the greater part of the Jewish intelligentsia was deprived of the possibility of earning a living in their own occupation' is greatly exaggerated.[57] It is true that members of the legal profession, lawyers and journalists or authors had difficulty in finding employment under the new regime. Quite often these professions were intimately connected with the former social-economic order and the prevailing ideologies in the Jewish community. It should be noted that much of the information on developments in Soviet-occupied territory came from people with such a professional background and hence, occasionally, a distorted picture was received. But the vast majority of Jews with professional or technical training of whatever kind were easily absorbed into the Soviet system. After a short period of transition and adjustment, the expanding Soviet administration, industrial enterprises, welfare and education services of various kinds willingly accepted the Jewish engineers, doctors, pharmacists, accountants, agronomists, teachers, etc.[58] Many who had no chance of getting a decent job in independent Poland were given the chance to work, develop talents and advance in their professional careers.[59]

The younger generation that in independent Poland had faced an extremely bleak future now took advantage of the opportunities offered by the new rulers. Jewish youth took literally the promises of equality and justice for all pronounced by the Soviets. Typical of the prevailing mood in the small shtetl was that conveyed by an Iwie resident: 'New and broad horizons were opened before the Jewish youth of the shtetl, living in conditions of economic degradation, deprived of any chance for social progress and economic success in anti-Semitic Poland. Jewish youth strived to study, to enter the universities, technical institutes and the scientific institutions of the great Soviet state.'[60] Jewish youth in the shtetl found life easier and more promising than ever before. The absence of former obligations and commitments facilitated their integration into the new system. Universities and other institutions of higher learning were opened up with the abolition of the *Numerus Clausus* that had limited the number of Jewish students in independent Poland.[61] Many vocational schools were established and special courses in professional training were offered to the young, e.g. courses for mechanics of different sorts, teachers, nurses, accountants, cooperative managers, laboratory technicians, and many others.[62] Younger people who were looking for more promising opportunities left the shtetl and moved to larger urban centers. This was a continuation of a trend noticed before the Red Army entered the eastern provinces, only now there were more incentives to move and study, and job opportunities in institutions of higher learning, professional courses, factories and administration became more abundant and accessible for the Jewish.[63] 'There were many enticing offers and quite a few of the young left the shtetl. They went to study, or to work or to far away Crimea . . . After a while only the old and children were left', related a Tuczyn resident.[64] This mobility and willingness to adapt and integrate, with all its attendant dangers of loss of Jewish identity, fostered the impression that 'a new generation had grown that believed that the new regime opened new horizons for study, improvement, progress. The youth literally bloomed.'[65]

The middle and lower-middle classes – owners of banks, factories and large estates, richer merchants, as well as self-employed small shopkeepers and independent artisans – who taken together constituted a majority in the Jewish community, faced difficult adjustment problems. They were considered by the Communist regime to be 'at best' non-productive elements and many were dubbed as outright 'class enemies'. What made the situation worse was the inability to escape one's class origin. It stuck to one by being included in the passport and was also transferred automatically to the children. Theoretically, people with a bourgeois background could get a job, yet the jobless, besides not having a regular salary, also faced the ever-present danger of being branded a 'negative element'. It was a vicious circle of being punished for your past and being prevented from changing it – the punishment for having been non-productive in the past prevented one from becoming productive in the present. But the Soviet system was not so consistent or efficient as to impose a uniform approach on all who had been property owners in the past. A major distinction was made between the large property owners and self-employed shopkeepers or artisans. The artisans, in particular, were treated more favourably than the others.

The group hardest hit was that of the larger property owners. Their property was confiscated during the first few weeks after the entry of the Red Army. The very rich who had been carriers of the defeated capitalist system were destined to disappear as a class from society. Quite a few were physically uprooted from the community and transferred to other places in the annexed territories or deported to labour camps in the interior of the USSR (see pp. 34–9). Their homes, furniture and other valuables were given to newly arrived Soviet officials from the east.[66] During the first few months, as we have seen above, many of the owners were employed in their former enterprises as advisers and assistant managers. With the end of the pseudo-NEP the former owners were replaced, mostly by arrivals from the east. The so-called *Gvirim*, very rich in relative terms, disappeared from the shtetl. Yet not all who belonged to that class fled the country or found themselves exiled or deported – the criteria for classification were not so clear-cut nor was the Soviet approach so efficient. It is obvious that many found a way to live with the system. There were those who kept a 'low profile' as assistants, or even as simple labourers in their former enterprises.[67] Others after being transferred to other places in the region, adjusted to changed circumstances, concealed their bourgeois origin and used their talents to earn a living.[68] Those who were not imprisoned or deported, and remained where they had always lived, looked for any job they could find to avoid the vicious circle of being branded as non-productive. Former wealthy members of the Jewish community became unskilled labourers, clerks, and manual workers.[69] 'One could meet respectable Jews who only yesterday had been great merchants and today were sweeping the streets of the Shtetl', recalled an inhabitant of Czortkow.[70]

The smaller shopkeepers, who were allowed to operate their stores during the pseudo-NEP, were, according to the designation of the regime a petty bourgeois element. As such they were destined to disappear in the new economic system. After their shops were emptied and new supplies did not arrive, the small stores closed one by one (see pp. 43–5). No attention was paid by the new rulers to that large group of Jews which had no profession and hence no readily available jobs. They certainly needed special training to adjust to the Soviet economic system. Left to their own devices they accepted any job that came their way, even if it was temporary, so as to earn a living and to avoid being stigmatized as 'parasites' and 'loafers'.[71] They looked for jobs that would legitimize their existence in the new society. The new supply networks of stores, warehouses and consumer cooperatives provided many jobs for Jews who had lost their stores or were formerly connected with commercial establishments.[72] Many thousands of Jews were absorbed into the Soviet marketing and supply system which was, like other branches of the economy, inefficient and labour intensive.[73]

The small workshop owner, or self-employed artisan, enjoyed special favour from the Communist rulers. Ideological and practical considerations combined to single out the artisans as a class for more favourable treatment than other lower-middle-class elements. Many of the Jewish artisans had found it difficult to make a living in independent Poland. Primitive working conditions, intense competition with their fellows, government restrictions and taxes brought many craftsmen to the verge of hunger. No wonder that many Jewish artisans could be considered proletarian as far as their standard of living was concerned. Many were among the poor of the community, and frequently their ideological inclinations reflected their low economic status. Therefore, when the Red Army occupied the provinces, Jewish artisans were among those who reacted favourably to the change of rule. To a large extent the favourable attitude was reciprocated by the new authorities. When asked what would happen to the small artisans and shopkeepers, the political commissar accompanying the advancing troops in eastern Galicia replied 'Don't worry, you will not be lost. Your life will be better than under Polish rule. Open the workshops and continue your work.'[74] The artisans were satisfied; they had heard about the artels (cooperatives of small producers) in the USSR. Their satisfaction was great when they heard that by joining an artel they could maintain the ownership of their workshops.[75] In a backward region, like the former eastern provinces of Poland, the artisans were a most important economic group. Many of the activities associated with the production of everyday consumer commodities, from the baking of bread to the producing of clothing and repair of machinery, were done by small artisans. This was another reason for more lenient treatment by the authorities. However, in the communist regime, the desired form of production was not the independent artisan, but the artel – the producers' cooperative. During the pseudo-NEP period the small producer continued to operate almost as before. There was no confiscation or decrees closing down independent workshops. But the great demand of Soviet personnel, shortages of raw material and high taxes frequently constituted an unbearable burden for the independent artisan.[76] Gradually the reserves of raw materials were used up and new supplies were scanty or absolutely unobtainable. This was the result of genuine shortages as well as government pressure.[77] The very high taxation imposed by the authorities was, according to numerous sources, the strongest incentive to join the new artels. 'The artisans were not forced to join or form cooperatives by the authorities, it was achieved by the tax burden', recalls a Stryj resident.[78] 'So high were the taxes on the independent single producer that he had to close down his workshop and join others in forming a cooperative. Eventually all the artisans in town joined', maintains M. Bromberg from Pinsk.[79] And from Semiatycz yet another artisan reports that 'the taxes imposed were so high, that private workshops were forced to close down one after another.'[80]

Producers' cooperatives began to be formed within a few weeks of the entry of the Red Army.[81] Unlike the small store-owners, who disappeared with the pseudo-NEP in the spring of 1940, the independent artisan continued to exist throughout the entire 21 months of Soviet rule. The establishment of new co-operatives and their formation from existing enterprises too went on throughout the same period. Organizing a new cooperative took time, thus a tailors' artel in Lipniszki was organized only at the beginning of 1941, 'when all the tailors of the shtetl with their sewing machines were concentrated in one place. There all of them worked together and the customer could choose any tailor for himself.'[82] The independent artisans usually tried to keep their private workshops as long as possible. They refused to join government sponsored artels, fearing collectivization and being reluctant to become what they dubbed 'officials'.[83] The Jewish artisans joined the cooperatives only when the pressures became unbearable. The authorities, on their part, tried to encourage the forming of cooperatives not only by fiscal pressures and by imposing difficulties in the receiving of new supplies, but also by using positive enticements. The central authorities for crafts and cooperatives of the Ukrainian and Belorussian republics provided the annexed territories with professional, financial and other material assistance.[84] The authorities on the spot took the initiative in bringing together those of the same craft, helping to organize management, to get suitable premises for the new cooperative and to finance the buying of equipment and raw material.

The Soviet Yiddish press devoted much space to the artisans and their cooperatives in what they called the western Ukraine and Belorussia. But, as on many other subjects of great interest, the Soviet press of the period is very meagre in precise information. Instead we find detailed reports on the gratitude to Stalin among the Jewish artisans. There are detailed descriptions of cultural and ideological activities that were taking place in the cooperatives. They had their wall news-sheets, 'Red Corners and Lenin Corners' groups for the study of Russian and Ukrainian for drama and choir, lectures on current affairs and, most importantly, almost all had study groups for the 'Stalin Constitution'.[85] From the fragmentary statistics and in between the lines of the over-zealous reports one can gain, occasionally, a view of the less glamorous side of the picture. Thus we find that from October 1939 to February 1940 in the western region of Belorussia 173 artels were formed with 4927 members. It was planned to establish, by the end of 1940, 370 new artels with 10,000 members.[86] We read that on 4 March 1940 the cooperative movement had reached the most remote places, but that it was still in its initial stages, and much had yet to be done. Many of the artels were still inefficient and needed help from the central authorities who had 'not yet lived up to their promises of help'.[87] And in the same tone we find complaints and criticism coming from Bialystok, where 'as a rule the artels have not yet succeeded in organizing their work efficiently and systematically in spite of their achievements.'[88] But from the scanty and very general information on the development of the producers' cooperatives which appeared in the Soviet press, even that in Yiddish, one can find very little on the specifically Jewish aspects.

The Jewish artisans as a group and as individuals fared relatively well under the Soviet regime. When compared to the conditions which had prevailed for many of them in independent Poland, there was probably even an improvement. Discrimination, and often cut-throat competition with fellow artisans characterized the former situation. Many lived in terrible housing conditions, with workshop and living quarters in the same shabby room. No wonder that Soviet and non-Soviet sources agree that the artisans' standard of living improved. 'Unrestricted competition characterized the life of the Jewish artisan under Polish government. Now under Soviet rule, with the establishment of the artels life became easier, more human', claimed a report from Grodno.[89] Interestingly enough, a resident of Grodno, in describing the situation of the Jewish community under Soviet rule during the spring of 1941, emphasizes that 'During the Pesach festival there was no shortage of traditional commodities . . . The material conditions of the Jews in general and of the artisans in particular were considerably better than under Polish government.'[90] The Jewish shoemaker was, for some reason, particularly favoured in the Soviet Yiddish press and one of the folk-heroes of the regime. A great many shoemakers or their sons occupied important positions among the Jewish cultural officials in the Soviet establishment. 'He was now a new man. Awakened to new life and creativity' – thus was described the shoemaker in an article entitled 'The Ascent of the Worker-Cobbler' 'Now, the cobblers of Grodno in large spacious halls, lighted and heated, produce. They achieve now what they have missed in the past.'[91] The tailor was yet another artisan hero of the regime. Therefore, the changes that took place in the life of 'Leibl the Tailor in his new apartment' were depicted in great detail. Under the Poles he had lived in a one-room apartment that was dark, cold and leaky, with hunger a frequent visitor. Now Leibl, from Nowogrodek, owns a two-room apartment, works lightly instead of 14 hours a day, his children attend school and are never hungry. Like other artisans he enjoys health insurance and gets paid when ill.[92] It should be noted that the description of the artisans' lot under Soviet rule, while couched in the highly exaggerated language of the Stalinist era, did not make unreasonable claims, and by and large corresponds to what is known to have been true. In a more restrained style, the Soviet claims are corroborated by other sources. There is no doubt that in relative terms the material situation of the Jewish artisans improved. What is more, there was a radical change in their social status. Now they were regarded as being close to proletarians in origin, which was no small matter under the new rulers,[93] whereas before in the former social order the artisans, particularly tailors, and shoemakers, were at the lower levels.

Life under the Soviet regime was difficult, even for people used to the low living standards which had prevailed in the eastern provinces of Poland.

There was a general reduction in the standard of living. It was particularly noticeable during the first few months of Soviet rule with dislocation of the supply and marketing organization. But even after the establishment of new supply routes and distribution systems and when Soviet salaries were finally paid, hardship did not completely disappear. The salaries were not sufficient and in order to maintain even a minimum standard of living, two members of the family had to work or 'supplement' their salaries from some other source.[94] We shall see later how people managed to earn more than their regular wages, yet it is important to emphasize that it was very difficult to get along with just one salary. The result, of course, was a decrease in motivation to work, and in production.[95] Soviet labour relations and discipline were yet another unpleasant surprise for the new citizens of the Union. Strict discipline, change of working place being barred without permit, enforced overtime even on rest days and meetings and indoctrination after working hours made life miserable for many. From the summer of 1940, following German successes in Western Europe, there was a general worsening of working conditions in the annexed territories as in the entire Soviet Union. On June 26 1940, the supreme Soviet of the USSR, decided to adopt a seven-day working week. The entire party and state apparatus was harnessed to increase production. The Soviet Yiddish press, like its counterparts in other languages, abounded with headlines such as 'The need to combat "disorganization" in production', 'Soviet laws have to be enforced', or 'A subject for prosecution', all relating to labour disciplines.[96] The next day were to be found headlines such as 'No effort is being made to improve production', 'For Bolshevik discipline in the Kolkhozes', 'There is no struggle against loafers.'[97] This being the general atmosphere in labour relations, it is understandable that local inhabitants felt oppressed in the proletarian state. However, there were compensations that somehow mitigated worsening conditions among the workers – numerous social welfare services were extended to workers in the new territories. Free medicine, the use of recreation facilities, very cheap theatre and cinema as well as free evening adult education courses, cheap books and libraries and other cultural facilities were made available for the local workers. Kindergartens provided child-care and enabled the parents to work. No wonder there were also those who claimed that, on the whole, there was an improvement of the standard and quality of life in the poorer strata of the Jewish community.

The evidence from many dozens of shtetlach all over the former eastern provinces of Poland, and of many people who lived through the period in the area, attests, in general terms yet unequivocally, that the Jewish community was integrating into the Soviet economic system. The Jews as individuals learned to survive, frequently at a lower standard of living, in the new economic environment. The first period, that of the winter of 1939–40, when remnants of the former order still existed, had its illusions and disappointments. They were the result of the dislocations caused by war, transition from one economic system to another and of ignorance as to the realities of the Soviet economy. This stage is reflected in many stories and news reports abroad.[98] But with the passing of time the Jews were absorbed into the emerging Soviet economy. 'We adapted very rapidly to the Soviet regime. Everybody found a suitable job. There were those who worked in the workshop, others in a cooperative, or government office. Within a short period all of us became government employees . . . Life took its normal course. We were satisfied with our lot and hoped to improve it further in the not too distant future', relates a resident of Stolpce.[99] 'Gradually people adjusted to the new regime. Life regained its normal appearance. People worked and earned a living. There were no luxuries, but there was also no unemployment, nor hunger. Many who were dissatisfied at the beginning, gradually accommodated to the new system', remembers a Janow inhabitant.[100] The rumours that reached the local Jewish community of the fate of their brethren in German territory convinced many to try and reconcile themselves with the Soviet regime. As a Sarny Jew explained:

> While life was not easy, all of us appraised correctly the situation and did not close our eyes to what was going on around us . . . Thus the Jewish population adjusted to the Soviet economic order.[101]

The same argument is heard from Kleck:

> Slowly and gradually we adapted to the new conditions. We had to accept gladly all the difficulties and hardships, we knew that Europe was a volcano erupting flames and fire and we were in a state of relative calm and well-being . . . There was no unemployment. The rich lost their fortunes but on the other hand the poor were satisfied with the new regime which had improved their lot.[102]

Whether based on actual fact or merely on subjective feeling, many thought that the poorer sections of the Jewish community had even improved their economic well-being in absolute terms.[103]

Their long historical experience of survival in adverse conditions, their willingness to integrate, as well as the fact that they were a mobile and flexible urban population facilitated the Jews' adjustment and integration. After a time the Jews of the eastern provinces became acquainted with the intricacies of the Soviet economy and its bureaucratic structure. They learned to use it to their advantage. 'The Jews really adapted. They learned all the combinations in order to be able to work and survive. Actually the officials who came from the East were the teachers of how to live under Soviet rule. They taught how to earn a supplement to the very low wages illegally' comments a survivor from Berezno.[104] People learned to 'get along' with the new system, to conceal their social background,[105] and to cooperate with the Easterners: 'The Jews of Stryj learned rapidly how to deal with their new rulers and employers. The new relations were based on the ancient rule of mutual advantage and aided by corruption, bribes and cooperation in embezzlement.'[106] Therefore, no wonder that in due course 'the Jews worked and earned a living in spite of the meagre salaries. Everybody has his supplement. Another salary, money saved in the past, food obtained by illegal means, etc.' as a Jew from Wolozyn related.[107]

Parallel to the official, legal, Soviet economy, existed the so-called 'black market'. Under this title were included, in popular usage, the illegal buying or selling of commodities as well as other economic activities that did not correspond to the literal observance of Soviet law. The basic reason for the emergence of the black market, which as we shall see later, was partially tolerated, and as such grey rather than black, was that demand exceeded supply. Supervision of prices together with shortages in consumer goods and services led to under-the-counter sales, and black marketeering.

There were many reasons and incentives to try to circumvent the economic restrictions and rules, particularly during the transition period, when the black market reached its peak. There were rules and orders which did not make sense to the local population and were difficult to enforce: very low wages that drove people to earn extra money by any means; a chronic shortage in the most basic consumer goods and services complicated by distribution problems and bureaucratic inefficiency; whole classes had been abolished by the new rulers, yet prevented from getting a decent job. The new ruling class itself was, probably, the major customer of the black market. From the very beginning, the orders issued by the Red Army to keep the stores open and not to raise prices, and the equal use of the Polish zloty and Soviet rouble, created an impossible situation for the individual storekeeper and also for his customers. He saw the fading away of his stock and its replacement by piles of potentially worthless money. The small shopkeeper tried by various means to get a higher price and hide away as much as he could of his merchandise. In a very short time the regular stores stopped their normal operation. People started hoarding almost everything they could lay hands on and the peasants refused to accept money for their products. Barter was replacing the regular money economy.[108] Thus, the massive purchasing by Red Army soldiers, Soviet civilian officials and the population at large, the inability to replenish stock, and the insistence of the peasants to be paid in kind, created shortages, queues, under-the-counter sales, and the use of barter, as well as the continual raising of prices – all illegal activities.[109]

Shortages, and frequently the complete disappearance of certain commodities from the regular official marketing centres, drove the inhabitants to the black market, where for much higher prices one could obtain everything. 'People were ready to pay any price. There was no sense in bargaining, you were just thankful for getting the goods'[110], related A. Zak from Grodno in the winter of 1939–40. Since shortages and lines for consumer goods did not vanish with time, the 'informal' supply methods remained, despite heavy punishment when one was caught.[111] Speculation, as the phenomenon was frequently called officially, was rampant all over the former Polish eastern provinces. 'In every town and village there suddenly arose illegal markets', writes D. Grodner in his impressions of the last months of 1939.[112] P. Shwarts, wandering through eastern Galicia from September to November 1939, noted that 'speculation was ever spreading. In the larger towns it reached the proportions of a plague of war profiteering. You could find it in the smallest shtetlach and in the major urban centers, which attracted many speculators.'[113] Speculation was rife and there were those engaged in illegal trading who had never before in their lives dealt with selling or buying. Zak noted 'It was no wonder that the entire community became businessmen. Even small children visited the market place. All the trading passed from the stores to private homes and apartments. Since the prices in the stores were supervised, for one kilo of sugar you could take only one zloty while at home – fifteen.' The temptation was very great, concluded the author.[114] Shortages in certain professional and technical services, as well as unequal distribution when certain commodities were in short supply in one place and abundant in another, were yet another cause for profiteering.[115]

The black market was no accidental, transitional or peripheral phenomenon that affected the deviant margins of local society. During the 21 months of Soviet rule in the former eastern provinces of Poland it became obvious that the black market was a widespread phenomenon. Almost every important section of the population took part in it to some extent, and it had the character of a supplementary economy that mitigated the rigours of the official, legal economic system.

In the Jewish community there were large groups who were forced to engage in illegal economic activities in order to survive. The declassed and expropriated, and those whose ideological past prevented them from getting jobs in state institutions or enterprises, had either to live on the earnings of their relatives, or more often by selling their personal belongings. Many of them were thus forced to join in the illegal economy because the system barred them from employment in a 'productive' job. Now they faced the danger of being punished for engaging in illegal activities; it was a vicious circle.[116] Another sizeable group that had recourse to illegal trading was that of the many thousands of Jewish refugees from German-occupied Poland. We shall see below how the refugees fared under Soviet rule. Here it suffices to note that most of them could not obtain stable employment. Illegal trading, using their personal belongings, or merchandise got by various means, became a major means of their material survival. 'Many of the refugees in the *Tolchok* were not traders at all. They simply brought to the market their personal suits of clothes in order to be able to finish the next week. The refugees were jobless, lacking even the minimal income', claimed Zak.[117] The refugees had the time, connections and incentive to trade in commodities which were in short supply, particularly those that came from the other side of the border.[118] Refugees spent whole days and nights in lines to buy consumer goods and then sell them in the market place. Illegal trading of one kind or another became endemic in the local population. Jews who survived the period attest that 'speculation was rampant in all sections of the Jewish community. Nobody was immune.'[119] The salaries were never sufficient, nor were there enough basic consumer goods. The result was that, parallel to the official economy, many were active on the illegal black market, which was long tolerated by the Soviet authorities.[120]

The black market would not have survived as long nor become such a widespread phenomenon had it not been tolerated and frequented by the Soviet personnel who flooded the annexed territories. The Red Army soldiers and officers as well as the civilian officials who came from the east were important customers of the illegal markets and quite often also instigators of illegal economic practices. The Soviet customers were eager to buy the products of the decadent capitalist West, particularly watches and fountain pens, which were a real obsession of Soviet citizens. Soldiers and officials were the main customers of the goods sold by the refugees or smuggled through the borders.[121] It seemed that the Soviet citizens were well supplied with local money and were willing customers, paying almost any price asked. 'You could frequently find in the market place Soviet officials of high standing', recalled H. Smolar, who was at the time the secretary of the Writers' Association in western Belorussia.[122] Red Army soldiers and civilian bureaucrats who came to supervise and administer the new Soviet citizens became major sources of corruption. 'The local Jews learned a lot from the officials who came from the East', claimed a Jew from Berezno.[123] In the same line a resident of Kostopol argued that 'the veteran Soviet citizens sent to instruct the new citizens of Kostopol in the new life engaged in speculation and black market business.'[124] Thus the personnel sent from the east helped the adjustment of the local population to the entire range of the Soviet economic system.[125]

The major meeting place for people engaged in black marketeering was the open market or *Tolchok* that originated in the civil war period.[126] One could sell in the market only one's personal belongings, not trade as a business. Thus each 'merchant' could sell only one item of each commodity. 'The *Tolchok* became the most popular word among the refugees and the local population. It is the legitimate child of the Soviet regime. In all the cities "liberated" by the Soviet army after a few days all the trading was transferred from the empty stores to the *Tolchok*', reads a contemporary report.[127] In the *Tolchok* one could acquire goods that had long before disappeared from the stores. Here also were sold commodities bought in other towns or in the lines of the official marketing centres or hoarded by former shopkeepers. The police conducted regular searches for illegal trading and smuggled goods, but without effective results. Soldiers were the best customers for the smuggled goods.[128] The *Tolchok* served also as the centre for selling smuggled goods. 'You could identify the smugglers by their huge rucksacks. These were the smuggler speculators. They crossed back and forth [over the border]. They know what to bring; frequently they receive "orders" for certain goods.'[129] Most of the smugglers were non-Jews, since they did not face the same dangers as did the Jews – on German as well as on Soviet territory.[130] In the shtetlach close to the former Soviet–Polish border, which continued as a boundary line limiting free movement, there was a lively traffic of forbidden goods to the east.[131] The veteran Soviet citizens bought any Western goods they could lay their hands on. There was one item that was smuggled from the Soviet territories into the annexed provinces – vodka. In Poland its manufacture was a state monopoly and the peasants had ceased to distil their own alcohol. Smuggling vodka was mainly a woman's occupation.[132]

The black market dealt with any goods imaginable, from food to weapons. There were consumer goods of the most elementary character, such as food brought by peasants, or by people who sold rations or what they acquired after spending whole days in lines. There was clothing and household equipment, whose origin was local people who sold their property, or refugees from the West. There were smuggled goods, usually luxuries which had disappeared completely from the local stores, whose main customers were Red Army personnel and Soviet civilian officials. Watches were the most important and desirable merchandise to the Russians and quite often this passion was exploited by swindlers, who sold dubious goods.[133] A very important item in the black market was foreign currency. The Polish zloty continued to be legal currency in the German-occupied territories after it was valueless in the Soviet provinces, and was smuggled in large quantities to the West.[134] But the most important black-market currency was the American dollar – its value was constantly rising. 'To exchange at the official rate was not only to lose money, but dangerous and complicated', argued a correspondent of the *Forverts*.[135] There were sophisticated methods of transferring currency from the German- to the Soviet-occupied territories. Zak, who escaped from Warsaw, used to receive money in Grodno, deep in the Soviet area, sent by his wife. She paid a sum in Warsaw and Zak received the amount for a fee from 'professional' dealers in Grodno.[136] The trading in foreign currency was recorded vividly by Mr Russel of the British Embassy in Moscow, on a visit to Lvov:

> The Jews are conducting a fine trade in foreign exchange which commands a fantastic price in Lwow today . . . The 'black bourse' operates more or less openly on the street at a point in the old town just behind the Hotel Bristol, where some half dozen small thoroughfares intersect. This place swarms from morning till night with a scrupulous crowd of kaftanned, bearded and side-curled Jews, who conjure up visions of the ghetto in some medieval German city.[137]

'The struggle against speculators' was the name given by the Soviet authorities to the attempt to stop the illegal economic activity. Soldiers and police conducted regular searches in market-places, trains and, private houses; the press conducted a regular and intensive propaganda campaign. Those apprehended for illegal trading or other criminal economic activities were severely punished even for minor offences.[138] However, the black market was as ever-present a phenomenon as the open and official economic activity. The illegal economic activity which was officially stigmatized and punished was tolerated, and Soviet officialdom, the new ruling class, was among its main customers. The illegal trading was of vital importance to whole classes of the population – without it the hundreds of thousands of Jewish refugees and thousands of dispossessed middle-class Jews would not have been able to survive economically. Under the prevailing conditions, they had no choice but to engage in what was considered illegal by the regime. The black market as a label for various illegal economic activities, was a pervasive phenomenon. People from all walks of life, salary ranges and social origins were affected by it. The sheer size of the black market and the number of people involved warrants its description as a parallel economy. As such, while illegal, it was to a large extent tolerated by the regime and could justly be called 'grey' rather than black. It fulfilled a vital function for the Soviet regime by mitigating some of the rigours of the system and enabled many to adjust to the economy of the socialist state.

The Jewish community of the annexed Polish eastern provinces after 21 months of Soviet rule was becoming part of the new economic order. The former economic order crumbled during the first few months. The initial adjustment was painful, with very high rates of unemployment. There was no special Soviet agency to deal with the particularly difficult economic problems of the Jews resulting from their socio-economic structure. They were left to manage alone, to adjust to the general economic transformation of the area. No positive effort was made to provide the Jews with 'productive' occupations after the destruction of the former economic order. Collectivization and industrialization together with an emphasis on developing the more easterly regions of the USSR were the prime methods used in integrating the Jewish masses in the USSR proper. In the annexed territories those processes had not developed to any considerable extent before the outbreak of the war with Germany. The adjustment had to take place within the boundaries of the region and in the economic conditions prevailing there. It was a process that varied from place to place and with age and social economic background. After a painful transition period, with its accompanying economic dislocations, the poorer masses of the shtetl Jews were finding their way into the emerging Soviet system. The younger generation was taking advantage of the new opportunities opened by the Soviet rulers and Jews were admitted to jobs and places that were closed to them in the former regime. The more affluent and the older generation, particularly in the major urban centres, found it more difficult to integrate into the new economy. However, though suffering from the general decline in the standard of living, the majority of Jews were learning to live with the Soviet economy. It is worthwhile noting that reports reaching the outside world during the first few months of Soviet rule, when the situation of local Jews was at its lowest, were responsible to a large extent for the somewhat distorted picture of Jewish economic adjustment.[139]

The Soviets' claim that they had come to change basic social and human relations was only partially justified. No doubt the new rulers had destroyed economic relations and structures that had lasted for many generations in the Jewish community. The few very rich as well as the small shopkeepers and most of the self-employed artisans disappeared from the shtetl and Jewish life. However, they were not replaced by a true Jewish proletariat. Jews still remained in marginal occupations. What was called 'productivization' in Soviet terminology, namely the employment of Jews in direct production in factories and farms, hardly took place in the territories. In one of the few revealing utterances in the Soviet Yiddish press concerning the Jews in western Ukraine and Belorussia, in an article entitled 'What happens to the former storekeeper?' the paper had to admit: 'In general the productivization of the *luftmentsch* is a very complicated matter. We have to admit that in this field very little has been done.'[140] The Jews of the former Polish eastern provinces were finding their way into the Soviet economy. They were able to do this because of their willingness to adjust and flexibility in doing so, yet their occupations continued to set them apart from the surrounding society.

6
Emergence of a New Culture

The transformation that took place in the Jewish community was intended to change the former basic structures and life-styles and replace them with new loyalties to the Soviet State and its goals. Sovietization in the cultural field meant an attempt to impose the Stalinist centralist monolithic model on the multi-faceted culture that existed before. The intention was to destroy primordial attachments to family, community and ethnic groups and replace former values with Soviet ones. As in other fields of government policy, in the cultural sphere there was no special agency that took care of the Jewish population. On the surface the same criteria and goals were applied by the authorities to Jewish culture as to that of other ethnic groups. However, because of consistent Soviet opposition to all manifestations of Jewish nationalism, the cultural policy in the annexed territories not only discriminated against the Jewish religion and culture, but actively brought about a radical destruction of all forms and institutions of Jewish religious and cultural activity. The goal of the new rulers was to reduce as far as possible all expression of Judaism, particularly those elements that were of a nationalistic nature, and substitute for them a denationalized Yiddish culture. The Soviet Yiddish culture served as a means of gaining the support of the Jewish population and of indoctrination and mobilization. Yiddish culture, Soviet style, was neither a viable nor an honest synthesis. It served only as a transitional stage towards the final aim of complete Jewish assimilation into the Soviet family of nations. The Soviet policy of de-emphasizing Jewish values exploited existing tendencies within the Jewish community. Secularization and assimilation were far advanced at the time of the Soviet occupation, particularly among the younger generation of the shtetl Jews. Soviet rule brutally accelerated the process of integration to the verge of the complete ruin of Jewish culture in the territory. Moreover, because of conflicting developments, the destruction of the former institutions and their replacement by Soviet cultural activities, the process, its direction and final goals, were not at the time obvious. Though the Jews saw massive destruction, they were quite frequently deceived as to its true nature and considered it only as a change in form and emphasis.

THE FATE OF RELIGION

The Jewish religion was the mainstay and fountainhead of Jewish culture and nationalism. In line with Stalin's Constitution, Judaism was formally tolerated, yet it was under constant pressure to reduce drastically the scope of its activities. There was practically no overt persecution for religious reasons, nor a pronounced policy of closing down religious institutions. Nevertheless, the well-known and widely propagated negative attitude towards religion, the general attitude towards all expressions of Jewish autonomy, as well as the Soviet value system and criteria for success, combined to bring about a radical reduction of all forms of religious practice and observance. The dissolution of the *kehilla*, which was the major monetary supply for many religious institutions and functions, delivered the mortal blow to organized Jewish religious activity. Thus the number of *mikvaot* (communal ritual baths), of *mohalim* (ritual circumcisers), *shokhatim* (ritual slaughterers), and most important, community rabbis, was drastically decreased. Community money was not forthcoming, and the institutions' major individual financial contributors either disappeared or aimed to become as inconspicuous as possible. The religious functionaries were left without their salaries and contributions and with very few fees for services rendered, because of the general decline in religious observance.[1] Rabbis could hardly support themselves by selling yeast and performing their duties for the faithful. The Soviet authorities attempted to decrease their number even further by imposing on them high income taxes, which they could avoid only by announcing publicly in the local papers that they had ceased to perform their functions as rabbis.[2] Shops selling religious prayer books and ritual items were closed down, since they were classified as engaging in religious propaganda, which was forbidden by law. Books on Jewish religion and law were confiscated and used occasionally for commercial and industrial purposes.[3] Jewish religious practices were not formally prohibited. Such practices as ritual slaughtering, circumcision, wedding and burial ceremonies according to the Jewish law were usually tolerated, but came under severe criticism as relics of by-gone primitive times, resulting in their drastic reduction in number.[4] Religious instruction was considered to be a form of propaganda, and as such was forbidden. The ramified system of traditional education which had existed in Eastern Poland for hundreds of years was wiped out almost overnight. Such famous centres of higher Talmudic study as the *yeshivot* of Mir and Wolozhyn were closed down, while their buildings became restaurants and clubs.[5] While organized and publicly supported religious-educational institutions disappeared, there is evidence of the continued functioning of private classes for children to study the Torah. The Soviet authorities were not too severe in persecuting the offenders and frequently closed their eyes to this private instruction.[6]

The Jewish holidays and *Shabat* had played a central role in the Jewish way of life, particularly in the shtetlach, where the Jews constituted such a large proportion of the population. Even the non-orthodox, who did not observe the Jewish laws, participated, at least passively, in the rhythm of life dictated by the rest days of *Shabat* and holidays. The Soviet authorities paid special attention to this subject in their anti-religious propaganda. It was obvious that the Communist rulers understood well the educational value of the Jewish holidays and appreciated their cohesive power for the community and traditional family. It would be no exaggeration to claim that the most important 'Jewish subjects' treated in the Soviet Yiddish press were those of the articles devoted to propaganda denouncing Jewish holidays. The main period for the publication of anti-religious articles was the spring and autumn months, close to *Pesakh* and the High Holidays of *Rosh Hashana*, *Yom Kippur* and *Sukkot*. Interestingly enough, *Pesakh* – celebrated as a holiday of redemption from slavery, as a symbol of freedom – became not only a symbol of Jewish reaction for the authorities, but also turned into 'a holiday not of liberty – but a holiday of enslavement',[7] a fine example of Soviet dialectic thinking. Since *Pesakh* was close to 1 May, which was a major Soviet holiday, the competition was seen by the new regime as too great, hence the many articles and letters to the editor with variations on the theme: 'Our Holiday of Spring is May 1!'[8] Now, maintained an editor, Jewish workers were free from forced unemployment during the holidays. Together with workers of other nationalities in the USSR, the Jews had worker holidays and were free of Jewish capitalists and rabbis. The High Holidays, a time for community and individual meeting and reflection, were sharply denounced by the authorities. 'The place of the working masses during the holidays is not in the synagogue, together with the Rabbis and remnants of the rich.' admonished B. Shulman, editor of the *Bialystoker Shtern*, 'their place is in the factory, in the cooperative. Here by their labour they will strengthen the USSR which has redeemed them and offered the opportunity to build a new life, a life without exploiters.'[9]

The papers regularly carried anti-religious articles as well as information concerning the anti-religious activities that took place in the annexed territories. It is quite obvious that the people in charge of changing some of the most basic attitudes, customs and allegiances of the local Jewish population faced a difficult job, in spite of the efficacy of their methods. Reports from schools after more than a year of Soviet rule express dissatisfaction with the anti-religious campaign. 'Children absent from school during the Jewish holidays, refuse to write or participate in competitions on *Shabat*', reads a report from Bialystok.[10] Teachers, as we read in another report, from Iwie, western Belorussia, played a major role in 'enlightening' not only pupils, but also their parents. In special seminars and lecture series for parents conducted by teachers, the themes discussed were on the reactionary character of *Shabat*, *Pesakh*, etc.[11] Yet in spite of special efforts, occasionally the Soviet press had to admit that 'the struggle against the remnants of prejudice is not yet complete. Particularly in the Western regions, large sections of the population still remain religious. There are many instances in school and home of observing religious law. There are shtetlach where one can find even a *Kheder* [religious private class].'[12]

Religious observance, particularly of holidays and *Shabat*, was not only the subject of propaganda attacks or denunciations in public lectures. Observance of the *Shabat* and holidays was, probably, the most conspicuous evidence for the communist rulers of religious attachment, and a sign of potential disloyalty in their new subjects. Sunday was the official rest day, and all were under pressure to conform. When in one of the factories in Pinsk, which had a majority of Jewish workers, the demand was made for the *Shabat* to be the rest day, the community leaders were arrested.[13] The *Shabat* thus became a regular working day and there was the threat of punishment for absence from work. Even those of the older generation who tried to maintain the old traditions, were forced to work on the *Shabat*.[14] In many shtetlach where Jews constituted a majority, at least among the businessmen and artisans, the Jewish rest days had in practice been rest days for the entire shtetl. 'All that changed completely when the Soviet ruled in our shtetl' related an inhabitant of Smorgon, Belorussia. 'The majority ceased attending services in the synagogue. People hardly knew when the *Shabat* came.'[15] There were real grounds for the elated mood of the Soviet reporter who, while on a visit to the shtetlach of the former Pale of Settlement, noted with satisfaction: 'Walking through the streets of Rowne on *Shabat* eve there were much less signs of *Shabat* than in the past. Only a few lighted candles could be seen in the windows; there were no children rushing from *Kheder*, and very rarely could you detect a Jew dressed up in his *Shabat* clothes.'[16] The fate of the holidays was not much better. There was a general and drastic decline in the observance of holidays. While there was enough *matsot* (unleavened bread eaten at *Pesakh*) in 1940, the number of *Seder* (Passover feast) ceremonies declined. 'The young and even older people refrained from making a *Seder*, even though there was no official pressure exerted', maintained a Dambrowica Jew.[17] To interfere with the Jewish holidays, which were obviously banned from all Jewish schools, the authorities organized special events to coincide with them, such as dancing parties and performances, to remove the children from the holiday atmosphere at home and synagogue.[18] There was much truth in the title of the article on *Rosh Hashana* eve in Bialystok over a year after the annexation which reported: 'It is sad in the synagogue – there is light and joy in the Club.'[19] The clumsy title, typical of the Soviet press, might have exaggerated the joy prevailing in the club, where a lecture on 'Jewish Autumn Holidays' was given. Yet there was probably little exaggeration in the description of the atmosphere of sorrow in the house of prayer, nor of its emptiness.

The synagogue had been in a way the spiritual centre of the shtetl community. It served as a house of prayer, a place to study Jewish law for young and old, and also as a centre for social community assembly and activities.[20] Religious education for the young was now considered a counter-revolutionary activity and as such had to be done in the private setting of the home. Only some older people still came together to study a chapter of the Jewish law (*Gmara*). The synagogue ceased, at least openly, to serve as a centre of the Jewish community life. The many different charitable and benevolent voluntary associations almost completely disappeared, as part of the disintegration of the old established fabric of Jewish life in the shtetl. Freedom of worship was, however, one of the highly acclaimed principles of Stalin's 1936 constitution. The synagogues in the shtetlach of the annexed provinces were thus left, at least in outward appearance, only with the function of a house of prayer.

Synagogues were not prohibited, as worship was officially tolerated, yet the negative attitude towards religious practice of any kind was well known. Attending prayers, while not banned, was considered almost an expression of hostility towards the official ideology, certainly an obstacle to success under the new regime. Officially the authorities did not order the closure of synagogues. However, without formal proclamations or decrees many houses of prayer throughout the former Polish eastern provinces were closing down. This was not mere accident. So, for example, in Stolpce, 'the Great Synagogue closed first. A cooperative for gloves was housed in the building. In response to "a request from the workers", the "New Synagogue" was shut down next and a theatre and club were installed on its premises. All the other small synagogues remained. Christian houses of prayer were not touched at all.'[21] In Dubno, the closing down of every synagogue and conversion of them into a cooperative or club, was done 'for some lofty purpose,' related one of the inhabitants.[22] Lipniszki's major house of worship became a military installation[23] and Iwie's old synagogue became a grain warehouse, in 'response to the requests' of the local Jewish population.[24] The same story was repeated in places like Lvov, Tarnopol[25] and Nisvizh, where an entire network of cooperatives was housed in Jewish houses of prayer.[26] Janow's synagogues became state stables,[27] while those of Lubcza stored state grain.[28] The local population was usually too frightened to protest or appeal against the systematic confiscations.[29] An important role in initiating the confiscation of synagogues was played by Jewish Communists or new converts to the official ideology.[30]

It is thus understandable that with the prevailing attitude of the authorities synagogue attendance shrank dramatically. 'Even synagogues that were always full to capacity in the past, stood almost empty now and it was difficult to assemble a *minyan* [a quorum of ten men] for prayers' recalled a Janow survivor.[31] The synagogue became a last refuge for the older generation, who had little to lose by being branded 'reactionary, clerical, or counter-revolutionary'.[32] Anti-religious propaganda was so acrimonious that people were convinced that their future could be affected even by occasionally attending the synagogue. Soviet policy exacerbated existing tensions between generations in the shtetl. Secularization, already prevalent in the pre-Soviet shtetl, won over the younger generation almost entirely within a very short time of the annexation.

The synagogue remained, however, the most important single Jewish institution in the shtetl. It became a melancholy place, almost empty of life, and under constant threats and pressures – some brutal, others subtle, all effective – to close down. Nevertheless it was a last refuge of Jewishness, an expression of religious and national continuity. Religious life went on with the stubbornness typical of an ancient religion and people. People came to the prayer-house to worship and to meet as Jews with fellow Jews in a setting tolerated by the authorities. It remained the only legal institution of Jewish autonomy and fulfilled functions such as a shelter and temporary home for refugees, and as a meeting place for underground Zionist activists.[33] The synagogue was the remnant of an elaborate Jewish religious institutional network. It was still formally tolerated, though under constant pressure from the regime and abandoned by the younger generation. The future looked bleak and threatening, especially for the faithful remnant.

THE NEW JEWISH CULTURE

On the face of it, the definition of Soviet Jewish culture should have been a simple matter. Since the USSR was a multi-national state its culture was supposed to be, according to official ideology, socialist in content and national in form. Hence the Jewish culture in the Soviet Union had to emphasize socialist themes yet was to be presented in the Jewish languages, mainly Yiddish and Hebrew, and in Jewish forms, in a way similar to the expression of the culture of other ethnic groups living in the USSR. However, the authorities were suspicious of Jewish nationalism in all its manifestations. The Jews, as we have seen above, were expected, given the proper conditions, to disappear as a distinct ethnic entity. Hence Jewish culture, in whatever form, could not really be encouraged. As the final goal remained assimilation, all the preceding stations were only transient. Applied to the former Polish eastern provinces, with their large Jewish population and far-ranging cultural activities and institutions, this meant that whatever positive cultural policy was pursued, it was of a temporary nature.

The destruction of the former cultural structure was a short, drastic action. Cultural institutions and organizations almost 'dissolved' by themselves, as did other manifestations of organized Jewish public life. 'We are living now in a time of liquidation. Things that took many many years to build are being ruined overnight' remarked the author P. Kaplan, when asked about Jewish culture in the new Soviet territories. 'All the activists hide in their corners, happy when left alone.'[34] After a short while the cultural area was clear of its former structure and the new rulers could pursue their plans.

It was obvious that the large Jewish community could not as yet assimilate into the cultures of the surrounding groups. It was also undesirable to force the pace and antagonize the Jewish masses, at a time when the new regime was looking for support. The solution was the development of a de-nationalized Yiddish culture. It was intended to bring to the Jewish masses the culture of Stalinist USSR in the Yiddish language, while never relinquishing the final goal of assimilation.

It was obvious from the very beginning of Soviet rule, that Jewish culture would not be treated the same way as the culture of other ethnic groups. The policy of Ukrainization and Belorussification brought with it discrimination against Jewish cultural needs. Publications in Yiddish were disproportionately fewer than those in other languages. The *Bialystoker Shtern* was the only Jewish daily to appear regularly in the entire annexed territory, replacing the many dailies and periodicals which had existed under Polish rule. *Der Roiter Shtern*, Lvov, appeared for a few weeks in June 1941. In spite of the pronounced policy of equality between the spoken languages, Yiddish did not have the same status as the other languages in formal usage.[35] Hebrew, the ancient tongue of the Jewish people, was completely prohibited in schools, cultural activities and publications. The struggle against Hebrew, dating from the twenties, was construed as a struggle not against a language but against an ideology: Zionism; and a class enemy: the Jewish international bourgeoisie.[36] The struggle against and animosity towards Hebrew went so far as to attempt to eradicate its influence on Yiddish by using a phonetic script and changing the accepted spelling of Hebrew words to blur their origin. The fact that there were quite a few people who knew Russian, particularly in the Belorussian provinces, mitigated the linguistic problem for the Jewish population.[37]

It looked, in the period immediately following the annexation, as if Jewish culture, albeit in Soviet form, would reach new heights of achievement. There was a very high concentration of Jewish authors, intellectuals, performers and artists of all kinds who left Warsaw and swelled the ranks of the local Jewish cultural elite. Most of them, as we shall see later, were ready in one form or another to integrate into Soviet culture.[38] The new rulers, on their part, were eager at this initial stage to mobilize the talents of this cultural elite to facilitate and ease the transition and integration of the new citizens into Soviet reality. Promises of generous assistance to all forms of artistic activity were aired with proclamations of equality for all ethnic groups residing in the provinces. The period lasting till June 1940 saw the growth of different expressions of Jewish culture and education, in Soviet form. As H. Smolar noted, it was spontaneous and without any official initiative.[39] After June 1940 came a period of gradual 'shrinking' of all Jewish cultural and educational activities. This was noticeable in official propaganda and political and administrative directives. The *Bialystoker Shtern* started to appear in a smaller format and only four times a week. Criticism of Jewish culture as being nationalistic and Zionist became more frequent. This trend became more pronounced and harsher until May 1941 when it began to turn into a purge against Jewish culture and activists.[40] A select few of the Jewish cultural elite were already aware in February 1940 that the current flourishing state of Jewish culture was temporary. 'The fate of Jewish culture in the western provinces would not be different from that in the eastern', warned Ponomarenko, the General Secretary of the Belorussian Communist Party, when he met Markish the famous Soviet Jewish poet, warning him not to encourage a culture that was destined to perish. Markish was on his way to visit the 'liberated territories', and in utmost secrecy related the message to a few of his old acquaintances from Poland.[41]

A large number of Jewish writers and artists, mostly from German-occupied Poland, were concentrated in the annexed territories. Among them could be found some of the more prominent cultural leaders of Polish Jewry, like A. Katsizna, S. Imber, I. Ashendorf, M. Grosman, A. Zak, M. Broderzon, Z. Segalowicz and many others. Quite a few were of leftist and even Communist orientation, and had been so even before the

Soviet annexation. They converged on the only two real urban centres in the region: Bialystok and Lvov. The new rulers saw the potential of this group, but were also suspicious of its ideological background. Even though there were no clear-cut plans for using this intellectual reservoir, the authorities provided some basic assistance in housing and food.[42] A special hostel and kitchen were provided for the refugee writers and artists. Special organizers came from the east to form new branches of the Soviet union of writers. Membership in the writers' union meant the chance to earn a living and to be able to publish. In order to become a member, one had to satisfy an ideological investigation and loyalty test.[43] Those who were not suspect ideologically had to conform to the prevailing standards of socialist realism and the cult of Stalin in its crudest forms. They had to write about the Soviet way of life, and their hopes for 'a happy future'. Their subjects were to deal with the proletarian struggle, Jewish cooperation with other Soviet nationalities, class antagonism in the shtetl etc.[44] The writers soon learned the true meaning of being Jewish writers in Stalin's USSR. They learned this through their own experience and from the 'brigades' of Soviet Jewish writers who came from the east to instruct the new citizens in the 'right way' and true faith. The story of the writers is the by now familiar tale of oppression, denial of freedom, hypocrisy and falsehood characteristic of the Stalinist period.[45] Most of the Jewish authors stopped writing either because they were not trustworthy enough and their work was unacceptable, or because they were more sensitive and could not adapt to the requirements of Soviet literary 'production'. They faced the ever-present danger of being accused of Jewish nationalistic deviations whenever they dealt with a Jewish-related subject. What hurt some of them most was the complete ban on any mention of the fate of the Jews under Nazi occupation. Those were the high days of the Stalin–Hitler friendship pact and nothing was allowed to blemish the relationship.[46] The net result was that most of the large reservoir of literary talent and its goodwill was dissipated and wasted, while the Soviet Yiddish press was reporting about the 'varied Jewish cultural activities' in the western provinces of Belorussia and Ukraine.

The only Jewish publication in the annexed territories, replacing a number of publishing houses, dailies and periodicals, was the *Bialystoker Shtern*. On the eve of the German invasion, on 1 June 1941, *Der Roiter Shtern* started to appear.[47] The Bialystok paper was published on the premises of a former Jewish daily, *Our Life* (*Undzer Lebn*), and also took over some of its former editorial staff. However, like other institutions in the territories, the *Bialystoker Shtern* was managed and supervised by officials who came from the east. From the beginning of 1940, B. Shulman was the Editor in Chief.[48] Many of its readers, unfamiliar with the workings of the Soviet system, thought that the *Bialystoker Shtern* and its editorial staff were playing an active role in shaping public Jewish life in the newly-acquired territories. But that was not the case. The newspaper was merely another organ of the regime, itself suspect and under supervision, and designed to extol the virtues and praise the greatness of Stalin and the socialist state. It served as a means of indoctrination and mobilization of the Jewish masses who could not read any other language.[49] By sending reporters as lecturers to factories and public institutions, the paper contributed to the propaganda efforts of the regime. Ever conscious of the danger of being accused of nationalist tendencies, the *Bialystoker Shtern* took special pains to watch over other Jewish cultural activities in the theatre, literature, and visual arts. 'Bolshevik Vigilance in Art', the headline of one of its editorials, was a major feature of the Yiddish paper.[50] Like other papers of the time, the *Bialystoker Shtern* reflected in the most crude forms the prevailing cult of Stalin. It contained little real information and less news relevant to its Jewish readers. The most urgent problems that concerned the Jewish world found no expression at all in this Yiddish Soviet newspaper. The fate of the Jews in Nazi Germany was not mentioned at all. The bombastic headlines, slogans, and pervasive festive tone were designed to conceal rather than describe and report actual events. The major Jewish themes were treated in the articles directed against Jewish traditional holidays, values and beliefs. Jewishness appeared in the paper mainly in a negative context, as a target for attack and denunciation. Thus the only Jewish publication in the former Polish eastern provinces could not serve as a source of inspiration or identification for the new Jewish citizens of the USSR.

The Jews were called 'The People of the Book'. Books and libraries were greatly valued in the life of the community and the individual. Every shtetl had its library, while every synagogue had its own books on Judaism and Jewish law. The Soviet regime had rather clear standards as to what were the proper books to be read by its new Jewish citizens. One of the first acts of the new rulers was the closure of all public libraries, which were re-opened after being cleansed of all suspicious material.[51] Special inspectors, sent from the east, equipped with the necessary instructions and assisted by local Jewish Communists or sympathizers, checked the local libraries. All books in Hebrew were, naturally, banned, regardless of content or author. The language in which they were written was sufficient proof for the authorities of the reactionary nature of these books. While Russian and Polish classics were approved, the criteria for the Jewish works were much more rigid. Thus Bialik and Sh. Ash were excluded because they had left Russia. Shalom Aleichem, Mendele and Perets were among the few who remained acceptable. The result was, for example, that out of tens of thousands of books in the library of Grodno[52] or Bialystok,[53] only a few hundred were left. The unacceptable books were sent to paper factories to be used as pulp, or occasionally transferred to closed research libraries. In the many shtetlach of the annexed provinces the libraries were closed, never to be re-opened.[54] Despite repeated reports in the Soviet Jewish press about an increase in the reading public, which was attributed to a growth in new facilities, we find in a Soviet Yiddish periodical as late as January 1941 that 'most libraries in the western Ukraine are still in the reorganization stage.'[55] Reorganization actually meant the closure of the libraries and purging of most of their Jewish content.

Soviet Yiddish literature was supposed to replace the 'decadent reactionary clerical' books in the libraries of the territories. The new books were to teach and encourage identification of the population with the ideology and goals of the socialist state. Soviet Yiddish authors and publishing houses did not fail to notice the huge potential reading public that was added to their domain. The major Soviet Yiddish publishing house, the Emes publishing house of Moscow admitted that 'There is a large group of consumers of our literature in the liberated provinces of western Ukraine and Belorussia. The demand for our books there is great. It might have been even greater had the distribution organizations cooperated with us.'[56] As became abundantly clear, the lack of an independent distribution network was a major, even insurmountable obstacle to the spread of Yiddish books. In Kiev, Minsk and Moscow, the location of the major Yiddish publishing houses and authors in the USSR, there was a clear awareness of the opportunities of disseminating Yiddish literature into new territories. Festive meetings, resolutions and plans were undertaken in the first months after the annexation 'to supply Soviet Yiddish literature' to the new areas. It was decided in Kiev to publish a series of brochures on 'life and people in the USSR',[57] and also to produce a series of political artistic books 'to relate to our brethren in western Ukraine the happy Soviet life'. Similarly, the Emes publishers decided to issue a brochure including songs, articles and illustrations in praise of the liberation. P. Markish was ordered to prepare a short film on the happy life of Soviet Jews.[58] Minsk was not far behind: the Belorussian state publishing house prepared special plans for publishing a series of political, literary and artistic books for the new Soviet citizens. The Jewish classics Mendele, Shalom Aleichem and Perets, as well as the Soviet Yiddish writers Bergelson, Markish, Akselrod and others, were to be included.[59] 'Books for the Masses in the Western Provinces' continued to be an important item reported in the Soviet Yiddish press, and also occupied the attention of both authors and publishers. It was reported that tens of thousands of books, brochures and pamphlets were actually sent to the provinces. They included the classics in Yiddish, Soviet Yiddish literature, translations from other Soviet tongues, political literature and thousands of copies of Stalin's constitution and other writings of the Soviet leader.[60]

The demand for Yiddish publications, with the cessation of local publishing, was indeed great. However, the Soviet Yiddish publishers could not meet the demand. Despite repeated requests from the towns and shtetlach of the western provinces the orders actually carried out through the distribution networks were very few in number, complained a correspondent of *Der Shtern* a few weeks before the end of Soviet rule.[61] Twenty months after taking over Eastern Poland, it should have been clear that it was no mere bureaucratic inefficiency, nor typical Soviet negligence. It was a reflection of a policy that had not yet become clear to the Jewish correspondent of *Der Shtern*. The Jewish masses in the shtetlach of the western provinces were increasingly denied even the de-nationalized literature of the Soviet Yiddish publications.

Increased denial of access to cultural and educational material having any Jewish national content formed the negative facet of Soviet attempts to bring about the assimilation of the Jewish population. The positive aspect was the attractions offered by the Communist State. These were many and appealed particularly to the poor shtetl masses and the younger generation. The attraction of socialism must be viewed against the background of the secularizing tendencies which had previously existed in the Jewish community together with the deprivation and discrimination of the previous regime. The masses did not care about, and certainly did not know or precisely understand, the goals of Soviet Jewish policy, not even its direction. Yiddish was anyway the language by far the most prevalent among the Jews of the annexed provinces, and hence its treatment by the new rulers was probably approved by many. Therefore the impression one gets from numerous reports that there was a Jewish 'cultural bloom' in the period following the Soviet conquest is justified by developments and the true sentiments of large sections of the Jewish population. Not only the Soviet Yiddish press reported about 'broad Jewish cultural activities in the western provinces of the Ukraine and Belorussia', but also many others who lived through that period. The shtetl Jew took advantage, probably to a higher degree than the non-Jew, of the broader-based cultural activity directed at the masses. This cultural activity is described by Y. Bromberg in an unpublished manuscript called *Pinsk under Soviet Rule*:

> The book stores were loaded with very good books in Yiddish, Belorussian and Russian and prices were very low. Every worker could acquire a library. The Yiddish newspapers, *Emes* and *Der Shtern*, and literary periodicals in that language were found in the stores. The cinema and theatre were packed with workers. Evening classes in different subjects became available as did amateur art groups. Various committees in the enterprises took care of the free time after work.[62]

In Lvov, there were organized associations of Jewish writers, performers, painters, exhibitions, clubs, etc. Yet what created a tremendous impression on the masses and intellectuals was the Yiddish hour that was broadcast on the local radio. 'We felt special satisfaction when we heard in the streets of Lvov, where not long before one had to be careful when using Yiddish, the Jewish words transmitted through loudspeakers from the state radio.'[63] In the shtetlach many shared the feeling that the communist regime was caring for the cultural needs of the population. 'There had been a noticeable increase in the activities of the different cultural fields. Clubs renewed their activity. Theatre performances became more frequent. A large library with a new reading room was opened to serve the local population', recalled a Lanin inhabitant.[64] In Dubno, 'one could recognize that the authorities cared for the cultural needs of the masses. There was an abundant supply of newspapers, films, performances, etc.'[65] And in Bransk, recalled one of its Jews, 'people rushed to study. Adults attended night classes. A town choir and an amateur drama circle were formed. Movies were shown twice weekly. A city park and dancing floor were built for the population.'[66] No wonder that the same narrator claimed that the 'Jewish population was happy during the 21 months of Soviet rule. They felt themselves to be free and equal citizens.'

One of the cultural tools most valued by the Soviet authorities was the theatre. It was considered a most suitable vehicle to indoctrinate and entertain large audiences, through the use of professional performers, as well as a convenient means of attaining large-scale participation in the many and varied amateur groups and drama circles. The network of Yiddish theatres in western Ukraine and Belorussia was indeed impressive. In the two major cities of the annexed territories Yiddish state theatres were established. In Bialystok it was headed by A. Moravski,[67] and in Lvov by Ida Kaminska, one of the most prominent figures in the history of Jewish theatre.[68] In forming the two state theatres, the organizers used several sources for performers and staff. In the annexed provinces there were many local troupes, some professional and many more amateur. The local artists were joined by many refugee actors from Warsaw, and Yiddish actors from disbanded Soviet troupes joined the theatres of Lvov and Bialystok.[69] In Bialystok, the so-called Miniature Theatre was also founded with the participation of the two most famous performers in Poland at the time, Dzhigan and Shumacher, and under the artistic and literary direction of the poet Broderzon.[70] Lower in status were several 'city theatres', which performed in their home towns and the immediate vicinity. Such theatres, at least during part of Soviet rule, were found in Tarnopol, Stanislawow, Grodno, Baranowicz, and Pinsk.[71] The professional theatres formed part of an elaborate broader system of theatrical activity that included amateur groups in many shtetlach and artels and drama circles in the Yiddish schools.[72] The actors served as instructors of drama for various groups. The Yiddish hour on the Lvov radio had a drama section that broadcast plays and discussions on theatrical subjects.[73] Together with the amateur drama groups were established many groups devoted to the other performing arts, such as choirs and folk music bands.[74] Frequent meetings and competitions took place to encourage the development of amateur groups and performers.[75]

A major problem faced by the new Soviet Yiddish theatres and actors was the ideologically proper selection of plays and their performance. N. Kompaniets, director of the culture department of western Ukraine, stated the problem bluntly: 'Our central task in all fields of the arts, theatre, orchestra, choirs, folk groups, painting, etc . . . is to create a new repertoire. We need a Soviet content to replace the old themes.'[76] The efforts dedicated to selecting ideologically suitable plays, cleansing them of undesirable elements, and always being on guard against slipping from the proper political line, were a great burden for performers brought up in a different atmosphere. Mistakes could be dangerous. D. Lederman, a former actor in inter-war Poland and at this time acting in the Bialystok theatre, recorded the theatre life under Soviet rule. The Soviet organizers, recalled, Lederman, emphasized the economic security now provided by state sponsorship of the Yiddish theatre. However, the price paid of the tight control imposed by political inspectors on every utterance was one of the most disturbing aspects of denial of artistic freedom.[77] As Jews, the performers were particularly hurt when forbidden to raise at all the subject of Nazi Germany. Any attempt to try to circumvent the ban on anti-German expression was bound to bring some severe punishment by the authorities. In spite of the strict supervision and censorship, the performances were received enthusiastically by the Jewish public. The plays offered were a combination of the accepted Yiddish classics of Sholem Aleichem, Perets, Goldfaden, and new Soviet Yiddish works written by Markish, Bergelson, Halkin and others. Thus, it was a blend of old and new that suited the taste of many.[78] No wonder that the theatre drew large crowds, since it was the only Jewish institution that remained active. In its many tours through the annexed provinces, the Yiddish theatre brought to many shtetlach a reminder of Jewish culture and created a definite impression that the Communist rulers cared for culture and entertainment for the broad masses.[79]

The Soviet regime was aware of the tremendous propaganda value of the cinema and radio. Hence the strenuous endeavour to introduce radio stations and cinemas, *Radiofikatsia* and *Kinofikatsia* as they were labelled in Soviet terms, into the annexed territories. Radio receivers were of course rare, expensive and difficult to control, hence the building of public loudspeaker systems.[80] Movies were among the first items sent to the new territories. Tickets were free or very cheap, enabling large numbers of people to attend performances. Many new cinemas were built in the shtetlach of the western provinces, while others were renovated and special efforts were made to ensure comfortable viewing.[81] Smaller places were served by dozens of mobile units brought over by the Red Army. Obviously the spread of cinema or radio was not specifically intended for the Jewish inhabitants of the area. Yet the availability of movies and radio enhanced the feeling among shtetl Jews that under Soviet rule more attention was being devoted to their cultural needs. The Jewish population took advantage of the opportunities made available by the Soviet state, thus participating in a broader integration into Soviet society.

During the period of Soviet rule, lasting only 21 months, Jewish culture and religion underwent radical change. Cultural and religious patterns that had lasted hundreds of years disappeared overnight. A much reduced number of synagogues, a few Yiddish theatres, and one daily were left of the elaborate religious and cultural structure that existed in Eastern Poland. The final goal of the transformation that took place was the complete assimilation of the Jews as individuals and the elimination of the Jewish community as a distinct ethnic and cultural entity. De-nationalization was the aim of the cultural policy pursued by the Communist rulers. They hoped to weaken and eventually to destroy the basic attachments and values of the Jewish community. Taking into account the prevailing conditions and ethnic composition of the annexed provinces, the authorities implemented their policy gradually and subtly. Therefore they replaced the former cultural establishment by a de-nationalized Soviet Yiddish culture as a transitional stage. This Yiddish culture, combined with the general growth of popular cultural activities characteristic of the communist regime gave some people the impression of a cultural flowering. Hence the confusion and contradictions often found in contemporary reports. Yet by the summer of 1940 it had already become abundantly obvious that an effort was being made to equalize the cultural situation in the annexed provinces with that of the USSR proper. It should be noted that the assimilatory trends made impressive inroads into the Jewish community. Imposed from above through an enthusiastic de-nationalizing policy, it was fostered from below by existing divisions and secularizing and modernizing processes within the Jewish population. That trend was particularly strong among the youth of the deprived, poverty-stricken shtetlach. Many were ready to abandon much of their ethnic identity in order to succeed in Soviet society. Yiddish culture and education, Soviet style, were not particularly attractive. They were definitely an impediment to success in the communist regime and gave very little in return. The destruction of the old order and its substitution by an anaemic Soviet Yiddish culture furthered the assimilation and atomization of the Jewish community and the emergence of the lonely Jewish individual.

7

Educating the New Soviet Citizen

A major means of integration of the annexed populations into Soviet society was the educational system. The massive increases in the number of institutions and in the enrolment of students of all age groups were the most obvious results of the regime's belief in the power of instruction. To prepare a productive, loyal and 'good' Soviet citizen was the goal of the educational system. It was designed to uproot the former value system and replace it with the one adhered to by the Communist regime. The schools were to become instruments for building up the Communist society, and of raising a generation able to accomplish that task.[1] For the Jewish population it meant progress on the road to full integration into the 'Soviet family of nations', in this case a euphemism for complete assimilation. Yet the approach was gradual, taking into account local conditions and limitations. The need to gain the support of the local population, as well as the effect of the policy pursued in the territories on the population in the USSR proper, determined actual developments in the area. A de-nationalized Yiddish educational system was formed in the annexed provinces as a temporary transitional phase, replacing the former structure.

A speedy return to the normal run of life in the occupied territories was behind the order to reopen the schools. All the former public and privately supported schools became state institutions. The other major principle put immediately into effect was education in the mother tongue of the pupils. This was determined by the parents. The application of the principle was designed to advance the Ukrainian and Belorussian populations and curtail the influence of the Poles. State education in the mother tongue was combined with a negative attitude towards Jewish nationalism and the

Hebrew language to provide the principles for rebuilding the Jewish educational system in the annexed provinces.

The educational system, more than other facets of Jewish public life in the territories, was used as the basis of and starting point for the Soviet system. The vast majority of Jewish children in the territories had been exposed to a Jewish national and religious education in one form or another.[2] It was done in the private or public Jewish schools, where instruction was carried out in Hebrew and Yiddish, or in the state-run schools where there were special classes on Judaism in the Polish language.[3] The major school networks were those of Tarbut, Iavne, Khorev, Tsisho, which taught in Hebrew, Yiddish and some subjects in Polish. Jewish education was also provided by private partial instruction and the many traditional *Kheders* and *yeshivot*. Within a period of several months, the entire Jewish educational system was rebuilt and reformed to conform to Soviet perceptions and goals.

The Soviet Yiddish school became, after a short while, the only legitimate Jewish educational institution in the annexed provinces. During the first few weeks there had been some misunderstandings as to the language of instruction. As in other fields, the orders were not always clear and much of what happened was the result of almost spontaneous development. All schools, except those teaching Belorussian and Ukrainian children in Polish, were ordered to continue to use the former language of instruction.[4] There were schools of the Hebrew *Tarbut* system that continued to instruct in the language formerly used.[5] This transition period lasted briefly, until the schools concerned were ordered, usually 'advised', to change to another language. Hebrew became a banished language for instruction. It was done without a formal governmental decree ordering the closure of the Hebrew schools or publicly prohibiting the use of the language. The entire episode was the result of the confusion during the first weeks of the Soviet conquest and of ignorance on the part of the officials in charge.[6]

With a few isolated exceptions, the Hebrew school system disappeared shortly after the occupation. There were those which were changed over to Yiddish by their own boards, which knew the attitude of the Soviet authorities towards Hebrew and Zionist national education. It happened almost spontaneously. Some Hebrew schools were re-opened after the summer vacation of 1939 and the German–Polish War. One way or another the Hebrew schools disappeared together with the language itself as a separate study subject. Yiddish became the instruction language not only in the former Hebrew schools, but also in other schools that in the past used other languages and had a Jewish majority. Even though there are no precise data available we have testimonies that such changes actually took place.[7] Formally such changes took place as a result of parents' initiative. In reality it was in response to Soviet policy and local official prodding. The nationalities policy pursued by the new rulers immediately after the occupation was designed primarily to decrease Polish influence in the area and promote the Ukrainian and Belorussian groups. It coincided with the aspirations of some sections of the Jewish community, who strove to promote Yiddish culture and schools.

> The authorities conducted a strenuous campaign to transfer Jewish children to Yiddish schools. The Jewish community in Poland had tried for a long time to be given the right to state supported schools in Yiddish and Hebrew, with limited success. Suddenly, the new regime granted the Jewish population rights long denied. We had few illusions as to the true nature of those schools. Yet, the mere fact that Jewish children would study together under Jewish teachers was a positive development that could not be missed

relates a Jewish teacher from Tarnopol.[8] Encouraged by government policy the *Bialystoker Shtern*, only recently established, conducted an active campaign and sent special groups to convince parents to demand Yiddish schools.[9] However, even at this stage, establishing Yiddish schools was only of secondary importance. The establishment of Ukrainian and Belorussian schools preceded that of Yiddish schools even in places that had a Jewish majority. Thus, in Grodno, which formerly had an elaborate network of Jewish schools, and a Jewish-Polish majority, the Yiddish school was built last – after the Belorussian, Russian and Polish. Jewish children were forced to attend the Russian school, since there were too few Russian students, while Belorussian children were brought from surrounding villages.[10] Eventually even the single Yiddish school was converted into a Russian one. The case of Kleck, as reported in the Soviet press, was instructive. Here the Jews constituted 70 per cent and the Belorussians 20 per cent of the population. But over 1,000 children attended the Belorussian and 720 the Jewish school.[11]

The encouragement of Yiddish schools was a temporary phase in Soviet educational policy. Even while it lasted it was not general, and was done half-heartedly. Already in the late spring and summer of 1940 there was a definite shift against Jewish culture and Yiddish schools. The policy of discriminating in favour of Ukrainian, Belorussian and Russian schools became increasingly obvious. Former Jewish schools were converted into those in which instruction was in Ukrainian, Belorussian and Russian. Official Soviet statistics, as published in the Jewish press, unmistakably demonstrate that the number of Yiddish schools decreased during the period under consideration. The *Oktiaber* of Minsk reported on 14 February 1940 that the number of Yiddish schools in western Belorussia was 197 out of a total of 5,071. On 5 May 1940 the same source reported 170 Yiddish schools and on 13 December only 150 out of a total that had grown to

5,685.[12] The trend is unmistakable: even in its watered down de-nationalized form the Yiddish school was considered to be an obstacle to the future plans of the regime.

A combination of several factors brought about the decrease in number of the Yiddish schools in the annexed provinces. No doubt the leading cause was governmental policy. For the local Soviet authorities it was one facet of the general acceleration of the pace of integration of the territories into the USSR that took place from the summer of 1940. The accelerated pace of Sovietization was accompanied by an attempt to gain the sympathy and loyalty of the Ukrainian and Belorussian populations. It meant an effort to make the state of Jewish culture and education in the new territories equivalent to that existing in the already established regions of Russia. There the trend in the thirties was one of a speedy decline of the Yiddish school system.[13] From non-Soviet sources we learn that from the summer of 1940 Yiddish schools all over the new provinces came under pressure to adopt Ukrainian, Belorussian or Russian as their language of instruction. In Tarnopol, the very same place where after the occupation an active propaganda campaign for Yiddish had been conducted, the situation now was as follows. The school principal was under pressure to introduce Ukrainian as the language of instruction. Regardless of the explicit desire of the parents to maintain the Yiddish school, it was turned into a Ukrainian institution.[14] In Grodno, yielding to the pressure of the local education department, the parents' assembly decided 'unanimously and freely' to turn their Yiddish school into a Russian one. Gradually the staff and student body were changed and Yiddish was removed even as an elective study subject.[15] We have similar testimonies from Dubno,[16] Nowogrodek,[17] Kowel,[18] Brisk,[19] Lvov,[20] and other places,[21] where, with the formal consent of the parents or by a simple administrative order, Yiddish schools were turned into Russian, Ukrainian or Belorussian ones. Typical were the cases of Kleck and Lubcza as illustrations of how the authorities applied the principle of providing every ethnic group with the opportunity to teach its children in their 'mother tongue'. In both the Jews constituted an absolute majority of over 70 per cent.[22] In Lubcza, at the beginning of the school year of 1940–1, the parents were assembled together and 'advised' to vote for the conversion of their Yiddish school into a Russian institution. Nobody dared to argue.[23] In Kleck, the decision was taken after some argument among the assembled parents.[24] The most frequently used argument for abandoning Yiddish instruction was that the graduates could not continue their studies in Yiddish at the higher institutions of learning.

The tendency to convert to other languages of instruction which was initiated and imposed from above had also the support of parents from below. While it is impossible to assess the precise number of parents willing out of conviction to educate their children in one of the majority languages, there is no doubt that they were numerous. This reflects the divisions that existed in the Jewish community before the Soviet occupation. Sections of the shtetl Jewish community were ready to sever any connection with the traditional way of life and pursue, if possible, the road of complete assimilation into the surrounding society. They saw no reason to instruct their children in Yiddish and thus put unnecessary obstacles on their road to success. Some of the parents could not find many advantages in the Soviet Yiddish school. It was not more 'Jewish' than other Soviet schools – actually less time was devoted to anti-Jewish themes in the non-Yiddish institutions. However, most of the parents' arguments against the Yiddish school were practical, even opportunistic. They saw no future for Yiddish in the USSR and the experience in the pre-annexation borders was proving them right. Higher education in Yiddish was impossible and the instruction itself was difficult because of a lack of teachers, proper books, teaching aids in different subjects, etc.[25] The Yiddish school, while for some being very meagre in Jewish content, demanded a high price from its students. Giving little emotional-national satisfaction, the Yiddish school was considered by many parents a real impediment to success in Soviet society. Hence when it became obvious that the authorities in charge favoured instruction in the majority languages or Russian, there were many parents who supported that move wholeheartedly.

The Soviet Yiddish school system was first and foremost Soviet in content and values. During the thirties, the Soviet Yiddish school was losing more and more of its Jewish characteristics. Yet it maintained two features that kept it apart as Jewish: the study of the Yiddish language and its literature; and the wholly Jewish composition of its student body. School had to become one of the major tools for indoctrinating the upcoming generation. It was considered an important means of undermining the hold of traditional Jewish values nourished by home and community. Opposition to Jewish religion and nationhood was a basic tenet of the Soviet Yiddish school. The Yiddish phonetic script used in school and in Soviet publications was designed to erase as much as possible of the Hebrew component in the Yiddish language. It changed accepted Yiddish spelling as part of an anti-Hebrew and anti-Jewish national effort. To blur national distinctions, Soviet schools did not usually bear names, but numbers, and one thus did not know from a school's number whether the institution was Jewish, Russian, or whatever.

To uproot religious beliefs and customs as well as Jewish nationalism was a major occupation in the Soviet Yiddish schools. Students were subjected to constant anti-religious propaganda. They were forced to attend school on *Shabat* and holy days.[26] Dancing parties, festivals, theatre performances, etc. were organized on the holidays to remove the younger generation from the home atmosphere. In spite of partial and limited opposition, gradually the Jewish children became used to attending school on *Shabat* and holy days, and participated in the various secular activities.[27] Promotion of Soviet values and norms figured prominently in the Yiddish school. The principles of Marxism and Leninism and Stalin's Constitution were regarded as major sources of inspiration. The struggle against national separateness and prejudice and the furthering of inter-ethnic cooperation and understanding were stressed on every occasion in word and deed.[28]

Destruction of class distinctions and attitudes was among the norms most valued in the Yiddish schools. 'Communist education in the Jewish schools', read an article in the *Oktiaber*, 'has to strengthen the value of labour instead of the inclinations towards business, that are very strong in the Jewish community . . . It has to uproot the still surviving negative attitudes towards physical labour.'[29] Moreover patriotism and love for the leader Stalin were the *sine-qua-non* of the entire educational system. These tenets and values stood at the base of the curriculum of the Soviet Yiddish schools.

The subjects that were included in or withdrawn from the curriculum and the teaching methods, as well as the extra-curricular activities, were designed to achieve the intended goals of the regime. In addition to Hebrew, Jewish history and the Bible as distinct instruction subjects were removed from the curriculum of the Yiddish schools. As in other Soviet schools, special classes were dedicated to the principles of Marxism and Leninism and to Stalin's Constitution. Yiddish literature was the only subject that related directly to the Jewish character of the school. It was taught up to the sixth grade, according to the accepted Soviet plan.[30] The selection from the rich nineteenth- and twentieth-century Yiddish literature was guided by 'revolutionary criteria', and consisted of authors who were revolutionaries or in whose works one could find 'revolutionary' material. The three Yiddish classics, Mendeli Mocher Sforim, Shalom Aleichem and I. L. Perets, albeit in censured form, were included.[31] Only selections critical of traditional Jewish life and values and those emphasizing social antagonism and class struggle were included. The selection also included Jewish writers of the USSR. Jewish history completely disappeared from the curriculum; in the elementary school (age 7–13) no mention was made of Jewish history even when general history was surveyed.[32] The Soviet Yiddish school did its utmost to stigmatize everything connected with Jewish nationalism, Jewish religion or way of life. 'They tried so hard to prevent any specifically Jewish manifestation in the life of the students that they prohibited the dancing of the *Sherele* [Jewish folk dance] in the regional competitions', recalled a teacher from Pinsk.[33]

Throughout their existence the Yiddish schools in the annexed provinces suffered from an acute shortage of Yiddish books. It was the result of the sudden duplication of the entire Yiddish school system in the USSR. The school year of 1939–40 was a particularly difficult time, and we have reports to that effect from all over the territories and throughout the entire year.[34] Teachers who had taught in the former Yiddish system helped in some places to improvise study material that was used by the students.[35] The Yiddish press carried reports of the planned publication of hundreds of thousands of new and out of print books in Yiddish to supply the increased demand.[36] But the shortage remained. It seems that the plans were never carried out in full. 'The Emes publishing house in Moscow promised to publish 27 text books for the school year of 1940–41. However, a month after the start of the year not a single book was published', complained *Der Shtern*.[37] 'There is a real chance that they will not be published at all. Why do the commissars for education keep quiet? Why do the Jewish schools which urgently need the books remain silent?' asked the Soviet Yiddish newspaper. It appears that the shortage was not only the result of bureaucratic inefficiency. Probably the shortage of books for Yiddish schools was yet another reflection of the negative attitude towards Jewish culture and nationalism.[38]

In the Soviet system the teacher served not only as an instructor, but also as a propaganda agent at school and in the community. Schools and teachers were important Sovietizing agents for the parents and the population at large. The same was expected of the teacher in the Yiddish school.[39] As a result of the sudden and marked increase in the number of Soviet Yiddish schools, the local authorities faced a difficult situation. They had to find suitable teachers and indoctrinate them in the proper creed. At first the former staff were asked to continue teaching, but in the 'Soviet spirit'. To ensure the 'correct' behaviour of the former teaching staff, they were under constant supervision from the education and security authorities. 'School inspectors were always on the watch as to the ideological fidelity of the teachers, which was checked repeatedly. The NKVD, too, often used to investigate the teachers' past and present whereabouts'[40], relates a teacher from Iwie. Teachers from among the refugees and local people with sufficient education were drafted to teach in the expanded system.[41] As could have been expected, many of the teachers lacked the necessary qualifications, background and ideological make-up. It is understandable, in view of the composition of the teaching staff, that the Soviet education authorities made a special effort to train new teachers as well as retrain the existing staff. Teacher seminars were organized in Lvov and Bialystok. Courses of various kinds were organized in Soviet teaching methods, Marxism and Leninism and Stalin's constitution, and in the Yiddish,

Russian, Belorussian and Ukrainian languages.[42] Courses in Soviet methodology and doctrine were held in various district centres and in the schools by inspectors of the Yiddish schools.[43] Winter and summer vacations were used extensively for instructing the teachers. The instruction covered Soviet teaching methodology and ideology as well as the Yiddish language and literature, and different general subjects and took place in different centres.[44] Several thousand teachers participated in the courses, thus being directly exposed to Soviet teaching methods. By contrast with other fields, the manning of the extensive and expanding educational system in the newly annexed provinces by people brought from the east was difficult. However, with the consolidation of Soviet rule, schools came under closer supervision and principals and teachers were replaced by more reliable elements, some brought over from the interior.[45] The purge and strict enforcement of the same methods and standards as in the USSR itself became the rule in the Yiddish schools in the territories from the summer of 1940.

Even to a much larger extent than in the field of popular culture it is justifiable to speak about an 'educational boom' under the Soviet regime. The decline of Jewish education was real and threatened the future of the community. However, for many, particularly the broader masses in the shtetlach and the younger generation, the developments in education had much to offer. Soviet education embraced many more students than the area had ever known before. Study was free at all levels, from kindergarten to university. It was offered to young and old in different institutions, and through night classes, and vocational training courses on a variety of subjects suitable for all. The regime conducted extensive extra-curricular and extra-scholastic activities, conducted during and after school hours. These, whether directly associated with the school or conducted by special extra-scholastic children's institutions, supplemented the school in educating the future generation of Soviet citizens. Great stress was laid in the extra-curricular activities on the inculcation of Soviet patriotism and the Soviet value system. Important roles in the organization of the extra-curricular programme were played by the Pioner and Komsomol organizations.[46] For the shtetl Jews these activities constituted to some extent foci of community activity and identification after the almost complete disappearance of the former Jewish institutions. The study opportunities offered by the regime were a temptation that could not be resisted by the deprived shtetl Jews, who overcame any reservations and qualms as to the content and norms of the education offered.

'It would be only fair to note also the positive side in the field of education during Soviet rule. Everyone studied and acquired new skills; the young in general in schools or vocational courses, the older in special institutions and various night classes. Sport played an important role for the young and the community at large and all this was free and paid for by the State' recalled a Kostopol inhabitant after complaining about the suppression of Hebrew culture.[47] The availability of study opportunities came with a radical change in the atmosphere surrounding the Jewish student. 'He straightened his back. The anti-Semitism that reigned in Polish education and the streets disappeared, at least on the formal level and on the surface. The Jewish student had his own distinct educational system, and he had a recognized status.'[48] Study in the Yiddish schools was only one possibility open to the Jewish students, and not necessarily the most desired. When it became obvious that the authorities were pressing for other roads of study many chose them. The majority of Jewish children studied in general educational institutions that were formally opened to them on equal grounds.

Like other ethnic groups, and being 'education-minded' probably to a higher degree, the Jewish population took advantage of the Soviet educational system. Yiddish schools very soon developed their extra-curricular activities and succeeded in becoming centres of community involvement. Student councils, with parents' participation; circles for arts and crafts that held open exhibitions; choirs and drama circles that performed to the whole community and participated in regional inter-ethnic competitions; participation in parades and holiday demonstrations – these were just a few of the varied activities promoted by the educational system and which involved large sections of the shtetl community.[49] Free education and adult literacy classes held a strong appeal for the largely impoverished shtetl population. This was noted with pride and satisfaction by the Soviet press and was also highly valued by the Jewish population.[50] Many children whose parents previously could not afford their studies and adults denied basic education were given the opportunity to study and thus obtained better qualifications for the future. The general expansion of educational opportunities contributed to the willingness to integrate and adapt into the Soviet system in spite of the resulting weakening of ethnic identity. This was typical particularly of the younger generation.

'Grave and hopeless was the situation of Jewish youth in Kostopol in the last years of Polish rule. Anti-Semitism was present everywhere. Those who were lucky and succeeded in getting a proper education could not find a suitable job. The future held no promise for the young' recollected a local inhabitant.[51] Kostopol was fairly representative of the prevailing situation and the mood among the teenagers and people in their early twenties in the Jewish community.[52] From shtetlach all over Poland came similar reports and complaints about the difficulties in being accepted for studies, getting a job, and about the lack of hope for the future. The young, many already far removed from traditional ways, felt more acutely than the older generation Polish haughtiness and anti-Semitism. There is no doubt that the Soviet regime, as long as it lasted in the area, represented a marked change for the younger generation. 'They brought to our shtetl a breeze of new air, a change of values. Jewish youth, eager for freedom, a sense of self-esteem, challenge and most of all for an encouraging government was largely carried away by the new environment', related a Lida inhabitant who was a teenager at the time.[53] The overt discriminatory policies of the former regime were abolished. Anti-Semitism was officially condemned and Jews considered to be equal citizens. Free education at all levels, without the blocking of the *Numerus Clausus*, became available. Jobs formerly beyond the reach of a Jew became, at least formally, accessible. The previous sense of hopelessness was now replaced by a feeling that there were unlimited opportunities to move to larger urban centres and that jobs, studies, entertainment and sports were easily available.[54]

Free access to education and the availability of jobs were the two strongest incentives for the Jewish youth to support the Soviet regime. 'The opportunity to pursue their high-school and university studies was the most attractive feature for Jewish youth. They flooded the institutions of learning. Now under Soviet rule Jewish youth could realize its strong desire for education and to study subjects previously denied', relates a Jewish student.[55] Free access for Jewish students to higher education, to universities and technological institutes, teachers' seminars, and a variety of courses in adult education on different topics, was the most obvious change that took place. Jewish students moved from the smaller shtetlach to larger centres, where study opportunities were more readily available. Even students who did not complete their high-school studies were accepted. Dormitories, free food and stipends were available for the student. That young Jews were drawn to support the regime may be understood. Jobs in the various branches of Soviet administration became accessible to the young who were willing to adapt and integrate.[56]

Attracted by new and ever-growing opportunities, the young generation in a very short time broke with many of the accustomed ways and long-established taboos. This was, of course, aided by the dissolution of the former institutions in the Jewish community. The extra-curricular and extra-scholastic activities – competitions, olympic games, entertainment events, etc. – attracted the Jewish youth away from home and replaced the former organizations. The Jewish youth, leaderless and disorganized after the dissolution of the Jewish youth organization, found it difficult to resist.

Not long after the occupation many of the best of our young people found themselves in the Komsomol. All the educational efforts of many years went down the drain. A shadow of doubt was cast over the whole of Jewish and Zionist education. Nobody was left that could find the right response to the new circumstances. As if all the leaders and instructors reconciled themselves with reality. They were occupied with their own problems. You could not seek advice or succour from them in an hour of stress that had no precedent

recalled one of the organizers of the *Hechaluts* (Zionist pioneers) movement in Szumsk.[57] The leaders either ran away, were in prison, or tried to hide. Another Zionist leader from Korzec expressed his amazement at 'how fast the young generation joined the Sovietization process and dissolved their old ties and acquaintances. They not only participated in, but frequently led, the process. People tried their best to obliterate all trace of past allegiances.'[58] In Grodno, when one of the leaders of the Zionist *Hashomer Hatsair* youth movement tried to convince local followers to go to Vilno, only one youngster was persuaded to do it. 'The others had many reasons not to leave. The truth of the matter was that new horizons and opportunities were opened up before the Jewish youth. They could study at any university or find a suitable job.'[59] Similar reports are available from other shtetlach in the annexed provinces.[60] Though there were those who tried to organize underground Zionist activity, to maintain their allegiance to Zionism and the Hebrew language, the majority availed itself of the new possibilities offered by the Soviet regime.

'Time took its course. In the summer and winter evenings, the great hall of what had been the Kleck *Yeshiva*, and was now a club, was filled with Jewish and Belorussian youth. Almost every evening had its own attraction. It was now a centre for entertainment and dancing. Theatre performances, movies, lectures, choirs, etc. took place before a mixed audience.'[61] Jewish youth in the shtetlach of former Eastern Poland was breaking away in increasing numbers from the traditional way of life.

Developments in the educational and cultural field were complex and frequently confused the contemporary observer. However, the general trend was clear and predictable. The former educational structure was destroyed and replaced by what looked to some to be a revival in the Soviet Yiddish system. Assimilation remained the real goal. School and the many varied extra-curricular activities and attractions were designed to bring about the weakening and eventually the destruction of the basic attachments and value system of the Jewish population. Soviet Yiddish education and culture were merely transitional phases. From the summer of 1940 on it was increasingly clear that the aim was to equalize the state of Jewish education in the annexed territories with that prevailing in the USSR itself. There assimilation was making ever larger inroads. In the former Polish provinces the 21 months of Soviet rule were too short a time to undermine long-established values and substitute the new loyalties for them. However, there could be detected definite changes in behaviour and allegiance, certainly at the public level. Among the poor masses and the young, one could notice a breaking away from tradition and a willingness to integrate into the surrounding society. But this was hardly brought about by the new rulers. It took place where the former culture and tradition showed clear signs of weakness and dissolution. Soviet rule and policies exposed existing trends of change within the Jewish community. For many, particularly the very young, Soviet education and its accompanying activities meant the escape from a marginal existence and an opportunity to tap the many possibilities offered by the modernizing Soviet State. The price for the attempt to succeed in Soviet society was separation from family and community, the shedding of Jewish identity and going it alone.

8
The Shtetl Changes its Face

The 21 months of Soviet rule could be considered the last stage of existence of the shtetl. Those were times of change in the external appearance of the small town, its Jews and their relations with the outside world. Streets and clothing, mutual relations and attitudes among Jews and non-Jews, holidays and the atmosphere in the shtetl underwent perceptible changes. Some innovations were drastic and rapid, the result of the brutal Sovietization policy. Others were subtle and slow, the consequence of slower processes of change and acculturation taking place within the Jewish community. The transformation that occurred in the socio-economic life of the Jewish community, as well as the negation of the Jewish traditional way of life, brought about perceptible changes in the shtetl and the life of its inhabitants. The Soviet economy, values and life-style, combined with the atomization of the Jewish community and its accelerated secularization, created different relations in the shtetl. Even sceptical observers who did not subscribe to the Communist claim of 'creating a new world' noticed that at least on the surface the shtetl and its Jews took on new forms and relationships.

Economic changes and the denial of traditional Jewish life were among the main causes of change in the external appearance of the shtetl and its Jews. The Communist regime was aware of the propaganda value of external trappings; hence the emphasis on public decorations. The shtetlach received what might be called a 'Soviet look'. Names of streets were changed and provided with suitable socialist and revolutionary names.[1] Symbols of Polish rule were replaced by Soviet signs. Posters carrying slogans and pictures showing the 'factories of Magnitogorsk, the oranges and limes of the Crimea and the peaches of Uzbekistan' were found everywhere.[2] Stalin's pictures and statues became a permanent feature of the main streets of many shtetlach, bearing witness to the transformation that occurred in the new Soviet territories.

There were shtetlach where the new regime had introduced electricity and others where street-lighting was extended for the first time. Loudspeakers were installed in the streets to carry the message of the regime. In many places the Soviet administration took care to clean the streets, repair the pavements, plant new trees and build new parks and squares. New cinemas were built in many shtetlach and 'Red-Corners' containing newspapers, books, games, etc. could be found all over the new provinces.[3] In numerous reports the Soviet press in Yiddish praised the regime's concern for the aesthetic side of socialist life and the changes that took place in that field in the shtetlach of former Eastern Poland. The emphasis was on the more ostentatious side: parks, squares, statues, fountains, etc.[4] Non-Soviet sources, less eager to report favourable changes, also corroborate the claim that the new rulers improved and developed the external appearance of the shtetlach, including their poorer sections.[5]

Economic change was, however, the major cause of changes in the face of the shtetl. The market street and the market-place had been the centre of life of the shtetl. They were also the geographic axis of the small town. This was the location of the shops, the stands, and the artisans' workshops. With the disappearance of private commerce, the forming of artisans' cooperatives and Soviet marketing, the old market and the buildings became redundant. 'The introduction of Soviet trade into the western provinces of Belorussia brought radical change in the external appearance of the streets' stated a report in the Soviet *Bialystoker Shtern*.[6] 'Almost overnight new big buildings were erected. They transformed radically the shape of the town. The small retail shop, narrow, airless and dark, vanished for good', continued the Soviet reporter. 'The market that served for hundreds of years as the source of livelihood for the shtetl Jews and the peasants was dismantled. It became a town park. In its midst was erected a huge stone monument to Lenin' related a Kolno inhabitant.[7] There are similar descriptions of other towns. The market and the surrounding buildings, for generations the centre of economic life of the shtetl Jews, disappeared. Squares, parks and statues of Lenin, Stalin, or other heroes of the Soviet state replaced the old structures.[8]

Secularization and the diminished influence of the synagogue and religion on the life-style of the Jews also had their effect on the external appearance of the shtetl. Previously the synagogue was not only a house of prayer, but also a centre of learning, assembly and conducting community affairs. It was thus a place of bustling life. Suddenly almost all social and community-oriented activities ceased. There was a drastic decrease in the numbers of those attending the services. Yet what most radically altered the vista of the shtetl and its peculiar 'Jewish' appearance was the decrease in the public observance of the *Shabat*, the holidays and the family celebrations. Because of the high proportion of Jews in many shtetlach, Jewish holidays of all kinds and the rest day of the *Shabat* became a most important part of shtetl life. Under the new rulers, even people who still observed the *Shabat* and celebrated the various holidays thought it wiser to keep their observances to the privacy of their homes. As we have seen above, the authorities made a special effort to attract the younger generation during the traditional holidays and *Shabat* nights. The communist regime tried to introduce its holidays and festive occasions to entice the youth away from the attractions of the traditional life-style. Sights of the *Shabat* and holidays, of festive streets and closed shops, of candles in the windows and Jews hurrying to the synagogue, all of these that were an integral part of the shtetl life almost completely vanished.

The 21-month period of Soviet rule could be seen as a long series of Soviet holidays and festive events: celebrations for 'liberation' from the Polish yoke followed by the referendum and annexation by the USSR, elections to different institutions like the local Soviets, Republic Assemblies, and the Supreme Soviet of the USSR, the day of the October Revolution, 1 May and in between birthdays or centennials of Stalin, Lenin and other leaders and heroes of the Soviet State. Reading the Soviet press of the period one may get the impression that the population was passing from one festive event to another. Soviet holidays were events that were seen in the streets. The shtetl was specially decorated with flags, posters, pictures of the leaders, and street slogans, stands, balloons, etc. Soviet holidays were not a one-day event. The masses were mobilized to participate in the various activities surrounding the celebrations themselves. Describing elections to the Republic's Soviet an inhabitant of Kleck noted: 'For many weeks before the elections the shtetl was flooded with special attractions. The entire town was under the impact of the elections. Regular activities in schools and other institutions ceased. Each and all had to contribute to the forthcoming event.'[9] The Soviet holiday was a community happening, an occasion to mobilize and indoctrinate the masses. Music, parades, decorations and special food supplies served to create a festive atmosphere in the streets. The ceremonies seemed like rites that served to strengthen loyalties and values of the regime.[10] This attempt to create a festive atmosphere of goodwill and satisfaction in the shtetl stood in stark contrast to the feeling of disintegration and despair one typically finds in an atomized Jewish community. However, the Jew as an individual tried, at least outwardly, to participate in the changed public events of the shtetl.

The sights of the shtetl changed also because people started to dress differently. Clothing reflected socio-economic differences, not just fashion and personal style. It was also proof of past and present wealth. 'Ladies with make-up vanished from the streets of our shtetl. So did furs and expensive suits. They were replaced by long black and brown coats and simple hats' relates a Czortkow Jew.[11] 'Instead of fur hats, ties, fur coats and fancy gowns, people wore short jackets and various shabby clothes. *Shabat* and holiday looked like regular days, one could no longer find the fancy *shtraimlach* (fur hat worn by *Khasidim* on *Shabat* and other holidays) and jewellery. The lustre disappeared from Jewish shtetl life' complained the narrator.[12]

The disappearance of *Shabat* and holiday clothing was an easily noted change in the external appearance of the shtetl. One felt as if there was no interruption in the drudge of everyday life. It added to the prevailing sense of shabbiness and lacklustre life found among the new Soviet citizens.[13] Coarse, shabby and, if possible, old and worn-out clothing replaced fancy dress. High boots, for some reason, were considered proper footwear in the socialist state. They looked more 'proletarian' than the more delicate and comfortable shoes worn under the former regime.[14] Rough and shabby clothing was the attire suitable for people belonging to the favoured classes, i.e. the peasants and workers. People with a 'suspicious' background were particularly careful not to reveal their past by wearing improper clothing.[15] Occasionally the result was 'a tragi-comic change in clothing. High boots replaced shoes. It was funny and regrettable to see people of standing walking around in high boots. There were those who without receiving orders to do so, and only to gain favour with the new rulers, took off their shirts with standing collars and put on Soviet-style khaki shirts.'[16]

New classes and different people rose to prominence in the shtetl under the communist regime. The former Jewish elite, based mainly on wealth and learning, lost its dominant positions overnight. Its members either fled abroad, were arrested or deported, or remained and tried to be as inconspicuous as possible. People with suspected backgrounds attempted to blur their social origins and to conform to the requirements of the new rulers.[17] There were the naïve who thought that 'by removing their silk ties and donning a "proletarian" shirt, they would become part of the new ruling class, or at least be left alone'.[18] Respectable leaders of the community were now under the constant danger of arrest. Former pillars of Jewish shtetl society did their utmost to gain favour with the new ruling class.[19] They tried to socialize with upstarts hardly known to them by name before.[20] While every small shopkeeper could be accused of being a capitalist, many with a suitable social background claimed that they were Communists in the past.[21]

In the backward impoverished shtetlach of the former eastern Polish provinces, one could hardly find a Jewish proletariat in the Marxist sense. Hence the class most favoured by the Soviet regime in the shtetl were the small artisans. They were now the 'important' people, praised and promoted to leading positions by the regime. They were honoured by all. For the first time, poor artisans were attending cafés and restaurants they never even entered before.[22] Having an artisan's origin put one in a most desirable social position. Now 'all the former *Gvirim* [rich] who despised the poor artisan and his family thought that . . . it might be a good idea to have one as a son-in-law, a safeguard against confiscation of their homes, and searches by the police,' commented a Soviet Yiddish author describing the changed social relations in the shtetl.[23] 'Highest in the new social ladder are now the artisans and the workers' claimed a report in the Soviet press from the annexed territories.[24] By and large this claim is corroborated by non-Soviet sources. 'We the artisans, who in the past were at the bottom of the ladder, all of a sudden became the most important people. The new rulers announced that we, as working people, living from our own labour, were more important than all the community notables – all the house owners, rabbis, learned and other "fine Jews"', recalled a Kostopol Jew, who became one of the six appointed policemen in the shtetl.[25] A new sense of value and self-esteem could be found among the poorer sections of the Jewish community. 'There was a feeling that the times of the wealthy and their rich houses had passed, and that the time of the downtrodden had finally arrived. They volunteered to serve in the militia, pacing the streets with a hitherto unknown confidence.'[26]

Whole classes and typical characters vanished from the shtetl townscape; the well-to-do disappeared and with them the sight of the *gvir* (rich man) of the shtetl. So did the small shopkeeper, independent artisan and pedlar. All were central and time-honoured figures of shtetl life. With the destruction of the former economic rule many shtetl occupations were also lost. The famous *luftmentsch* (literally 'air man', – a person without a profession or steady occupation) was not seen any more.

> Almost completely gone from the shtetl scene was the Jew holding a piece of straw in his mouth, a walking-stick in his hand, checking out peasants' carts to make a bargain. Gone were the professional loafers that you could find in the past around the market place . . . On first sight one could detect that a transformation had taken place in the behaviour of the shtetl Jews: the nervousness and irritability of the past were gone,

related a Soviet reporter.[27] One could doubt the extent of the accuracy of the descriptions of the 'changed shtetl Jew' that appeared frequently in the Soviet Yiddish press. However, there was much truth in the claims of the changed shtetl townscape, and its Jews.[28]

Outwardly, there was a considerable change in the relationship between the shtetl Jew and the surrounding non-Jewish society. The breaking up of the former order resulted in the disappearance of long-established barriers between the Jews and their neighbours. The atomized Jewish community, stripped of almost all its particularist organizations, came into much closer and more open contact with the non-Jews than ever before. At work, in school, in the club or army, Jews found themselves mingling with Ukrainians, Poles, Belorussians and Russians. Formal equality, access to jobs that were closed before them in the past, the official ban on anti-Semitism which was recognized as a punishable crime, combined to create a different setting for the more frequent encounters with non-Jews. Long-standing patterns of behaviour, attitudes, prejudices, etc. had not changed during the 21 months of Soviet rule. However, one could easily detect new elements in the relationship between Jew and non-Jew in the shtetl.

The announced Soviet policies of equality, solidarity and opposition to overt discrimination were most important in determining the nature of inter-ethnic relations in the annexed provinces. We have seen above that equality had its limitations in that there was a policy of preference of Ukrainians and Belorussians. Nevertheless when compared to the Polish regime, the Jews were granted equality on a scale unheard of before. In the eyes of the law, in schools and universities and above all in access to jobs, it was a genuine revolution. While being denied access to the highest ranks, Jews still enjoyed many and varied opportunities for work and career. This was particularly true in the shtetlach, those small urban centres where they constituted such a high proportion of the population. 'Jews, in large numbers, occupied positions of responsibility in both the administration and municipal government. It was a dream that could not happen in independent Poland,' remarked a Borszczow inhabitant.[29] 'The Soviet authorities used many Jews in their administration and services . . . A considerable number of young Jews were employed by the Communist party', claimed a Zulkiew resident.[30] 'There was no discrimination against anybody . . . and the attitude towards the Jew was favourable' came the testimony from Lomza.[31] And so on. For the first time Jews 'felt that they were citizens with equal rights. Some held jobs of importance in government service. They participated actively in cultural life. One could find Jews as teachers, principals, inspectors. In almost every office you could find Jews.'[32] At the same time, on every occasion Soviet propaganda and educational policy emphasized the value of international solidarity and equality of all ethnic groups. Strife between national groups was described as a tool of the former Polish regime to divide and rule.[33] In the regular school curriculum and on special occasions like meetings with artisans and literary evenings, the principles of solidarity were propagated among the citizens of the new provinces.[34]

Among the Poles, Ukrainians and Belorussians, the prevailing opinion was that the Jews enjoyed a most privileged position under the Soviet regime. It was a Jewish government in the eyes of many.[35] That view was particularly strong among the Poles, as emerged from numerous reports from dozens of shtetlach from all over the territories.[36] The non-Jewish population resented the new conditions of relative equality of the Jews and their occupation of positions of authority in the Soviet administration. The Poles in the territory were offended by the changed situation and the loss of their dominant position. To accept a job from the occupying power was regarded almost as an act of treason. The Ukrainians and even the Belorussians did not easily accept the changed status of the Jew. Whether in response to Nazi propaganda or as the continuation of prevailing stereotypes, the 'Jew' was identified with the Soviet regime and, usually in silence, resented for it. 'People were waiting for a suitable moment to settle accounts', recalled a Targowica resident.[37] For many non-Jews it was difficult to accept a situation of formal Jewish equality.[38]

Anti-Semitism as policy, in its violent and brutal forms, disappeared under the new regime. 'During the Soviet rule we had never even once encountered an expression of anti-Semitism and discrimination' recalled a teacher from Kleck.[39] This statement is corroborated by many others from different shtetlach and from people with varied backgrounds from former Eastern Poland.[40] The Soviet authorities realized that anti-Semitism was frequently a guise for opposition to the regime. Violent expressions of anti-Semitism were strongly suppressed because of their danger to the rulers.[41] But anti-Semitism among the local non-Jewish population had not disappeared; it might even have increased in intensity. 'Open anti-Semitism went underground. Our neighbours thought that the Jews were the favourites of the new rulers. Anti-Semitism was illegal, but the population identified the Jews with the regime and every wrongdoing was attributed to the Jews. In due course, they promised to avenge themselves', recollected a survivor from Stolpce.[42]

It had been difficult in particular for the Poles to get accustomed to the changed conditions and new status of the Jews. 'The relations between Poles and Jews are at present markedly worse than before the war' maintained a Polish report from Stryj.[43] 'The entire Polish population adopted a negative attitude towards the Jews because of their blatant cooperation with the Bolsheviks and their hostility against the non-Jews ... The people simply hate the Jews', asserted the same report. Similar descriptions are available from other places.[44] Among the Jews, one could note a sense of relief and even defiance towards their former rulers. 'I have to admit that we were quite happy to see them [the Poles] in their present condition ... Our rulers of yesterday were made small and humble. Only yesterday we were second-rate citizens,' commented a Mir Jew about the transformed relations.[45] Any attempt by the Poles to regain some of their lost pride by abusing the Jewish population was put down by the Soviet authorities. No wonder that one could find Poles trying to gain favour with the Jewish population. 'They believed that the Jewish government had arrived and sought Jewish friends and friendship' claimed a report from Pinsk.[46] Neither did the Ukrainians reconcile themselves easily to the changed conditions. While the Poles resented the loss of power, the Ukrainians complained that they did not get enough and had to share some jobs with others. Thwarted national aspirations drove the Ukrainians to oppose the Soviet government and the people associated with it. Ukrainians, to an even greater extent than the Poles, tended to brand the communist state as 'Jewish, ruled by a Jewish government and where all the central positions were occupied by Jews'.[47] Anti-Semitic stereotypes were strengthened among the Ukrainian peasants by intense Nazi propaganda that equated Soviet rule with Jewish dominance.[48] Violent or even verbal public anti-Jewish outbursts by Ukrainians were strongly repressed by the authorities.[49] In the many shtetlach of the newly annexed provinces the Jewish community found itself in a dire predicament: how should they behave in a multi-ethnic environment and with what nationality should they cooperate and identify? The option of pursuing a separate Jewish national line had been prevented by the regime. When the Jews opted for cooperation with the Soviet authorities and with the ruling Russian nationality it aroused the strong resentment of the local nationalities and exacerbated long-standing anti-Semitic sentiments. On the eve of the war with Germany one could clearly detect the strong rumblings of anti-Jewish feelings seeking an outlet.[50]

As long as the Soviet rule lasted the emphasis was on solidarity and cooperation between the nationalities of the new territories. No doubt the shtetl Jews were quite eager to change the nature of the relations with their non-Jewish neighbours. They stood to gain personal and physical security and were ready to pay for these in terms of losing their separate identity and by breaking long-established taboos. On the surface, at least, one could notice a change in relations. The Soviet authorities initiated many programmes that brought together Jewish and non-Jewish children, youth and adults. Conferences, meetings, games, performances, etc. were organized to bring about the intermingling of people from the different ethnic groups. In the smaller shtetlach in particular schoolchildren went to common schools and were exposed to the preaching of Soviet notions on solidarity among the nations.[51] It was mostly the youth of the different ethnic groups that was affected by the breaking down of former barriers as a result of the dissolution of the old order. At school and at work youngsters could meet as never before. A Jewish youngster recalled:

> During the Polish rule no friendships were formed between Jews and Poles. There were constant tensions between the two groups. During Soviet rule the barriers disappeared. There was a feeling of togetherness and people came closer to each other. Friendships between Jewish and Polish boys and girls were formed for the first time in the history of our shtetl.[52]

Soviet entertainment brought Jewish and non-Jewish youth together in the clubs and cinemas and on the dance-floors built by the new rulers. 'Time took its course. In the long winter evenings and bright summer nights Jewish and Belorussian youngsters filled up the former *yeshiva* hall.'[53] 'Jewish and Ukrainian boys and girls, as never before, sang and danced together with utter abandon on summer evenings', recalled a former Lanowce resident.[54] Barriers that existed for many generations, based on deep-seated taboos of relations between Jew and non-Jew, were undermined.[55] The shtetl was changing ancient norms of behaviour. 'Jewish Dereczyn changed drastically within a very short period. Traditions that lived with many generations vanished suddenly. The younger generation did not attend the synagogue and did whatever it pleased. It became a fashion to speak Russian, to assimilate into the new Russian environment . . . A new life-style emerged in the Jewish community', lamented the narrator from Dereczyn, himself a rabbi's son.[56]

The Soviet press abounded with descriptions of the joyful atmosphere prevailing in the shtetlach of the new Soviet territories. One can find equally as many opposite accounts of the shtetl mood.[57] Outbursts of spontaneous joy that met the Red Army on its entry soon vanished. The shtetl of Eastern Poland before September 1939 was not really a joyous place and it did not become one under the new rulers. The realities of Sovietization and the Communist regime determined the atmosphere of the shtetl. Destruction of the old order, arrests and deportations, constant anxiety felt by many about personal safety and livelihood, the ever-present lines and worry to get the basic necessities were not incentives for high spirits among the new Soviet citizens. There were those who benefitted from the new rulers. Yet the majority, even people favoured by the regime, lived under the constant threat of the secret police and the oppressive atmosphere of the Stalinist regime at its peak.

The dissolution of the former order with its institutions and intense community life created a void that no Soviet initiative could replace. Shtetl intimacy and closeness were replaced by a sense of loneliness and detached suspicion. 'Soon after the Soviet occupation all normal social and cultural life ceased. All usual social intercourse among people stopped overnight', related a Baranowicz survivor.[58] Zak, who lived in Grodno, complained that

Everyone was living by himself and for himself. The Jews maintained very little contact with each other. It was as if all friendships were frozen, as if people suddenly lost confidence in each other. One could feel a sense of reservation everywhere. They had taken a Jewish town and emptied it of any Jewish content . . . It looked as if the town lost its will to live.[59]

People were preoccupied with providing the basic daily needs. 'The only real interest in every home was the daily concern to get the basic commodities, and that was not an easy task', claimed Zak.[60]

Even before the onslaught of the large-scale waves of arrests and deportations, with the first sporadic apprehensions of local leaders, an air of suspicion and fear descended on the shtetlach of former Eastern Poland. People broke off their former social ties, abstained from new acquaintanceships, were afraid to meet strangers, etc.[61] It was, however, just a foretaste of the depressive atmosphere that reigned in the territories after the beginning of the large-scale systematic deportations. 'It became dangerous to contact your close friends', recalls a survivor. 'The Jewish population lived in a nightmare. People felt like living dead: grey and monotonous lives.'[62] No wonder that after the deportations of February 1940 'the Jewish population and its non-Jewish neighbours never regained their peace. Streets were full of anxious faces. People lost any sense of security during the day and few had a restful sleep at night.'[63] 'Terror reigned in the streets and people ceased to talk about anything but the weather. They refrained from meeting even relatives, did not visit friends or host any.'[64] The intensity of the terror and its effect on daily life and moods decreased after each peak in the arrests, yet it never disappeared. It was a dominant and pervasive element in the everyday life of the shtetlach of the former Polish eastern provinces.

After 21 months of Soviet rule, for better or worse, there emerged a markedly different shtetl. Stripped of market and synagogues, many of its traditional characters and sights were gone; it was still very much a small backward town. Remaining were the shabby houses, dirty streets, the poverty and negligence of generations. Gone was the shtetl with its close and intimate Jewish communal life, the *Shabat*, holidays and family celebrations. Soviet-organized holidays and mass events were poor substitutes for old-time joys. A deep-seated feeling of loneliness and fear descended on the small towns of the new Soviet territories. Organized anti-Semitism and the threat of pogroms had disappeared, yet the Jews were still afraid of a sudden knock on the door at night, of unexpected arrests. The shtetl was still there, but much of its Jewish character had gone or changed.

9
Refugees*

Former Eastern Poland became a refuge for a sizeable group of Jews who escaped from German-occupied territory. Their presence was felt in the larger and smaller urban centers, augmenting the numbers of the maladjusted and frustrated among the local Jewish community. The refugees and their fate contributed to the depressing atmosphere that prevailed in the annexed territories. They were always on the move, restless, nervous, uncertain about the future, and subject to continuous police supervision. Their mere presence enhanced the sense of frustration and uncertainty among the new Soviet citizens.

Hundreds of thousands of Jewish refugees sought homes free from Nazi persecution during the period between 1933 and 1941 preceding the extermination of millions. Hitler's rise to power in Germany and the extension of Nazi rule over large parts of Europe were accompanied by sharp increases in the number of Jewish refugees to non-Nazi countries. Prior to the outbreak of the Nazi–Soviet War in June 1941, German authorities allowed and even forced the Jews living within their borders to leave. The real tragedy was that most of the other countries either closed their doors or sharply limited the numbers which they were prepared to accept.

A general international apathy concerning the fate of the Jewish refugees from Nazi-occupied territories prevailed among most of the member governments of the League of Nations and outside that body.[1] The policy of the League amounted to a refusal to deal with the problem, despite the fact that a High Commissioner (James G. McDonald) was appointed to take care of refugees, Jewish and others, coming from Germany. However, the

Commission did not receive its budget from the League, and its achievements were very limited. 'The victims of Nazism met with resistance almost everywhere. Many countries stiffened their immigration requirements in order to prevent the entry of those doomed people into the Western hemisphere.'[2] A conference was convened in Evian, France, in July 1938; representatives from 30 countries who responded to President Roosevelt's initiative participated, but effected no real changes in the policies adopted by the non-Nazi countries.[3] In a way, the policy of appeasement applied to Germany during the 1930s was transferred to the Jewish refugee problem.

There are no exact figures concerning the number of Jewish refugees who were able to find temporary or permanent homes outside the Nazi territories. Jacques Vernant estimates that by May 1939 the number of Jewish refugees from Germany, Austria and Czechoslovakia was 401,000, of whom 194,000 emigrated to countries overseas and 207,000 found refuge in Europe.[4] Arieh Tartakower and Kurt R. Grosman maintain that during the years 1938–1942 the number of Jews who were able to leave for countries overseas was about 213,000. They could not, however, ascertain the total of refugees leaving before or after the outbreak of the war.[5]

Taking into account the general background of the refugee problem, as well as previous Soviet policy on the subject, the presence of several hundred thousand Jewish refugees in Soviet-occupied Eastern Poland after September 1939 created something of a paradox and deserves more attention than it has hitherto been given.[6] About 10 per cent of the largest Jewish community in Europe found refuge in Soviet territory by leaving those parts of Poland which were occupied by the Nazis. This group became the largest remnant of European Jewry after the Holocaust.

Even though the Soviet constitution included a special article which offered asylum to foreign citizens who were persecuted for political reasons,[7] the USSR was not among those countries which absorbed any meaningful number of refugees from Nazi territories. The Soviet government did not cooperate with the High Commission established by the League of Nations and, together with Germany, tried to curtail the Commission's activities. The Soviet government was afraid that the High Commission would support anti-Soviet refugees.[8] In addition, internal developments such as collectivization, rapid industrialization and the purges of the mid-thirties did not create a favourable environment for the acceptance of or any attraction for the victims of Nazism. The Kremlin viewed the Evian Conference as a 'plot to encourage the sabotage activities of the Trotskyist emigrés', and therefore refused to send its representatives or to participate in the Intergovernmental Committee for Refugees which the Conference established.[9] Only after the occupation of Eastern Poland did the Soviet government directly encounter the Jewish refugee problem, and on a massive scale as well.

Two major waves of Jewish refugees in flight from Nazi occupation reached Eastern Poland: the first started before 17 September 1939, when the Red Army crossed Poland's Eastern border, and lasted until the official incorporation of Eastern Poland into the USSR; the second wave started after 30 October when the border between the German and Soviet zones was officially closed, and lasted almost until the outbreak of hostilities between Germany and the Soviet Union.

The first group of refugees, who arrived in Eastern Poland without encountering difficulties in crossing the border, did so both before and after the demarcation of the new Soviet–German border line. Among them were those who were in the area when occupied as well as those who were admitted later by the Soviet authorities. This distinction is of importance when dealing with the problem of Soviet policy toward those Jews seeking refuge from Nazism. Most of the refugees found in Eastern Poland at the time that the Soviet troops entered had come there as a direct result of the German – Polish War. The systematic attacks on purely civilian targets, particularly large cities, were an integral part of the blitzkrieg tactics, intended to destroy the morale of both the civilian population and the Polish army. The fact that the cities contained a relatively high proportion of Jews made the Jewish community more nervous about Nazi intentions. That, however, was not the major reason for the massive flight of Jews to the east. German atrocities perpetrated against the Jewish population deeply affected the Jewish community, and tens of thousands of Jewish men left Warsaw and Lodz.[10] The flight from Warsaw was accelerated after 7 September when an official decree was published ordering all men eligible for military service to move to the eastern provinces where a new army and line of defence would be established. The Polish government itself was retreating from the capital to Lublin and organizing special convoys for selected groups.[11] It should be noted that a very high percentage of those fleeing east were men and women without families. 'There were among the younger people those who intended to cross the Soviet border in the case of a total German victory. Members of the Zionist organizations fled to towns close to the Rumanian border, hoping to reach Palestine via Rumania.'[12]

The final border between the USSR and Germany was drawn on 28 September; until that date no clear-cut delineation between the two had existed. The Soviet authorities, therefore, inherited the Jewish refugees remaining in Eastern Poland as part of the local population. It hardly required a policy of generosity toward victims of Nazism to let the refugees stay where they were found. More complicated is the matter of Soviet policy towards those Jews who were permitted to cross the border without hindrance, mainly in October 1939. Should this be considered as a policy designed to rescue Jews from Nazi persecution? The evidence available does not warrant such a conclusion. Soviet policy was determined by general considerations that had very little to do with the fate of the Jews in Nazi Poland. Moscow insisted on maintaining the fiction that the Soviet Union came to 'rescue and liberate the oppressed Belorussian and Ukrainian population'. In line with this policy, the Soviet authorities in Poland organized elections to constitutional assemblies which decided, unanimously, to join the USSR.[13] During the period of preparing the elections, the Soviets had every reason to be liberal in order to prove that not only the local population but also the people from German Poland preferred to live under Soviet rule.[14]

During the month of October the Soviet authorities did not object to the German practice of forcing entire Jewish communities to cross into Soviet Poland. Thus the Jews of Sokal, close to the new border on the Bug, witnessed the arrival of many Jews from Belz, Kristiampole, and Varzh. Among them was also the famous Rabbi of Belz.[15] All the Jewish inhabitants of Ostroleka were forced to cross the border at the same time. When they reached the first Soviet outpost 'the Russians received us cordially, offered us cigarettes and candies', related one of the refugees.[16] Przemysl, in Galicia, became a major center for entire Jewish communities who were forced to cross to the Soviet side during the month of October.[17] The Soviets were still ready to accept thousands of Jewish refugees, both those who had been expelled and those who were fleeing on their own.

The second major wave of Jewish refugees started reaching Soviet territory after the official incorporation of Eastern Poland into the Belorussian and Ukrainian Soviet Republics, at the beginning of November 1939. This wave lasted, although numbers reduced very quickly, almost until 21 June 1941. The refugees were now fleeing from territories where the massacre had already begun to a country that promised to be at least a refuge. The Soviet authorities required special permits from people trying to enter their territory, or those qualifying according to the population exchange agreement with the German government on 16 November 1939. The crossing of the border without mutual consent involved great hardship and the risk of death. The local German authorities continued their practice of forcing entire Jewish communities to cross the Soviet border, but now the Soviet guards refused to admit the victims of persecution. Those caught were shipped back to the Nazi border. German guards in turn fired at anyone trying to re-enter. Thus, quite frequently, thousands of refugees had to stay for days in the no-man's land along the border.[18]

A rather bizarre episode was the attempt by the Germans to use the agreement with the Soviet Union of 16 November 1939 to transfer 'legally' Polish Jews across the Soviet border. According to that, the undersigned parties had agreed to the exchange of Ukrainians and White Russians living in German territory for Germans (the so-called Volks-Deutsche) living on Soviet territory.[19] The German authorities tried to register Jews as 'Ukrainians of the Mosaic faith'.[20] The Soviets refused to accept that arrangement. Moscow tried to stop the flood of expelled refugees by requesting the direct intervention of the German Foreign Ministry. Violators of the prohibition to cross the frontier were threatened with three years' imprisonment. On 15 November the Soviets officially protested Germany's action of forcing Jews to cross their border.[21] State Secretary Weizsäcker reported the complaint of Colonel General Keitel, in a memorandum dated 5 December 1939, stating that the Jews expelled across the Russian border were being forced back by Soviet commanders. Keitel asked the Foreign Ministry to take up the matter with the governor general of Poland in order to prevent possible future friction.[22] In response to Soviet objections as well as to changes in the policy towards the Jews in the Nazi territories, the practice of expelling thousands of Jews across the Soviet frontier ceased at the beginning of 1940.

Despite the dangers involved, the stream of Jewish refugees continued throughout the winter of 1939–40. Thousands fled from towns and villages close to the border. Here entire families, including children and the elderly, attempted to reach the Soviet side. Many were killed in the no-man's land and some, who succeeded in crossing the border, were tried for espionage. Nevertheless, one has the impression that the Soviet border was not yet tightly sealed to those seeking refuge.[23] The attitude of the Soviet guards differed from place to place. Occasionally hundreds and even thousands were allowed to cross the border.[24]

The number of Jewish refugees decreased in the spring of 1940 and ceased almost completely during that summer. The difficulties in crossing the Soviet frontier prevented many from even attempting the venture. At the time when increasing numbers of Polish Jews were drawn into ghettos in the summer of 1940, the Soviet border became even more difficult to cross. The reasons for the closure of the Soviet border to Nazi victims, like those for its openness in the preceding months, had little to do with Soviet policy concerning the fate of the Jews under German occupation. The summer of 1940 saw a general tightening of the Soviet policies in the newly annexed territories. The free movement of people across the border created a genuine security risk, and it was too complicated to control every crossing. Beginning with the summer of 1940, the border between the 'friendly' countries became a fortified line. Not only Nazi collaborators but also Nazi victims had to be prevented from crossing the frontier.

The exact number of Jews from Nazi-occupied Poland who found refuge on Soviet territory is not known; nor do we have reliable data concerning the proportions among the various waves of refugees. One may doubt whether the absolute figures of refugees under Soviet jurisdiction could be found even in the Soviet archives. The chaos that reigned in the area for quite a while after the entrance of the Soviet troops, and the transfer of many refugees across the borders and within the boundaries of Eastern Poland, complicated the problem of census-taking. The speedy collapse of Soviet rule after the outbreak of the war with Germany probably destroyed much of the available material. Those studying the problem from outside the Soviet Union must rely on secondary sources, and therefore their statistics amount to rough estimates at best. The range of differences in estimates might give us an idea of the problem's complexity. Thus, Avraham Peteshnik estimated the number of refugees as one million,[25] while the journal *Jewish Affairs* maintained that their number did not surpass 200,000.[26] Bernard D. Weinryb, using a variety of sources and testimonies tends to accept 300,000 as the approximate number of Jews who found refuge in Soviet Poland.[27] Other investigators of the period tend to accept Weinryb's estimate.[28] Refugees constituted about 20 per cent of the Jewish population of Soviet Poland; therefore, sheer numbers of refugees alone created an important problem for the Soviet authorities in Eastern Poland.

These hundreds of thousands of Jewish refugees were one of the most problematic groups in adapting to the Soviet way of life. They were difficult to direct, and Eastern Poland lacked the economic capacity to absorb them. For the Soviet authorities, the refugees became a political, administrative and economic problem. The authorities had very little regard for the refugees' unique situation, particularly in its human aspects. A contradiction existed between the goals and attitudes of the Soviet authorities and those of the Jewish refugees. Their mutual relations went through several phases reflecting changes in Soviet policy towards the local population, and also the differing reactions of the refugees themselves.

During the first stage, which began after the Soviet army had entered Eastern Poland and which lasted until the formal incorporation of the area into the USSR, the local authorities exhibited a rather liberal attitude towards the refugees. At this stage, the victims of war and Nazi persecution were allowed to adapt and to find their way in the new system with little interference and even with some help from the authorities.

The local Jewish communities, themselves experiencing the painful process of adaptation to the new regime, their autonomous organizations dismembered, tried their best to offer help to their brethren. One gets the impression that the shtetl communities showed greater concern and devoted more energy to helping the refugees than one could find in the larger towns. Thus in Sokal, a special committee was established to take care of the refugees. The entire community contributed to the establishment of a public kitchen, while private homes, synagogues, and schools were used to provide housing.[29] 'Almost every Jewish family housed some refugees from Nazi Poland', relates an inhabitant of Dereczyn, a town in Belorussia.[30] The Jewish community of Janow, near Pinsk, mobilized all its resources to provide first aid for the refugees: 'After a short while all the refugees found housing with local families. All of us felt a moral obligation to offer help to our destitute brothers', recalled a survivor from that little town.[31] In Lutsk, 'every Jewish home had at least one refugee. The hospitality was spontaneous and natural . . . It amounted to a huge effort to provide first aid to hundreds of homeless Jews.'[32] This is just a sample illustrating the generous behaviour of the shtetl in time of need. Refugees with special skills were able to find employment in both the smaller towns and the larger centres. Teachers, engineers, technicians, accountants and physicians were in great demand.[33]

On the other hand, the situation was particularly acute in the larger cities. The Jewish populations of Lvov and Bialystok were almost doubled, adding tens of thousands of newcomers.[34] Within a very short time all houses and rooms were rented. New arrivals were forced to use schools, synagogues, theatres, railway stations and parks. Those who were lucky enough to find a vacancy needed a special permit from the local authorities.[35] The Soviet administration was reluctant to provide housing for the refugees, since it needed the limited housing facilities for its personnel arriving from the USSR. One finds numerous, identical descriptions of misery and the problems of housing and unemployment which afflicted thousands of refugees in Eastern Poland. The local authorities opened some public kitchens in the major cities to provide food for the refugees, but the food was poor and the number of kitchens insufficient.[36] During the first months of Soviet authority existing Jewish relief institutions were not abolished, but could not handle the situation. Later, the Soviets simply let them run out of funds. In Bialystok and Kovel the Joint Distribution Committee (JDC) was able to offer some aid.[37] In Lvov 'food relief was organized as long as the financial resources lasted. When the money ran out the Soviet authorities made it clear that they were against philanthropy', reported one of the Jewish community leaders.[38] When the JDC sent 150,000 zlotys for relief work in Lvov, the Soviet authorities refused to permit the opening of public kitchens.[39] After 1 January 1940 the Polish zloty was no longer legal currency in Eastern Poland. This regulation affected those refugees who had not exchanged their savings in time and who, therefore, became penniless overnight.[40]

Finding a job was one of the major concerns of the refugees. The local Jewish community could not take care of a problem of such magnitude even in normal times. As mentioned earlier, some refugees found employment in the professions, in local institutions, factories, cooperatives and the expanding educational system. A small, but important group, which attracted the attention of the Soviet authorities, was that of Jewish intellectuals – poets, novelists, journalists, and artists – who found refuge in Lvov and Bialystok.

The Soviet authorities paid special attention to the 're-education' and indoctrination of the new citizens of the Soviet State. The relatively large group of Jewish intellectuals assembled in Bialystok could potentially serve that purpose well, provided, of course, that those with an ideologically suspicious past had been duly eliminated. The rest had to adapt themselves to the official thought and style. During the first few weeks after the occupation the authorities provided a special home for refugee artists and writers.[41] Those who were suspected of having had some past connection with either the Bund or the Zionist movement stood no chance of being accepted, and looked instead for safer occupations.[42] Others, who could not force themselves to follow the official line and to remain silent in face of the tragedy of their brothers in the Nazi territories, stopped writing.[43] Dozens of poets and novelists who were ready to serve the regime 'produced' poetry according to the prevailing Stalinist style. The pages of the *Bialystoker Shtern*, the *Oktiaber*, *Der Shtern*, and other Yiddish papers were filled with their literary 'products'.

With the passage of time, special branches of the Soviet Union of Writers were established in Bialystok and Lvov.[44] Thus, in January 1941, the *Ofboi*, a monthly published in Latvia, could print an article entitled 'Broad Jewish Cultural Activity in Western Belorussia'.[45] The paper reported that 'in Bialystok there are many Jewish writers who previously lived in Warsaw. In Bialystok, as in the entire area formerly under the rule of the Polish Pans, where any cultural activity could barely exist, intense creative cultural activity is now going on . . . The cultural production of the Jewish writers has increased tremendously.'[46] The same paper reported that David Bergelson, the famous Soviet Yiddish writer, had met with the editorial board of the papers *Der Shtern* and *Oktiaber*. During that meeting Zelig Akselrod, a member of the *Der Shtern* board, talked about the publication of a series of books by the refugee writers.[47] The Yiddish writers from the Soviet Union played an important role in 're-educating' the refugee writers. Their frequent visits to the new territories were designed to influence the Jewish masses and to enforce the official line on the newcomers. Yitzhak Fefer from Kiev was particularly active in the western Ukraine, while western Belorussia was visited by two special 'Writers'

Brigades' with Peretz Markish and David Bergelson heading the one, and Leib Kvitko and Yehezkel Dobrushin the other.[48] The more complex question about the interaction between the Yiddish writers from the Soviet Union and the Jewish Polish writers deserves a more detailed analysis that would be beyond the scope of this book. Suffice it to say that the influence was by no means one-sided.[49]

The Soviet authorities employed some refugee writers and actors in the Jewish state theatres that they formed in the annexed territories. The Jewish Drama State Theatre was established in Lvov. Its literary manager was Alter Katizne, and its most important actress was Ida Kaminska.[50] Bialystok was even more active. A Jewish Drama State Theatre, whose members were mostly actors from Warsaw, performed mainly in Bialystok and the major cities of western Belorussia. A 'Wandering Theatre' was organized to cover the smaller towns and to 'provide culture to the large Jewish masses in the provinces of western Belorussia'.[51] But the most 'illustrious' contribution was the Jewish Miniature State Theatre under the literary direction of Moshe Broderzon, with Shimon Dzhigan and Shumacher serving as art directors. It was formed in November 1939 and took extended trips throughout the Soviet lands. Its repertoire consisted mainly of short satirical sketches.[52]

Only a small fraction of the refugees could find suitable employment in Eastern Poland. For the vast majority the authorities found another solution: they were offered jobs in the USSR itself. As we have seen, special employment offices, 'labor departments' in western Belorussia and 'labour bourses' in western Ukraine, tried to persuade those seeking employment to accept jobs in the interior of Russia.[53] The registration for work in Russia had already begun during the months of September and October, after the final demarcation of the border.[54] There are reports of pressure being put upon the refugees to accept the jobs offered in the interior of Russia as early as September 1939.[55] Central Asia, the Caucasus, the Urals, and the Donbass were among the places offered to the refugees who were looking for jobs. Those who agreed to go were immediately given free transportation, advance payment and tempting conditions. While the majority refused, there were thousands who stood in line for registration.[56] 'Many wanted to leave Bialystok, where they find it increasingly difficult to get housing, food, fuel . . . They register to go to the Caucasus, the Urals, to sunny Tashkent', recalled Moishe Grosman, a refugee writer who lived in Bialystok at that time.[57] The exact number of refugees who actually left is unknown. D. Grodner maintains that 'In Bialystok alone 20,000 registered in one week; in Brest-Litovsk, 10,000.'[58] The Soviet press in Yiddish carried frequent reports on thousands of refugees being sent to various parts of the Soviet Union for work.[59] Representatives from different Soviet enterprises visited the major refugee concentrations in an effort to recruit them for work.[60]

Those who registered for work left with great fanfare – flags, orchestras and patriotic speeches accompanied the outgoing trains. The receptions were equally enthusiastic and were confirmed by letters from the registrants, some of which were published in the local press.[61] But the honeymoon was a rather short one. Most of the refugees were unskilled and therefore employed as simple labourers. The work was hard, housing conditions inadequate, and the pay very low, compared to the accustomed standards of the refugees.[62] Many tried to go back to Eastern Poland, and quite a number reappeared in Bialystok and other towns after a few months.[63] Through placards on the walls and newspaper advertisements, those who returned were invited to register for free food and work. The returnees who came to register were immediately arrested.[64]

The Soviet attempt to provide employment and to 'productivize' the people (a term used by the Soviet Yiddish press to describe the registrants) was a complete failure. Only a small proportion of the refugees did register, and quite a few among them came back. What might have been considered by the Soviet authorities to be a generous offer of conditions equal to those of their own citizens was believed by the refugees to be an offer of hard labour that they were not accustomed to performing. The Soviet failure to transfer a sizeable part of the refugees who were concentrated in the larger cities made the question of the refugees' status in Eastern Poland even more acute. The presence of many thousands of jobless persons reluctant to adapt to the new regime was a problem that the Soviet authorities could not tolerate. They would try to resolve it together with the problem of the refugees' legal status.

On 29 November 1939 the Soviet Citizenship Law was extended to Eastern Poland. According to that law, all Polish citizens who were living in the territory when it was incorporated into the USSR (on 1 and 2 November 1939) automatically became Soviet citizens. The same status was given to persons who came to the Soviet Union in accordance with the population exchange agreement with Germany of 16 November. Automatic Soviet citizenship was also granted to people who left Vilno, which was transferred to Lithuania on 10 October 1939.[65] People living in Eastern Poland not included in the above-mentioned categories could become Soviet citizens because of the existing naturalization law of 1938.[66]

There is no doubt that the Soviet government intended to convert the Jewish refugees into Soviet citizens. It should be added that certain limitations were included, as will be shown later, in the citizen status offered to the refugees. It would be wrong to attribute this policy merely to humanitarian considerations. General imperatives of the control and

Sovietization of Eastern Poland were the more dominant motivation. Whatever the rationale behind the Soviet policy was, it received a negative response from the vast majority of Jewish refugees. Most of them considered their stay under Soviet rule as temporary. They thought that the war would be short and hoped to return to their former homes. There were those who tried to emigrate to the United States, Palestine, or other non-European countries. Some simply refused to become citizens of a regime they hated.[67] Many refugees refused to accept Soviet citizenship considering it to be an act formally and finally severing their connections with their families living in Nazi Poland: 'Most of the refugees left their wives, children, closest family on the other side; how could they accept Soviet citizenship, an acceptance that would mean remaining in the Soviet Union forever! To say farewell to home, to the dearest forever?!' – that was the cruel dilemma that faced the majority of the unfortunate, as it was eloquently expressed by one of them.[68]

The fact that the refugees received Soviet passports containing the so called 'paragraph 11', contributed its share to their reluctance to become Soviet citizens. Paragraph 11 imposed certain restrictions on residence and freedom of movement; only small towns and villages located no less than 100 kilometers from the border were open to people carrying such passports. They needed special permits to leave their place of residence. For most refugees it meant leaving the larger cities, where they had at least some chance of finding employment.

Some time during the spring of 1940 the Soviet authorities decided to take drastic steps either to force the refugees to accept Soviet citizenship or to resolve the problem by other means. While we have no direct evidence concerning such a decision, the events that followed make it abundantly clear that such a decision had been taken as part of the general hardening of Soviet attitudes towards the local population. Special commissions of the NKVD were established in April and May 1940 to register the refugees. Those who registered were faced with two alternatives – either to become Soviet citizens or to declare that they were ready to return to their former homes, now under Nazi occupation.[69] Most available sources deny that any pressure was put on the refugees to register one way or another.[70] The vast majority decided to register their intent to return. Among them were people holding jobs and those who were aware that Jews were being driven into ghettos in Nazi Poland. The registration, considered a test of loyalty by the Soviet authorities, had dire consequences for the refugees.

A strange and rather tragic episode occurred about the same time. Jewish refugees tried to register to return to Nazi Poland with German commissions that operated in the Soviet territory. A certain misunderstanding of that episode exists in the scholarly literature on the subject.

Thus Weinryb maintains that, in conjunction with the general registration, 'those who registered with the NKVD had to register again with a German commission operating in Soviet-occupied Poland in April–May 1940, in accordance with the Russian–German agreement of April 1940 on exchanges of population. But only a few Jews were admitted by the German commission.'[71] Solomon M. Schwartz contends that Weinryb and Grodner are wrong: he finds no documentary evidence that any population exchange agreement was signed between the Soviet Union and Germany in April 1940. 'However, some kind of a new agreement was signed ... This is confirmed by many testimonies of the operation, on the basis of a Soviet–German agreement, of commissions to register refugees to return to their former homes.' Schwartz concludes: 'Probably the agreement dealt not with population exchange, but only with the repatriation of refugees.'[72] Yosef Litvak tends to dismiss the entire matter as 'an episode around which rumours and gossip ... abound', a fabrication without foundation.[73]

On the basis of the available evidence, several conclusions can be drawn concerning the issue. Throughout the period there were Jewish refugees who tried to return, and some who even succeeded in returning, to their former homes in Nazi Poland.[74] Economic conditions in Soviet Poland, fears of imprisonment and deportation, family connections, ignorance of the real situation and dangers facing the Jews in the Nazi territory, were all reasons why the refugees tried to return. There are no doubts about the operation of German commissions on Soviet territory at the time, in April and May 1940. These commissions were invariably designated as the 'commissions of population exchange', and registered those who wanted to be repatriated.[75]

An interesting confirmation about the entire episode is found in Nikita Khrushchev's memoirs. Recalling some of the events of the time Khrushchev, then in charge of the Ukraine, writes that there 'was an exchange agreement whereby people on German-occupied territory who wanted to return to their homes in the former Polish territory now occupied by the Soviet troops were allowed to do so; and likewise, anyone in the Ukrainian population on Soviet territory who wanted to return to German-occupied Poland could do that'.[76]

The commissions operated in several cities such as Bialystok, Lvov and Brisk. The last location served also as the place of departure for those returning to German territory. There is little evidence to justify Weinryb's assertion that those who registered with the NKVD, 'had to register again with the German commission'. Most of the evidence seems to indicate that the two commissions operated separately and that quite a few Jews wanted to register with the German commissions without any Soviet order to do so. In Bialystok, many Jewish refugees waited for hours to register with the

German commission.[77] The refugees did not know the exact nature of the agreement between the states, but they had learned very quickly that the Germans refused to register Jewish refugees. Some tried to bribe the German representatives for a chance to be reunited with their families.[78] Lvov was one of the major centres for registration, and many refugees had to wait for days to reach the commission.[79] Khrushchev also relates 'that most of the people standing in line for registration were Jews'.[80]

The Soviet authorities interpreted the efforts to register with the German commissions as an overt act of disloyalty. The attempts of many Jews to cross the border and their willingness to live under a regime that publicly announced its hatred toward Jews were considered, correctly, as dangerous to the prestige of the Soviet government. Thousands of Jews who assembled in Brisk, hoping to sneak aboard the trains moving West, were arrested by special NKVD units.[81]

The following authentic story demonstrates better than any analytical exposition the tragedy of Polish Jewry living on both sides of the border. At Biala Podlaska, the first station on the German side of the border, the train carrying refugees east encountered the train moving west. 'When Jews coming from Brisk saw Jews going there, they shouted: "You are insane, where are you going?" Those coming from Warsaw answered with equal astonishment: "You are insane, where are you going?"'[82]

The Jewish refugees in Eastern Poland presented a problem for the Soviet authorities which they were neither able nor willing to solve in a way satisfactory to both sides. The Soviets considered the refugees to be a security risk since they showed a particular interest in the developments in the German area, had family connections across the border, had made repeated attempts to sneak through the frontier to visit relatives, and had often expressed the desire to emigrate overseas. This increased Soviet distrust and the refugees were considered as likely candidates for espionage. The refusal of most to accept Soviet citizenship, coupled with their overt declaration to return to German-occupied Poland, drove the Soviet authorities to a radical resolution of the problem – massive deportation of the refugees. During the spring of 1940, there were signs that the Soviet authorities were prepared to institute this plan as the answer to the refugee problem. It was part of a general shift towards a policy of removing entire social groups from Eastern Poland. It replaced the more selective and individual character of the previous imprisonments and deportations.[83]

The first to be deported were refugees without families who had registered to return, refusing to become Soviet citizens. 'The first arrests did not create any panic among the refugees. At worst, some thought, they will be sent to the interior regions of the USSR, where they could get employment and wait until the war would end', recalled a witness from Pinsk.[84] It soon became obvious that those were mere illusions; the deportations extended to the entire refugee population in Eastern Poland, and the destination of the trains moving east were the labour camps of northern Russia and Siberia.

During the second half of June 1940 most Jewish refugees were removed from Eastern Poland. The operation lasted only a few days. The secret police were assisted by the entire Soviet governmental apparatus and the members of the Communist Party in that area. The deportees were told, at least during the first stage of the operation, that their refusal to become Soviet citizens and registration to return to German territory were the reasons for their deportation.[85] The refugees were 'picked up' by the NKVD, which used its lists of those who had expressed their wish to return. When the refugees started to hide and to change their places of residence 'they were simply kidnapped while walking in the street, dragged from their homes, separated from their families', recalled a witness from Pinsk.[86] In Lvov the entire operation lasted only four days and nights. It involved the total mobilization of the secret police, party members, and higher administrative personnel.[87]

It was evident that every detail was planned in advance: trucks were waiting at the intersections; from certain concentration points, the deportees were transferred to long trains moving east. The disinformation section of the NKVD was very active in preparing and executing the deportations – the victims had to be unprepared, taken by surprise, and led to believe that nothing bad would happen to them. False announcements, deceptive rumours and misleading information were among the methods used.[88] In Lvov the police shifted its focus of attention from individuals to families. When the latter began to hide, those without families thought that the danger had passed and started returning to their homes. They were immediately picked up. The result was that each group in its turn was caught unawares.[89] The drivers mobilized for the operation in Bialystok were told that they would have to 'collect' arrested prostitutes – only later did they learn that the wives and children of those who had already been deported were their cargo.[90] After some initial success, the police found it increasingly difficult to trap their victims. The disinformation section was reactivated. Rumours were spread that people were being sent to nearby places: that at Minsk, the capital of Bialystok, for instance, the families were being reunited. When asked the destination of those deported, the police replied that Kiev would become the refugees' permanent home. There they would receive profitable employment and nice housing. Others were told that they were going to be transferred to the Nazi zone.[91]

The Soviet deportation machine was well-prepared for its job. Years of experience in uprooting and hunting down thousands of helpless victims bore fruit. Acting in accordance with General Serov's detailed instructions, most of the refugees were deported in June 1940.[92] Among the deportees were also people employed in Soviet institutions and even some who had accepted Soviet citizenship. The deportations continued after June 1940, although on a much smaller scale. The last large convoys of refugees left Pinsk on 20 June 1941, two days before the outbreak of war with Germany.[93] Trains with deportees passed through Lida on 22 June 1941.[94]

While it is impossible to ascertain the exact number of deported refugees, there is no doubt that the vast majority of the refugees were exiled. There was an inherent incompatibility between the Jewish refugees and the Soviet authorities in Eastern Poland. The refugees could not sever their ties with the past, their families, and their hopes; they did not adapt to the Soviet way of life. A complex human problem became an administrative question for the Soviet government. They resolved it by using a method with which they were familiar – mass deportation. The deportees were victims of Hitlerism, as they were victims of Stalinism. The deportation to the interior of the Soviet Union saved the lives of most of the refugees after Eastern Poland was conquered by Germany. It was the ultimate irony of history.

10

Why Did They Stay? The Strength of Stereotypes

Soviet rule over the eastern provinces of Poland ended all of a sudden. Most of the area was occupied by German troops within the first few weeks after 22 June 1941. The vast majority of the Jews living in the area came under Nazi occupation. Circumstances beyond their control prevented mass evacuation of endangered populations to the Soviet interior. Yet, the most astonishing fact was the reluctance of the majority of Jews even to try to join the retreating Soviet army. German rule had not appeared that dangerous, nor did the Soviet sanctuary seem that appealing. Generations-old images and stereotypes blurred the vision of many. The Jews of the new Soviet provinces became victims of a lethal combination of circumstances beyond their control and understanding.

During the Soviet occupation the Jewish community was deliberately cut off from all sources of information on Nazi attitudes towards the Jews. This was the direct outcome of the Molotov–Ribbentrop Agreement of 23 August 1939. The pact between Nazi Germany and communist Russia necessarily led to a change in public references to the Nazi regime and its leaders.[1] Hitler soon became an honourable figure and Nazism a legitimate ideology against which it was forbidden to fight. Moscow stopped publication of anti-Nazi material and communist parties all over the world hastened to align themselves with the new policy.[2] The new atmosphere created in the wake of the pact made the Jews even less aware of the dangers inherent in Nazism. None of the reports reaching the Soviet Union on events in Nazi-occupied territories were presented in a hostile way. It should be noted, however, that internal considerations contributed to this policy. Anti-Semitism reached unprecedented peaks in the USSR itself at the time, particularly in the new Soviet western provinces where it had deep historical roots.

Reports of Nazi atrocities committed against the Jews in their territories were completely absent also from Soviet Yiddish publications intended for the Jewish population. Absolute silence was forced upon Jewish writers and artists concerning the most urgent subject of Jewish life at the time. The constant stream of refugees coming from German-occupied Poland brought updated information on Nazi atrocities – accounts of yellow stars, ghettos, executions. Yet the Soviet authorities prevented any mention of the subject in public. 'It was forbidden to write or even speak about it. The stories of mass executions, murder of children and old people by the German allies of the USSR were told in secret', relates Sh. Broderzon, the poet's wife.[3] Not a single word was reported in the *Bialystoker Shtern*, the only Yiddish daily appearing in the provinces. When M. Grosman, who worked for the paper, tried to insert an article on the plight of the Jews in Nazi-occupied Poland, he was told by the editor: 'The supreme authorities did not permit its publication. This is the current line and comes from overriding necessity.'[4]

When the friendship between Stalin and Hitler began to cool and the Western press and radio began to warn the Soviet people of an imminent German attack, there was no change in the situation. Jews and non-Jews were left in the dark as to the real dangers of Nazism. There is no doubt that the Soviet authorities knew of the fate of the Jews in Nazi territories, and could have warned the Jewish population.[5] However, until the actual German attack, the Soviet government refrained from any deed that might have offended its German friends.

At the outbreak of the war, the Jewish community was certainly ill-informed about Nazi deeds and policies. 'To an amazing extent, the Jews are remarkably ill-informed about our attitude towards them', reports a German intelligence officer on 12 July 1941 concerning the situation in the Belorussian provinces.

> They do not know how Jews are treated in Germany, or for that matter in Warsaw, which after all is not so far away. Otherwise their questions as to whether we in Germany make any distinction between Jews and other citizens would be superfluous. Even if they do not think that under German administration they will have equal rights with the Russians, they believe, nevertheless, that we shall leave them in peace if they mind their own business and work diligently.[6]

One does not have to accept the above report at face value. It does indicate, however, that there was widespread ignorance among Jews about Nazism. The silence of Soviet media and the concerted effort to depict their allies in favourable terms contributed to a slackening awareness of the danger in the advance of German troops. This undoubtedly contributed to the unwillingness of the Jews to join the retreating Soviet army while there was still time and a chance to reach the interior safely.

Official silence added support to the prevailing image of Germany as a civilized country. Among the Jews living in Eastern Europe the long-established stereotype of Russia was of a backward, anti-Semitic country, traditionally associated with rioting mobs, unruly Cossacks and government-instigated pogroms. Germany meant for many the West and culture, the rule of law and hence security. People who remembered World War I were full of praise for the correct and helpful behaviour of the Kaiser's troops as opposed to the rioting Russian soldiers. The Jews of the shtetlach of the annexed territories were historically prepared for the worst from Russia, while expecting from the German army a strict observance of law and order. It is interesting to note that almost without exception the survivors refer to the Soviet authorities as 'Russian' rather than Soviet, thus revealing a deep-seated conviction that nothing had changed since the Revolution. This attitude is particularly surprising in view of the information that was available to many Jews. There were no overt anti-Semitic activities by Soviet authorities or soldiers. On the contrary, as we have seen, many noticed the civilized behaviour of the Soviet soldiers and how different they were from their predecessors. At the same time, despite the complete ban in the official information channels, many did know that Nazi Germany was not in any way the Kaiser's Germany in its attitude towards the Jews. Nevertheless among many, particularly the older and more orthodox sections of the Jewish population, the old stereotypes persisted and convinced many to stay.

'People were saying that the Germans were a well-organized and disciplined nation. They knew how to impose order and pursue a policy of law and justice', recalled a Pinsk survivor.[7] 'People thought about the German army of World War I, trying to recollect the image of "their" good Prussian who brought them food in time of need . . . There were those who even rejoiced that finally the Russian rule was over, that the "barefooted" were retreating and there would be an end to the lines for food.'[8] Many Jews were acquainted with the German language and culture and could not believe that there would be real danger to Jewish life. They had no doubt that people willing to work would not find it difficult to survive.[9] Some hoped that the former economic order would be restored and that they would regain lost properties. 'There were among the Shtetl's *gvirim* [rich] many who believed that the Germans would return their confiscated properties, that things would be restored to what they had been in the past and that they would again run their businesses', recalled a Korzec Jew.[10]

Twenty-one months of Soviet rule had not endeared the USSR to the

Jews of Eastern Poland, nor had it made the Soviet lands an enticing refuge. The Jewish middle class, the most important social group, had suffered economically and culturally; many were deported or faced the constant danger of arrest. Even those who nourished few illusions about German rule could not, in view of limited information, easily choose to look for refuge in Stalin's Russia. 'For the Orthodox Jews Russia was a threat to their souls, while Germany, at worst, threatened their bodies, and they chose what appeared the lesser evil.'[11] Thus strong reservations about Soviet rule joined the traditional image of a civilized Germany to hold back many Jews from trying to flee.

The more affluent people refused to listen to the awful stories of the refugees who reached Wolozhyn from the German occupied territories. They treated the stories as yet more Soviet propaganda, as sensational news invented by sick minds. World War I was for them the primary example. The German army had already ruled Wolozhyn in 1918 and no Jew was hurt. It was impossible that within one generation they would change such as to want to destroy the Jewish people. There was no good reason to be scared of the advancing German army.[12]

Thus went the argument of many Jews who refused to flee. They expressed relief for what they thought would be the end of food shortages, confiscation of property and arbitrary arrests. The stereotype of Germany as a civilized country proved for many stronger than reports of German atrocities that reached the new border provinces of the USSR.[13]

The majority probably stayed for a combination of reasons. A perceptive observer of the events that took place in June 1941 in the provinces noted with astonishment that the majority of the Jews, while frightened and apprehensive about the future, nevertheless did not join the Russians. 'They did not believe that the disintegrating Soviet administration would be able to defend or safeguard their existence. Nor could the Jews foresee the savagery of the advancing Germans.'[14] Lack of sympathy towards the Soviets combined with the absence of a correct perception of the Nazis.

Most Jews understood that they would suffer under German rule, yet they could not imagine it would mean complete annihilation. They had large families, many children and small babies. It was impossible to carry them into the unknown. There were those who reached complete apathy after many months of scarcity and suffering under the Soviet regime. They were exhausted and did not care to exert themselves and run. And there were the believers . . . who maintained that God would not forsake his people.[15]

Thus faith and prejudice joined with aversion of the Soviet regime. Physical and mental exhaustion were strengthened by simple human inertia; reluctance to become a refugee and attachment to birthplace made people stay and await, frequently with terror and deep anxiety, an unknown future.[16]

The actual number of Jews who fled to the Soviet hinterland was determined by two variables: the willingness of the Jews to escape, and the availability of evacuation facilities. As the war went on, relatively greater numbers of Jews escaped, especially in the easternmost regions of the newly-conquered Nazi territory. This was the result of the improved Soviet evacuation facilities and the greater awareness within the Jewish community of the danger to its very existence.[17] In the former eastern provinces of Poland the majority for one reason or another were reluctant to escape, while those who tried to do so faced the most difficult obstacles.

Evacuation and spontaneous flight of the civilian population from the attacked territories were most adversely affected by the blitzkrieg strategy of the German army. Deep encircling pincer movements of armoured units, continuous bombing of communication centres and transport facilities, and deliberate attacks on civilian centres and refugee convoys directly affected the flight of the civilian population.[18] Organizing the evacuation of material resources and the civilian population became one of the most important tasks of the Soviet government. But it took time to organize the evacuation apparatus and the former eastern Polish provinces were too close to the border to benefit substantially from the Soviet evacuation efforts. The surprise of the German attack and the unpreparedness of the Soviet units led to the speedy collapse of the Soviet lines and authority within the border regions. Utter confusion and disintegration reigned in the areas under imminent German onslaught.[19] Under such conditions, Soviet troops found it most difficult to retreat and any planned evacuation of the civilian population was extremely unlikely. Evacuation from the immediate border territories was highly limited and poorly organized, even according to Soviet official history.[20] The fact that the chances to escape were slim further immobilized the Jewish population, reducing the number of people trying to flee.

From the available evidence it is clear that those who wanted to be evacuated were mostly Jews associated with the Soviet regime, particularly the younger generation. Members of the Communist Party, employees of Soviet institutions and enterprises and those who had reason to fear the vengeance of the local population were among those escaping. 'Only thirty-five Jews joined the retreating Russians. They were active in the Soviet administration and knew that they would suffer from the change in government', relates a Jewish police officer from Lanowce.[21] 'We ran for our lives, while the entire Jewish community of our shtetl refused to move', emphasized the police officer. 'Few Jews joined the Russians in Dubno. Only several dozens of youngsters, members of the Communist youth movement, were evacuated together with the retreating authorities.'[22] In Kostopol approximately 400 out of a population of 7,000 Jews joined the retreating Red Army.[23] Among those who fled were people who served the regime, members of the Komsomol and avowed sympathizers of Communism. Most of them were young and could face a long journey into the unknown.[24]

Confusion and chaos reigned in the front zone of the annexed territories. Local authorities were frequently left without instructions on what to do or reliable information on what was happening. Soviet administration collapsed together with the disintegration of the many illusions held by the Red Army. They failed in many instances to evacuate even many of the Soviet institutions and personnel.[25]

As a rule, Soviet officials and their families, the so-called 'Easterners' (*Vostochniki*), had first priority for the limited evacuation facilities. Difficulties in communication and coordination as a result of the sudden attack left much to the discretion of the local authorities and military command. The results were contradictory. There were instances where Jews were encouraged to flee at one place,[26] and prevented from doing so in another.[27] An atmosphere of despair and helplessness reigned among the Jews – the result of the absence of guidance and reliable information. The general disarray of the different branches of the Soviet administration during the last days of Soviet rule brought into tragic relief the effects of Soviet policy. There was no leadership or organization of the Jewish community, both had been dissolved by the Communist regime. The Jews faced the unfolding events not as a collective or a community but as an atomized society that lacked any means of collective consultation or action. Personal courage and wit were the only means the individual Jew could rely on when deciding whether to escape or to stay. Those who decided to look for refuge had to depend on themselves. Many who tried to flee did not make it to the Soviet interior; scarce evacuation facilities, encircling German units that prevented further movement and local collaborators who blocked roads cut off the retreat routes. Many found their death on the roads, in the trains, or at the railway stations that were bombarded mercilessly from the air.

There were marked differences from place to place. Lvov and Bialystok, the two major urban centres in the annexed provinces, came under attack with the outbreak of hostilities. The local authorities could hardly manage to organize the evacuation of their own personnel and families. The civilian population was left to its own devices as far as its flight was concerned. A Lvov Jew recalled:

> Lvov came under severe bombardment from the very beginning and within a few hours the entire governmental apparatus collapsed, it simply disappeared. There were no leaders, no managers . . . Each one thought only about his personal lot: how to leave town with his family and the first to flee were those who came from the East, party members and their families . . . After a few hours we were left without any authority.[28]

Panic stricken, only small numbers tried to flee by whatever means they could get. Several hundred youngsters who were drafted by the Red Army with the outbreak of hostilities succeeded in escaping.[29] Many of those who tried to reach the Soviet interior returned after a few days, exhausted and in despair. The sight of the retreating Red Army, disorganized and demoralized, brought many back to Lvov to stay with their families.[30] Almost the entire Jewish population of Lvov, which numbered at the time approximately 160,000 fell into the hands of the Nazis. Bialystok's fate, with the second largest Jewish community of almost 100,000, was not much different.[31] There the authorities were a little more successful in organizing the evacuation of their personnel,[32] and formed a special convoy of writers and artists living in the city.[33] Quite a few of the Jewish literati when given the opportunity to join a retreating convoy refused. They had had enough of the Soviet regime. But even those who left the city were not sure they would reach safe ground. Many of the fleeing were either caught by the encircling German troops or fell victims to the continuous strafing and bombardments of German planes.[34]

The majority of the Jews in the annexed provinces, those living in the numerous shtetlach, had been from the outbreak of hostilities completely cut off from reliable information and major roadways. Panic, rumours and lack of transport facilities precluded any real attempt by the Jewish community to escape. People wandered aimlessly in a futile attempt to escape. 'Rumours spread about roads strewn with dead, hunger, closed borders, etc. Even those who wanted to flee decided that they might as well stay home', reported a Rokitno survivor.[35] 'The authorities fled immediately and the Jews did not know what to do. Should they run? Where to? And meanwhile the advancing German troops cut off the roads leading East,' remembers a Ratno Jew.[36] 'People moved aimlessly on the highways. The Soviet radio was announcing German penetrations, promising speedy victories. Yet German troops were seen everywhere and were met with enthusiasm by the Ukrainian peasants,' recalled a Dereczyn inhabitant.[37] Isolated, bewildered and frequently removed dozens of kilometers from railways or major roads, the shtetl Jews were left to face a grim future under German occupation. The few who tried to escape had to walk long distances to the nearest station. Many of them were forced eventually to return, finding their road cut off by advancing German units.[38]

The role of the Soviet authorities in the crucial days of June and July 1941, in facilitating or hindering the flight of Jews, was dubious at best. There was no attempt whatsoever to encourage or to prefer Jews during the retreat or where any organized evacuation could be detected. While there was no doubt that the Jews were among the more threatened elements of the local population, nothing had been done to facilitate their escape.[39]

Soviet personnel in the shtetlach tried their best to evacuate their own members. On the first day of hostilities they started packing, even in the places not under immediate attack.[40] It looks as if in many places the only authority still exercised by the disintegrating administration was the power to issue transport permits. For a few days the police authorities refused in many places to issue permits that would enable free movement with the retreating Red Army across the border. Permits were granted only to the Jews who were active in the party and administration. All the rest who wanted to escape were denied for a few crucial days the licence to do so.[41] There were marked differences in the actual attitude of the authorities towards Jews trying to flee. Because of the collapse of regular communication lines, the local authorities did not know what attitude to adopt or what advice to offer. In Rowno, the local party chief advised the Jews to remain in their place. Those who refused to accept the advice could not anyway go too far in the absence of sufficient vehicles or trains.[42] In Nowogrodek retreating Soviet troops agreed to make room in their convoy for some Jewish youngsters. But many were killed on the road or had to return because German troops cut off their route.[43] Baranowicz fell after five days. Many Jews tried to flee with the troops, but the masses of civilians and soldiers that packed the roads were all caught between the pincers of German armoured units that moved quickly eastwards.[44] 'Soldiers in army trucks enabled women and children to join the retreating convoy . . . Trains stopping at the station attached wagons loaded with local Jews', relates a Lida survivor.[45]

An unexpected obstacle for thousands of refugees running east was the crossing of the former border between the USSR and Poland. That border was not abolished completely even after the official incorporation of the provinces into the Soviet Union. Former Polish citizens could not cross without a special permit. With the outbreak of hostilities, when thousands of refugees tried to reach the Soviet interior, the same prohibition continued for the first few days. The prohibition was not general and reflected the confusion that existed in the front region at the time. It was maintained most strictly in Belorussia and in the eastern sections of the former Baltic states, while the border in the Ukraine remained mostly open to free movement. Only those who were Soviet citizens before 1939 or carried special permits from the police could cross the restricted borders. It was a rather bizarre episode: 'in the midst of a disintegrating administration when German troops advanced hundreds of kilometers and the Red Army retreated in utter confusion jamming roads and railways by the thousands – yet it did not affect the guarding of the eastern border and this prevented thousands of refugees from escaping the German threat'.[46] Thousands of refugees who flocked to the border station at Rodoshkevich on the road to

Minsk were greeted with a large signboard warning people crossing without a permit that they might be shot, to the embarrassment of the guards.[47] They were waiting for new instructions, explained the guards. The result was that many had to turn back.[48] There were, however, many more who, when they learned about the situation, refused to try and escape. In the border shtetlach, like Lanin and Mikszewicz 'many families spent day and night in the open fields in a futile attempt to enter Soviet territory. Watching the stranded refugees near the closed border deterred others from even trying to escape', noted a Lachwa Jew.[49] When the barriers were finally lifted and people could move eastwards freely, the three or four lost days were of dire consequences for many thousands. The time wasted near the border while trying to evade the Soviet patrols was used by the German army to move further east, trapping many of the refugees or killing them by air attack.[50]

For a generation that is painfully aware of the Holocaust, that knows what happened to the hundreds of thousands of Jews who stayed in the former eastern Polish provinces, the act of staying behind requires an explanation. However, when we study the history of the Jewish community in the fateful days preceding Nazi conquest we have to look for the causes of its behaviour in what people knew at the time. They decided to stay or to flee according to what looked right or convenient at the time, without being able to surmise the more distant future. Total and systematic annihilation of the Jewish people, as attempted by the Nazis, was beyond the historical experience or comprehension of all. Therefore, when the vast majority of Jews stayed they did so not simply out of blindness to impending events, but also through choice of what they thought was the lesser evil. The objective circumstances of the blitzkrieg and collapse of the Soviet authorities made it extremely difficult to flee eastward, had they been willing to do so. But most of the Jews did not even try to flee. Elemental human inertia was probably the basic reason for that. Even a people famous for its 'rootlessness', for being a 'wandering nation', does not leave its place of birth, the place of its forefathers for many generations, that easily. It was extremely difficult for large families, the typical family in the provinces, to decide to become refugees with an unknown future. This basic reluctance to leave home was strengthened by an existing stereotype of Germany as a civilized country, an image that tended to weaken the impact of reports of German atrocities. The short period of Soviet rule had not overcome the traditional image of Russia as a barbarous country. On the contrary, for many the prospect of moving deeper into the USSR became even more repulsive. Those who were associated with the regime, generally younger people, made up the majority of those who fled. The rest stayed behind, even when many were not absolutely sure that they were doing the right thing. They were victims of their own inertia. Only a perceptive leadership could have moved at least parts of the Jewish community of the new Soviet provinces, but in the hour of trial the Jews stood without any leadership. The original leadership had been in one way or another completely eliminated by the regime. More than that, for the first time in history, and in their most difficult hour, the Jews of Eastern Poland faced the future as atomized individuals, without any collective institutions to consult and be guided by. This was just one consequence of Sovietization, and not the least important.

Conclusion

The USSR ruled the former Polish eastern provinces for over 21 months. Soviet presence ended as abruptly as it began, by war and invasion. Less than two years is usually too short a time to effect radical change in the structure of society, economy or other spheres of social activity. However, one can safely argue that the Soviet case was different. The transformation introduced by the new rulers fell short of Communist claims to change basically the pre-existing social structures and human relations. Nevertheless, Communist ideology, combined with Stalinist methods and ruthlessness, radically changed some of the essential features of the previously Polish provinces in spite of the short duration of Soviet presence. The attempts to destroy the old order, to change the former way of life and force the adoption of new forms were part of the Communist rulers' efforts to integrate the annexed territories into the Soviet State and make them conform to the existing regime in the USSR at the time. Sovietization as practised by Stalin meant an attempt at a total structural transformation of society in the new Soviet territories. It included not only politics and the economy, but also the intellectual and cultural sphere. It meant the adoption of new attitudes, norms and ideologies that would foster integration into and loyalty to the Soviet State.

Sovietization affected the entire population inhabiting the area. All the ethnic groups underwent change and some measure of destruction, development and adaptation. Historical relations do not easily lend themselves to clear-cut categories and do not provide us with clear-cut distinctions between development, change, destruction and adaptation. There are fine transitions from one to another, as well as dialectic tensions not easily discernible. Nevertheless, coercion and speed of change, as well as stated goals of wiping out former structures and supplanting them with completely new forms, do turn development, change and voluntary adaptation into destruction. Sovietization of the provinces, even in its Stalinist form, was, in the final count, an uneven blend of accelerated development of processes begun before the beginning of Soviet rule, gradual change, voluntary adaptation and brutal destruction of centuries old forms of social existence. It affected the different ethnic groups unevenly, depending on differences in Communist policy applied to the various groups as well as their own idiosyncrasies.

Sovietization found the Jewish community in a state of change and struggle between the traditionalists and those who tried to adapt their way of life to the modern world. The Jewish community itself underwent a variety of transformations. Soviet policy, when superimposed on existing social-economic and ideological divisions within the Jewish community, affected different groups and aspects of Jewish life diversely. For the first time in the history of the region the Jews as individuals were granted formal equality, that was also implemented to a high degree. However, for the Jews to become Soviet citizens and maintain at the same time their Jewish ethnic identity was an even more difficult problem than that encountered by other Jewish communities when faced with emancipation. But the new Soviet citizens were given little choice. It was made abundantly clear that the price would be the loss of a distinct and separate Jewish identity. Stalinism meant reluctance to recognize social, ethnic or any other idiosyncrasies that deviated from the monolithic model. It meant a complete denial of the peculiar economic structure, national character, traditions and needs of the Jewish community. No special agency, like the Jewish sections of the Soviet Communist Party (CPSU) of the twenties, was formed to facilitate the transition of the Jewish population to its new status. While destroying the old order, the Communist rulers took very little positive action to aid the transformation.

Various sections of the Jewish community faced the challenge of Sovietization in different ways. The more affluent, the propertied class, and the political and cultural elites, found it most difficult to adapt to and integrate into the new system. Communism considered these groups as 'class enemies' and ideological foes that had to be eliminated. They constituted a threat to the re-education of the new Soviet citizens and were largely removed, on one way or another, from the community. Other social groups in the Jewish population fared differently. While radical changes were introduced in almost every major sphere of life, old structures eliminated and supplanted by Soviet substitutes, many and particularly the less affluent, the shtetl Jews and the younger generation found, on an individual basis, their place in the new system. Formal equality replaced the traditional institutionalized anti-Semitism of the old regime, and Jews as individuals availed themselves of the new opportunities opened before them. New jobs in government and public organizations became available for the first time. Higher education institutions located in the new territories and even in the USSR itself opened their gates before Jewish students. To many Jews the Soviet regime offered new and undreamed of fields of action and progress in the material world. This was the mood of the community, particularly among the young. But the price was the destruction of the centuries old institutions that expressed and preserved Jewish ethnic identity.

Equality for the Jew under the Soviet regime in the annexed territories stopped where the collective ethnic identity was concerned. Even under the Stalinist regime, when an attempt was made to impose one monolithic culture planned and controlled from above, no one denied the existence or legitimacy of a Ukrainian, Belorussian or Polish nation. When nationalist tendencies were suppressed by the Soviet authorities they did not question the rightful existence of the nationalities in the USSR, but promoted their cultures. This was not so with the Jews. In line with ideological assumptions that preceded the October Revolution, Communism prescribed the end of the existence of the Jewish community as a distinct and separate ethnic group. They were destined to assimilate into the surrounding nationalities. Stalin's policy in the thirties ruthlessly followed that goal in the USSR itself and expanded it into the new Soviet territories. All the autonomous institutions and organizations, as well as the elaborate network of cultural and religious organizations, were eliminated within a short period after the invasion. There were no Soviet substitutes to express Jewish ethnic identity as there were for the other nationalities. A de-nationalized school system that used Yiddish for its language of instruction, one daily newspaper and a few theatrical groups – these were the only remains of Jewish identity. Even they were of a temporary nature, destined to disappear with time. The Jewish religion, while officially tolerated, as were other denominations, suffered from the open hostility of the regime to any religious activity. Hence the drastic decline of religious observance in private and public alike. The synagogue drew mainly the old who expected very little from the new rulers. All the tools for continued Jewish ethnic existence were thus completely abolished. The continuance of the Jews' very existence as a distinct ethnic group was in doubt. A lonely Jew faced on his own the challenges and dangers of the new situation without any collective tools to deal with them. These developments were most strikingly demonstrated in the shtetl communities.

Even a casual observer touring the hundreds of shtetlach of the former Polish provinces in June 1941 could have easily detected important changes that had occurred in its townscape. They were still shabby settlements, with poor connecting roads and sanitation. Their basic economic role did not change and they continued to serve a poor agricultural countryside. However, the imprint of the Soviet regime was felt all over. Demographically, the shtetl hardly changed. A few left to find their fortune in the larger urban centres, yet these losses were balanced by the arrival of Jewish refugees from the German-occupied territories. Jews still constituted a majority in many shtetlach, in others they were still the largest single ethnic group. But now there was more social contact between Jew and non-Jew in common enterprises and organizations. The small town lost many of the external Jewish traits that had characterized it only 21 months earlier. Most Jewish public institutions ceased functioning. Many synagogues were converted into warehouses, stables, clubs etc. Those that still functioned were poor reminders of their former glory. They struggled on as if the life was draining out of them. For the old who attended them, the synagogues became a last refuge of Jewishness. But the young could not be found in these institutions of the 'reaction', as they were dubbed by the Soviet rulers. The smaller prayer houses together with the *kheders*, the *mikvaot* and Jewish slaughterhouses disappeared from the shtetl townscape. Public manifestations of Jewish customs and religiousness, which were so prominent in the past, almost completely vanished. *Brith-mila* (ritual circumcision), *Bar-mitzvah* and weddings, when performed according to Jewish law, were carried out in the privacy of home, away from the watchful presence of the authorities and their informers. The *Shabat* and Jewish holidays ceased to be public events in the shtetl and no longer affected the rhythm of economic activity. They became regular working days. Special efforts were made by the Communist authorities to attract the schoolchildren and the young on Friday nights and holidays to activities organized by the Komsomol (Communist youth movement). Conspicuous manifestations of the Jewish religion and ethnicity connected with the holidays such as *Sukah* (booth), during the feast of Tabernacles; *Khanukah* candles lit in almost every home and displayed in the window for everybody to see; the festive celebrations and street performances on *Purim*, as well as other festive occasions that used to be seen in the shtetl streets and demonstrated the Jewish presence, disappeared almost completely. *Shabat* and the holidays became a private affair for those who still practised them. They ceased to be visible events in the shtetl streets.

New sights, holidays and noises were becoming part of the shtetl townscape. The market-place and its surrounding small shops and artisans' workshops, the economic centre of the small town, disappeared with the economic changes introduced by the Soviets. Quite frequently the market-place became a square or turned into a park adorned with statues of Soviet heroes, most frequently of Stalin. Flags, placards, posters and slogans written on cloth became prominent marks of the shtetl streets, particularly before and during the many festive Soviet occasions which included official holidays like 1 May, 7 November (day of the Bolshevik revolution), election days, birthdays and anniversaries of the USSR's leaders etc. Parades, demonstrations, speeches and special meetings were organized on such occasions. The shtetl population considered it wise to attend the meetings and march with the demonstrations. Loudspeakers that transmitted news, patriotic slogans and songs were installed in many places and became conspicuous in the small town. So did the never-ending lines before the shops, due to the constant shortages.

Not only buildings and streets looked different, so did the people. The more affluent ceased to wear their 'better' clothing and jewellery so as to conceal their bourgeois past. Jewish traditional attire, prevalent before the Soviet occupation, became a rarity, limited almost entirely to the old and devout. So did other visible signs of attachment to tradition and religion, like *peyes* (side-locks), and beards. If one wanted to succeed in the emerging Soviet society, one had to conform to its norms of appearance and dress. To display openly attachment to tradition and religion meant giving up any chance of getting ahead in the new system. People wore what they thought was 'proper' Soviet clothing, usually shabby, old fashioned and coarse. Thus the 'proletarian-looking' Jew lived in a shtetl that had lost many of its former Jewish marks and peculiarity.

Changes in the external appearance of the shtetl reflected more profound transformations that took place in the life of its community. Squares instead of markets reflected the new economic reality. Shopkeepers became cooperative clerks, simple labourers, or unemployed. The shops were closed or demolished. Independent artisans were herded into producers' co-operatives or factories and government plants. It should be noted, however, that while many shtetl Jews changed occupation, they still remained in service branches and did not become peasants or factory labourers – true 'productive' occupations according to Soviet terminology. The shtetl Jew remained, by and large, in the service occupations for the surrounding agricultural population, his traditional role for centuries. In fact, the quantity of services supplied by the new regime was much larger than that of its Polish predecessor. It meant more jobs for shtetl inhabitants. People spent more time in work and in endless lines to obtain the most basic necessities of life, yet it should be kept in mind that the standard of living under the former regime was also very low. Many families barely survived and managed only by relying on charity. The shtetl Jews, on the whole, found their place in the Soviet economy.

Conspicuous buildings and public ceremonies connected with the Jewish religion and Jewish customs became rather rare in small towns of the former Polish provinces. It was in line with identical developments that took place among the other religions in the region. Polish Catholic clergy and churches were certainly under more severe constraints, for the obvious reason of being suspected of fostering Polish national opposition to the Soviet invader. The Jewish religious establishment suffered from the regime's view that all religions were mainstays of reaction and bred opposition to the Communist State. However, shtetl Jews, and particularly the young, did not abandon religious observance only with the entrance of the Red Army into the region. Secularization had been rampant in the small towns for decades. Religion still played a prominent role in shtetl public and private life, but its hold was definitely weakened. Soviet presence brutally and drastically accelerated the secularization of the shtetl and in particular removed religion almost completely from the shtetl streets. When practised at all, it was in the privacy of home and family.

The transformation that took place in the various forms of cultural activity and education was radical. The multi-faceted educational and cultural activities that were found in the small towns of Eastern Poland expressed and fostered the ethnic identity of the shtetl Jew. Prescribing assimilation of the Jewish community as the final goal, the Soviet authorities destroyed the former structure. Instead of varied cultural activities, all of them testifying to the vitality of Jewish identity, whether in religious or secular-nationalistic forms, the new rulers introduced into the shtetlach Soviet-style cultural activities containing as little Jewish content as possible. Actually the amateur theatre groups, the 'purged' libraries, the different extra-curricular activities for the young and old when offered in Yiddish served mainly as tools of anti-Jewish indoctrination. They certainly were not aimed at encouraging the development of a genuine Soviet-style Jewish culture. The case of education was not much different. Instead of many and varied educational establishments, so typical of the shtetl, all in their own way designed to strengthen Jewish identity and its continued existence, a new Soviet system was created. At first sight it appeared that the new Yiddish schools embraced even larger numbers of pupils than the former network. But an analysis of the content of the curriculum and purposes of the Soviet Yiddish school clearly reveals its true goals. Yiddish was used as a language of instructing Jewish pupils against their own ethnic identity. It became quite obvious to many parents that the schools had very little positive value for their children. Their Jewish content was very meagre and graduates found it difficult to pursue their studies in general institutions of higher learning that used other languages for instruction. Even during the 21 months of Soviet rule the Yiddish school system showed clear signs of decay. The Communist authorities considered the existence of the Yiddish cultural and educational institutions formed in the new territories to be a transitional phenomenon. They were destined to shrink and eventually to vanish together with similar institutions in the USSR itself.

Most drastic was the transformation introduced by the Communist rulers in the ethnic and social cohesion of the shtetl Jewish community. The vitality and intensity of Jewish life as well as the intimacy and strength of social intercourse – a prominent characteristic of shtetl life – were demolished. In these fields Soviet actions amounted to the destruction of centuries old structures, attitudes and relations, that had been mainstays of Jewish existence. As noted above (pp. 92–101), the external manifestations of the change were the disappearance of most of the many and varied institutions and organizations from the shtetl landscape. Gone was the *kehilla* and its subsidiaries together with the dozens of voluntary societies that bound together the shtetl Jewish community with an intricate network of social intercourse. The many political parties with their youth movements, whose activities and bickering had been an integral part of shtetl life, vanished never to return. With them disappeared the entire elite that provided leadership and management for the autonomous Jewish establishment. Even people who had not held leadership positions in the past, yet could potentially become nuclei of opposition to the re-education of the new Soviet citizens, were removed from the community. The result was the emergence of an atomized community. Of course, it was not unique to the Jews in the shtetl – other ethnic groups were also denied their former institutions and leaders. But for the Jews it meant the destruction of the tools that enabled their continued distinct ethnic existence. The constant threats of arrest and deportation created an atmosphere of terror, fear and suspicion, drawing people away from each other, instead of the openness and intimacy of the past. It was the antithesis of the centuries old experience of the Jewish community. Thus even in the shtetl with its relatively large and cohesive Jewish population the individual faced the challenges of the present and the dangers of the future alone. For the first time the shtetl Jews lacked collective instruments to deliberate, consult and decide in times of emergency.

When in June and July 1941 German troops conquered the hundreds of small towns scattered in what were once the eastern provinces of the Polish Republic, they encountered a different shtetl and a radically transformed Jewish community.

Appendix: Encounters with Soviet Jews

After being separated from them for 25 years, the former Polish Jews had the opportunity to meet directly their Soviet fellows. The impact of the encounter could be detected in the attitudes of the Polish Jews to the new regime. It gave them a certain sense of confidence as to the place of the Jew in Soviet society and a foretaste of what might be expected of the future. Soviet Jews, whether they admitted this or not, came away from the renewed contacts with a heightened sense of Jewish identity.[1]

Annexation of the territories of Eastern Poland by the USSR did not bring free movement of people in both directions. To enter the new territories the Soviet citizen needed a special permit, although some were sent there to perform particular jobs. Former Polish citizens, wanting to visit relatives long separated by artificial borders, found it difficult to get permission to move east. Thus the encounter between the two Jewish communities was limited in scope and nature. Most of the Jews encountered by the new citizens were Soviet officials of one kind or another, at first mainly soldiers and officers of the Red Army. Then came the numerous Jews who took part in the administration of the territories. Quite a different group of Soviet Jews that came to the area specifically to see and meet the local Jewish community were the Soviet Yiddish cultural elite of writers and performers. They were used by the authorities to help indoctrinate and integrate into Soviet society the large Jewish population and its intelligentsia in particular. The last, and occasionally most revealing, group were Jewish visitors who came on some official business and used the opportunity to meet local Jews.

We can identify the whole gamut of human sentiments in the reactions to these encounters. There were those among the Soviet Jews who were reluctant to identify themselves as Jews or even outrightly hostile to the idea. There were those who refused to have any contact with Jews. Yet, by and large, the dominant sentiment was one of mutual curiosity, interest and desire to learn about and help each other. The encounters took place usually on two different levels. On the formal public level the Soviet Jew appeared in his official capacity, representing the authorities, propounding the official line. The local Jews appeared as subjects ready to be instructed in how to behave, and what to do. However, there was also the informal encounter, when, away from public attention, the two sides could be a little more outspoken. Then the Soviet Jew could provide more accurate information as to the true meaning of Jewish life in the USSR, and reveal his interest, concern and even solidarity with his brethren in Poland and other countries.

For the local Jews who were willing to integrate, particularly the young generation, the mere presence of Jews in commanding positions in the Red Army and administration, was of great importance. It proved that Jews could succeed in the Communist State and this facilitated their integration into the Soviet system. 'There were many Jewish officers among the Red Army soldiers stationed in our town. There were officers of our kind, and local Jews from all walks of life used to turn to them with love and admiration', recalled a Jew from Lida.[2] Such encounters took place also in other shtetlach where units of the Red Army were stationed. It should be noted, however, that the Jew serving in the army, despite expressions of sympathy towards foreign Jews, behaved like other Soviet citizens. Typical was the answer given by a Jewish officer when told about German atrocities against the Jews – he replied: 'It is terrible. Really terrible! We did not know. I advise you: Write to comrade Stalin! Write to him, he will help. Write to Stalin!'[3] When encountered by local Jews, the Jewish soldier or officer serving in the annexed territories was friendly and sympathetic, thus contributing to a sense of security and confidence among his local brethren.[4]

Soviet Jews were present in large numbers in the different branches of the civil and economic administration. They were plant managers, school teachers, commercial agents, investigators in the NKVD, etc. There were those who refused to have any contact with the local Jews and would not even admit that they themselves were Jewish. It seemed that they were reluctant to become involved in friendly relationships with an unknown and suspect population.[5] Occasionally some of the Jewish Soviet officials were even more hostile than warranted, in an attempt to show ideological orthodoxy. These were, usually, young Communist intellectuals who all of a sudden found themselves in positions of authority. But more often 'the Jewish Soviet officials who came from the east had close and friendly relations with the local population. They were ordinary folk – people who spoke willingly with the local Jews in their mother tongue, Yiddish.'[6] In Nowogrodek 'many of the officials turned out to be Jews. It became obvious that in spite of the long separation they still had a strong attachment to their brothers abroad. With few exceptions, the Jewish officials were willing to assist other Jews, when asked.'[7]

The informal, casual meetings that took place between Jews of the annexed provinces and Soviet Jews during mutual visits gave both sides a unique opportunity to look into actual life beyond official propaganda. Interestingly enough the contacts between Jews from the two sides of the border were initiated by the authorities themselves. Following the conquest many Jews received identical letters and telegrams from relatives and acquaintances congratulating them on their 'liberation'.[8] Yet the border remained closed. Only a limited number of permits were issued to visit or study in the USSR. The authorities were not over-eager to show how people really lived in the land of socialism.[9] Among the visitors to the newly acquired provinces, which for a while preserved some of their former character, one could detect the Jews produced by the Soviet State. For them a visit to Eastern Poland was a visit to the West with all its luxuries. The visitors, usually people with some official standing, denied the existence of anti-Semitism and stressed the equality and opportunities open for Jews in the USSR.[10] 'The Jews are now different from what they used to be' claimed three Soviet Jews on a train to Baranowicz.[11] 'Instead of the sickly, pale *luftmentsch* of the past, the Jew is now strong as an oak. He has left the old ways of his forefathers', boasted the Soviet officials. But watching how the visitors from the USSR bought literally any merchandise they could lay their hands on, observing their frightened looks and suspicion and their insatiable hunger, showed that not all was well with the Jewish Soviet citizens. When asked why they ordered so much cake, milk and other beverages in a Bialystok café, eating it all on the spot, the reply was: 'Wait until you are long enough in the USSR and you will know the answer.'[12] Such encounters gave some, albeit vague, idea of what the future might hold.[13]

Soviet Jewish 'cultural workers', as the writers and performers were designated, frequently visited the annexed provinces. They were sent officially as Soviet Jews to meet specifically the Jewish population. Doubtless many were eager to meet the large and warm Jewish audiences of Eastern Poland. Officially the purpose of the visits of Yiddish Soviet troupes and writers' brigades was to bring to the 'broad Jewish masses the message of Soviet culture'. To the Jewish intelligentsia they brought the 'true line' in literature and the arts. The Jewish theatres of Kiev and Minsk extensively toured the annexed territories. Though they performed adapted Soviet and classical Yiddish plays, they were met with overpacked halls and enthusiastic crowds.[14] 'The mere name, *The Jewish State Theatre*, contains a message to the liberated Jewish worker', claimed M. Goldblat, the manager of the Kiev theatre. 'For the first time in the history of our people, and this under Soviet government, is Jewish culture and the Jewish theatre in particular a matter of state concern. It is supported materially and morally to the full . . . It represents Stalin's slogan – National in form, Socialist in content', explained the Soviet Jewish director to his 'liberated' brethren.[15] If the local performers needed any detailed instructions about the arts in the state they had newly joined, the message of the visiting Jewish theatre was sufficient.

Visits of Jewish writers were among the subjects most covered in the Soviet Yiddish press. The Jewish literati were probably the most important single vehicle used to spread Soviet ideology among the new Jewish citizens. From the first days of the conquest the Jewish writers were mobilized to spread the true word. They wrote special songs, articles and stories directed at the new public. Individually and more frequently in 'writers' brigades' they visited the annexed provinces. Those were the years of the great diminution of all forms of Jewish culture in the USSR. Soviet Yiddish writers met in Eastern Poland the kind of public that was fast disappearing in their own country. Hence press reports of capacity crowds enthusiastically receiving the representatives of Yiddish culture reflected the true sentiment of the population.[16] The writers visited schools and factories and toured the shtetlach of the region. The authors read from their works and lectured on Soviet literature. Meeting local Jewish writers was a primary goal of the visits. The official public appearances were strictly dedicated to indoctrination and instruction. 'The local Yiddish writers learned a lot from meeting with their Soviet colleagues. The long evenings were for the local writers a great school to learn and get acquainted with Soviet Yiddish literature', reported *Der Shtern*.[17] The public message delivered in festive meetings with local writers was simple and clear: the new Soviet citizens were to become acquainted with the new reality, and write accordingly. The content, style and tone of the official presentations of the Soviet guests made it abundantly clear it was the heyday of Stalin's cult of personality.[18] I. Fefer, the famous writer, warned his audiences not to adopt Soviet themes too soon. They were to develop gradually, naturally.[19]

Informally, the interaction between the Soviet Yiddish writers and their colleagues in the annexed provinces was more complicated than a simple one between instructors and pupils. Many of them had a common background and origin. They shared common concerns for the future of the Jewish people and culture in the stormy days ahead. Yet, to reveal their true feelings and apprehensions, the two sides used esoteric hints, concealing their true meaning from the ever-watchful NKVD.[20] Publicly the Jewish writers never dared to deviate from the official line or take a stand against any official action. When asked to intervene to prevent the closure of a Yiddish high-school in Lvov, two Soviet Jewish writers replied 'we have full confidence in the nationalities policy of the Soviet government. Whatever the government does is certainly right.'[21] However, in private or by hints when they felt secure that their intentions would not be revealed, or in a moment of absent-mindedness, the Soviet Yiddish writers unveiled some of their true feelings. Thus, carried away after a few toasts, two of the visiting poets stood up and raised their glasses 'to the life of the great and suffering Jewish people', a rather unusual gesture in the USSR of 1940.[22] In private and secret conversations or in symbolic spontaneous gestures, in the annexed provinces or in Moscow when hosting colleagues from the western regions, the Soviet Yiddish writers revealed their attachment to the Jewish people and culture.[23] Even the poetess R. Koren, a strong sympathizer of the regime, when recalling her visit to Moscow in February 1941 was left with the nagging impression that not all was well with Yiddish writers in the land of socialism. 'While outwardly the writers exuded success, one could detect in their hearts deep seated anxieties and a strong desire for things Jewish', recalled Koren.[24] It was certainly not an encouraging omen for new Soviet writers.

From among the large group of Soviet Yiddish writers, two are worthy of special mention: P. Markish and Z. Akselrod. The first because of his keen artistic and Jewish perception, the other because of his daring and his final fate. Markish was considered at the time the foremost Yiddish poet in the USSR. On his visit to the annexed territories he was received with great honour and adulation by the population and his local colleagues. His suite became a place of pilgrimage for admirers.[25] Markish's warm personality, politeness, and intimate acquaintance with some of the refugee writers and performers (dating back to his life in the early twenties in Warsaw) created an opportunity for a close look into his deeper sentiments. When meeting alone with Lederman, a refugee actor in the Bialystok theatre, Markish revealed his deep anxiety as to the future of Jewish culture in the Soviet Union.[26] The same apprehension as to the future of the Jewish people, not only in the Soviet Union, was expressed by Markish in his poem 'To the Jewish Dancer'. It is yet another example of the so-called 'drawer literature', since it was not written to be published at the time. Markish likens the Jewish people to a dancer, relating selected chapters from the history of Jewish martyrology and expressing his fear of the danger of extinction. The poem was read to a chosen few, and shocked the audience by revealing a Markish entirely different from his public persona.[27] Being always forced to hide his true sentiments and follow carefully a prescribed line created extremely difficult situations for Markish. He was aware of the intention eventually to curtail Jewish culture in the new territories and tried by sarcasm to deliver that message to an eager, sensitive and apprehensive gathering of writers. What the Soviet Union needed were cobblers and tailors, productive people, not the many writers from a disappearing world, the Soviet Yiddish poet remarked sarcastically.[28] However, much of his public, amazed and angered and misinterpreting his manner, deeply resented the words of the poet.[29]

Z. Akselrod was affectionately and gratefully regarded because he was among the rare few who did not always toe the line and occasionally dared to express their deepest Jewish sentiments. A poet, and one of the people sent from Minsk to help establish the *Bialystoker Shtern*, and a branch of the Belorussian Writers' Union in the new provinces, Akselrod was always willing to meet the refugee writers. He had a warm word for everyone and expressed genuine interest in Jewish life in Poland and abroad.[30] His language was simple and straightforward, as were his feelings. During a performance by the famous cantor Kusevitski, Akselrod asked him to sing *Kol Nidrei*, the *Yom Kippur* prayer, instead of Italian opera songs.[31] He tried unsuccessfully to publish a news item on the execution of 53 Jews in the German-occupied territories.[32] Such expressions of Jewish solidarity were considered dangerous deviations from the proper line. He was accused of Jewish nationalism and Zionism. Late in the summer of 1940 Akselrod disappeared from Bialystok without explanation. It became known much later that the outspoken Soviet Yiddish poet was executed in the Minsk prison on June 26 1941, when the German troops were approaching the city.[33] Akselrod's fate was a grave warning to the local intelligentsia and writers as to the prospects for Jewish culture and artists in the USSR.

Notes

INTRODUCTION

1 B. D. Weinryb, 'Polish Jews Under Soviet Rule', in P. Meyer (ed.), *The Jews in the Soviet Satellites*, Syracuse, 1953, is the most extensive treatment of the subject.

1 JOINING THE SOVIET FAMILY OF NATIONS

1 R. J. Sontag and J. S. Beddie (eds), *Nazi–Soviet Relations: Documents from the Archives of the German Foreign Office*, Washington DC, 1948, p. 78.
2 *Pravda*, 18 September 1939.
3 Sontag and Beddie, *Nazi–Soviet Relations*, pp. 90–6.
4 N. P. Vakar, *Byelorussia*, Cambridge, Mass., 1956, p. 156.
5 N. Khrushchev, *Khrushchev Remembers*, Boston, 1970, p. 146.
6 *Documents on Polish–Soviet Relations, 1939–1945*, London, 1961, pp. 104–5, 541.
7 According to the contentions of the Polish government in exile, out of 13.199 million people living in the Soviet territories, 5.274 million were Poles, 4.125 million Ukrainians, 1.123 Belorussians, 1.109 Jews, 0.0134 Russians, 0.084 Lithuanians. See file A-9-III-1/1 p. 9, from the archive of *The Polish Institute and Sikorski Museum*, London. The files belonged, mostly, to the Polish Government in Exile situated in London. The archive contains valuable material for the study of the period 1939–45.
8 Thus in Tarnopol, Brody, Stryj and other places, Jews were district physicians, while a Ukrainian carried the proper title. See P. Shwarts, *Dos iz geven der onheib*, New York, 1943, pp. 312, 316; *Sefer Stryj*, Tel Aviv, 1962, pp. 162–3.

9 H. Smolar, 'Hakhaim hayehudiim bmaarav Belorussia hasovietit, 1939–1941: prikhah vshkiah', *Shvut*, 4, Tel Aviv, 1976, p. 126.

10 *Sikorski*, file A-9-III-26/3 p. 10. The file contains a summary of reports presented to the Polish Government in Exile, summarizing the first year of Soviet rule.

11 *Sikorski*, file A-9-III-2a/21. Intelligence reports for the Polish government noticed that Poles were now welcome to jobs formerly open only to Ukrainians.

12 *Sikorski*, file A-9-III-2b/4, 'Reports from the Soviet occupied territory for the period to February 1, 1941'.

13 *Sikorski*, file A-9-III-2a/33. Summary of reports to the government presented by the Polish embassy to the Vatican, covering the period to June 1941.

14 Ibid., also file N-1954/78/38. Summary of interviews of arrivals from Poland, end of 1941.

15 R. S. Sullivant, *Soviet Politics and the Ukraine, 1917–1957*, New York, 1962, pp. 237–8.

16 K. K. Dubina (ed.), *Istoriia Ukrainskoi SSR*, Kiev, 1969, vol. 2, p. 471; T. S. Gorbunov et al., *Istoriia Belorusskoi SSR*, Minsk, 1962, vol. 2, pp. 384–5.

17 'Regional committees were formed mainly from people who came from the Soviet [eastern] Ukraine, while district committees were drawn largely from local party activists', *Khrushchev Remembers*, p. 143.

18 See *Sikorski*, file A-9-III-2c/37, pp. 5–7. The file referred to contains a study by M. Rogoyski, *Gospodarka Sowiecka Na Ziemiach Polskich, 1939–41* (*Soviet Economy in Polish Lands, 1939–41*).

19 An eyewitness described the situation in the first few weeks as almost catastrophic: 'One could see repeatedly the same sight: long lines waiting for food . . . People got up early in the morning to line up for the food store', *Shoat Yihudei Polin*, Jerusalem, 1940, p. 34.

20 *Sikorski*, file A-9-III-2c/37, pp. 46–7. The zloty maintained some of its value as long as it could be smuggled into the German-occupied territory.

21 *Sikorski, ibid.* pp. 55–6.

22 *Shoat Yihudei Polin*, p. 27: 'We have plenty of everything in our country', claimed the Soviet citizens, who bought anything they could lay their hands on.

23 See *Pinkas Kleck*, Tel Aviv, 1959, pp. 88–9; Vakar, *Byelorussia*, p. 164.

24 Dubina, *Istoriia Ukrainskoi*, p. 480; Vakar, *Byelorussia*, pp. 166–7. Dubina reports that until the spring of 1940, 155 Kolkhozes had been formed, in September there were over 400 and on 1 June 1941 there were 2,589.

25 *Sikorski*, file A-9-III-2a/21, reports dealing with Soviet deportations from the eastern Provinces.

26 *Documents on Polish–Soviet Relations*, p. 572. 'It was our view that these arrests served to strengthen the Soviet state and clear the road for the building of socialism on Marxist-Leninist principles', *Khrushchev Remembers*, p. 146.

27 *Documents on Polish–Soviet Relations*, p. 573–4; also *Sikorski*, files A-9-III-2b/3 and A-9-III-2c/58.

28 *Sikorski*, files A-9-III-2b/3 and A-9-III-2c/58. The number given is among the lower estimates. For a detailed discussion of the subject see *Special Report No. 1 of the Select Committee on Communist Aggression*, House of Representatives,

83rd Congress, Second Session, Washington DC, 1954.

29 On the methods used and techniques employed during the purges, see chapter 8.

2 SHTETL JEWS

1 S. Etinger, *History of the Jewish People, Vol. III, Modern Times* (Hebrew), pp. 232–5.

2 Based on the calculations of B. D. Weinryb in 'Polish Jews under Soviet Rule', in P. Meyer (ed.), *The Jews in the Soviet Satellites*, Syracuse, 1953, p. 331. The British Foreign Office arrived at the figure of 1.175 million Jews residing in the area, see FO 371–24470. S. Schwartz in *Evrei v Sovetskom Soiuze s nachala vtoroi mirovoi voiny*, New York, 1966, p. 20, estimated that 1.309 million Jews lived in the area at the time of occupation.

3 FO 371–24470.

4 B.-C. Pinchuk, 'Jewish Refugees in Soviet Poland 1939–1941' in *Jewish Social Studies*, vol. 40, New York, 1978, p. 145.

5 H. Rabinowicz, *The Legacy of Polish Jewry*, New York, 1965, pp. 120, 121.

6 Weinryb, 'Polish Jews under Soviet Rule', p. 332.

7 Ibid., p. 333. Over 90% of the Hebrew-speaking schools in Poland were in its eastern provinces. See also C. S. Heller, *On the Edge of Destruction: Jews in Poland Between the Two World Wars*, New York, 1977, pp. 222–31.

8 Heller, *On the Edge of Destruction*, 25, 155–8.

9 According to the 1931 Polish census, 41.9 per cent of the urban population of the eastern provinces were Jews. R. Mahler, *Yihudei Polin bein shtei milkhamot olam*, Tel Aviv, 1968, pp. 25, 33.

10 Heller, *On the Edge of Destruction*, p. 72.

11 Schwartz, *Evrei v Sovetskom Soiuze*, p. 21.

12 Weinryb, 'Polish Jews under Soviet Rule', p. 331. Compared to 58 per cent of the businesses and 24 per cent of the crafts in Poland as a whole.

13 Heller, *On the Edge of Destruction*, p. 5.

14 Ibid., pp. 216–32.

15 According to the 1931 census 12 per cent named Polish as their mother tongue, 79 per cent Yiddish, and 8 per cent Hebrew. Heller, *On the Edge of Destruction*, p. 8.

16 Heller estimated that over one third of the entire Jewish population of Poland was traditional orthodox. The proportion was higher in the shtetl, in the east and in the older generation, ibid., p. 232.

17 For a detailed anthropological study of the traditional shtetl Jew see M. Zborowski and E. Herzog, *Life is with People: The culture of the shtetl*, New York, 1952, pp. 71–124.

18 On the economic backwardness and stagnation of the Kresy and eastern Galicia, the Soviet share in the spoils, see A. Polonsky, *Politics in Independent Poland, 1921–1939*, Oxford, 1972, p. 5; J. Taylor, *The Economic Development of Poland, 1919–1950*, New York, 1952, p. 79.

19 Mahler, *Yihudei Polin*, pp. 28–36.

20 See for example *Sefer Dereczyn*, Tel Aviv, n.d., pp. 27–9; *Korzec: Sefer zikaron likhilatenu shealah Aleha hakoret*, Tel Aviv, 1959, pp. 75–90; *Sefer izkor likhilat Sarny*, Tel Aviv, 1966, pp. 21–7; *Sefer zikaron likdoshei Lanowce shenispu bashoat hanatsit*, Tel Aviv, 1970, pp. 20–1; *Sefer izkor likhilat Luboml*, Tel Aviv, 1973, pp. 61–4; *Sefer zikaron likhilat Iwie*, Tel Aviv, 1968, pp. 92–133. The books mentioned above are just a small sample of many memorial books of small towns of the region that note the same phenomenon.

21 *Sefer Sokolka*, Jerusalem, 1968, pp. 257–62; *Sefer zikaron likhilat Turka al nahar Stryj*, Haifa, 1966, pp. 75–81; *Sefer Radzin*, Tel Aviv, 1957, pp. 47–50; *Lebn un umkum fun Holszany*, Tel Aviv, 1965, pp. 24–6; *Korot aiarah akhat Sopotkin*, Tel Aviv, 1960, pp. 98–100.

22 *Sefer izkor lehantsakhat kdoshei khilat Czortkow*, Tel Aviv, 1961, pp. 12–18; *Sefer zikaron likhilat Augustow vhasvivah*, Tel Aviv, 1966, pp. 130–67; *Pinkas Byten*, Buenos Aires, 1954, pp. 58–70; *Sefer Jezierzany vhasviva*, Jerusalem, 1959, pp. 60–90; *Sokolka*, pp. 97–122.

23 *Izkor buch Pulawy*, New York, 1964, pp. 64–78; *Sefer Ostroleka*, Tel Aviv, 1963, pp. 60–78; *Pinkas Krynki*, Tel Aviv, 1970, pp. 117–30; *Sefer Kostopol: Khaieha umotah shel khila*, Tel Aviv, 1967, pp. 150–74; *Sefer Stryj*, Tel Aviv, 1962, pp. 75–105; *Radzin*, pp. 149–57; *Luboml*, pp. 111–22; *Korzec*, pp. 153–6.

24 On education and culture in the shtetl see *Sefer zikaron Dubno*, Tel Aviv, 1966, pp. 317–42; *Korzec*, pp. 111–33; *Dereczyn*, pp. 40–1; *Sarny*, pp. 178–98; *Pulawy*, pp. 102–48; *Iwie*, pp. 365–87; *Kostopol*, pp. 107–36; *Holszany*, pp. 69–77.

25 *Ostroleka*, pp. 110–53; *Sarny*, pp. 198–211; *Turka*, pp. 91–133; *Dubno*, pp. 249–78; *Stryj*, pp. 139–59; *Radzin*, pp. 182–207; *Iwie*, pp. 393–431; *Sefer Jezierna*, Haifa, 1974, pp. 111–26.

26 For an overview of the economic situation see Mahler, *Yihudei Polin*, ch. 8, pp. 189–95, entitled 'Dalut vdildul' ('Poverty and Impoverishment'). On individual shtetlach see *Dubno*, pp. 213–28; *Korzec*, pp. 157–66; *Dereczyn*, pp. 38–40; *Czortkow*, pp. 174–89; *Byten*, pp. 147–52; *Radzin*, pp. 162–81; *Jezierna*, pp. 91–107; *Kostopol*, pp. 139–48; *Sopotkin*, pp. 18–21.

27 Heller, *On the Edge of Destruction*, pp. 91–125.

28 R. Mahler concludes his economic and social study of Polish Jewry in the inter-war years with a chapter named characteristically 'Poverty and Impoverishment', which summarizes his conclusions: Mahler, *Yihudei Polin*, pp. 189–95.

29 Ibid.

3 THE SHTETL MEETS THE RED ARMY

1 The atrocities perpetrated by the advancing German army against the Jewish population in cities such as Czestochowa, Vishkov, Krasnoshelts and others brought a massive wave of refugees to the eastern provinces. See, M. Prager, *Yiven metsulah hekhadash*, Tel Aviv, 1941, pp. 28–9.

2 Reports from eastern Galicia found in the *Central Zionist Archive*, Jerusalem, file

S5/642. See also *Sefer Nisvizh*, Tel Aviv, 1976, p. 363 – the author describes the situation of lawlessness in the town between the two regimes; *Pinkas Ludmir*, Tel Aviv, 1962, p. 337; *Sefer Dereczyn*, Tel Aviv, n.d., p. 261.

3 *Central Zionist Archive*, file S5/642; also *Sefer zikaron likdoshei Wysniowiec*, Tel Aviv, n.d., pp. 119–20. Jewish self-defence rescued the Polish church from destruction.

4 *Ludmir*, p. 337.

5 See *Yad Vashem Testimonial*, Jerusalem, file G-225-3046 on Szumsk. Also *Kehilat Lanin sefer zikaron*, Tel Aviv, 1957, p. 47; *Pinkas Byten*, Buenos Aires, 1954, pp. 196–8.

6 *The Sikorski Historical Institute*, London, file A-9-III-2a/19.

7 *Central Zionist Archive*, file S5/642 reporting from east Galicia. Also *Yad Vashem*, file II-85-14/9 from Lvov and vicinity; *Sefer Przemysl*, Tel Aviv, 1964, p. 374.

8 *Przemysl*, p. 374. 'There will be a new regime, but there will be peace in the town. The endless fear will stop. The ever-present anxiety for mere survival has passed . . . There was no end to our joy, as if the Messiah's times have arrived', relates an eyewitness from *Dereczyn*, p. 247, and pp. 260–303; also *Yad Vashem*, file K-290-3385 (Lida); file S-109-3219 from (Hancewicze); file S-118-3548 (Baranowicz); file G-226-3047 (Szumsk).

9 Z. Segalowicz, *Gebrente trit*, Buenos Aires, 1947, p. 95. The author stayed as a refugee in Rowno.

10 Ibid., p. 96.

11 *Pinkas Slonim*, Tel Aviv, 1962, p. 18.

12 *Yad Vashem*, file K-147-1659 (Mizocz) – 'The Russians came to help us', announced the Polish mayor. Also *Sefer Budzanow*, Haifa, 1968, p. 157; *Sefer Borszczow*, Tel Aviv, 1960, p. 172.

13 See the numerous reports in *Sikorski*, file A-9-III-2a/19.

14 The Soviet Yiddish daily *Der Shtern* (Kiev) carried headlines such as 'Brotherly Meeting' (18 September 1939), 'Enthusiastic reception of the Red Army' (20 September 1939), 'Days of Happiness and Enthusiasm' (23 September 1939). And the *Oktiaber* (Minsk), 'The Red Army is Met with Joy and Songs' (19 September 1939), 'From Slavery into Bright Socialism' (20 September 1939), 'Greeting the Liberators' (20 September 1939).

15 *Oktiaber*, September 22, 24, October 2, 5, 6, 7 1939; *Der Shtern*, September 23, 26, October 5, 7 1939.

16 *Der Shtern*, September 23 1939.

17 *Oktiaber*, 2 October 1939. The same theme of rescuing the Jews from Polish oppression and pogroms and offering them the benefits of Soviet equality is reported in *Der Shtern*, October 23, 24, 28 1939.

18 *Sikorski*, file A-9-III-2a-19/6.

19 M. Sne, Kleinboim at the time, was one of the important leaders of Polish Jewry who reached Palestine at the beginning of 1940 and reported his impression in *Shoat Yihudei Polin*, Jerusalem, 1940, p. 35.

20 S. Schwartz, *Evrei v Sovietskom Soiuze s nachala vtoroi mirovoi voiny*, New York, 1966, p. 230.

21 *Sefer Izkor Likhilat Sarny*, Tel Aviv, 1966, p. 78; *Sefer zikaron Dubno*, Tel Aviv, 1966, p. 234; *Yad Vashem*, file N-13-705.

22 *Yad Vashem*, file N-13-705 (Galicia); file SH-204-2275 (Lida); file N-13-705 (Lvov); Schwartz, *Evrei v Sovetskom Soiuze*, pp. 228.
23 See for example Schwartz's vivid descriptions of the buying craze of the Soviet soldiers, *Evrei v Sovetskom Soiuze*, pp. 225–30. Also *Shoat Yihudei Polin* p. 35; *Yad Vashem*, file N-13-705; file SH-204-705. When questioned about the buying craze the uniform answer of the Soviet soldiers was: 'We have plenty of everything at home.'
24 F. Zerubavel, *Na vanad*, Buenos Aires, 1947, p. 74.
25 Ibid, p. 75.
26 *Sefer Kostopol*, Tel Aviv, 1967, p. 185; *Pinkas Kolomyja*, New York 1957, p. 268; *Nisvizh*, p. 361.
27 *Sefer zikaron shel khilat Lipniszki*, Tel Aviv, 1968, p. 133.
28 Zerubavel, *Na vanad*, p. 75.
29 *Sefer izkor lehantsakhat kdoshei khilat Czortkow*, Tel Aviv, 1961, p. 222.
30 T. Fuks, *A vanderung iber ukupirte gebitn*, Buenos Aires, 1948, p. 44.
31 *Nisvizh*, p. 122.
32 'We were sentenced to death, now it was commuted to life imprisonment' was the often reported joke among the Jews, *Shoat Yihudei Polin*, p. 34.
33 *Byten*, pp. 196–198; *Wysniowiec*, p. 119; *Yad Vashem*, file SH-191-2131 (Luck).
34 *Sikorski*, file A-9-III-2a/19. The file contains reports from eastern Galicia arranged according to the Polish administrative subdivisions.
35 Ibid.
36 *Czortkow*, pp. 221–2; *Sefer Dambrowica*, Tel Aviv, 1964, p. 687; *Yad Vashem*, K-247-2963 (Berezno).
37 *Dereczyn*, pp. 385–6; *Dambrowica*, Tel Aviv, 1964, p. 685; *Bransk: sefer hazikaron*, New York, 1948, p. 248.
38 *Sikorski*, file A-9-III-2a-19, reports from Galicia.
39 M. Grosman, *In Farkishuftn Land Fun Legendern Dzugashvili*, Paris, 1950, vol. 1, p. 28.
40 *Bransk*, p. 247.
41 *Yad Vashem*, file V-195-3485 (Buczacz); file G-147-1908 (Radziwillow); *Bransk*, p. 248; *Sefer Jezierzany vhasviva*, Jerusalem, 1959, p. 281.
42 *Sikorski*, file A-9-III-2a/19 (Lubaczow and Dobromil), also file A-9-III-2c/58 contain numerous reports from all parts of the Soviet-occupied areas emphasizing the role of Jews in building the Soviet administration. Also *Yad Vashem*, file L-28-313 (Mlynow); file G-225-3046; file G-226-3047 (Szumsk); file R-240-3597 (Molczadz); file SH-191-2131 (Luck); *Nisvizh*, p. 125.
43 Schwartz, *Evrei v Sovietskom Soiuze*, pp. 281–3.
44 *Korzec: Sefer zikaron likhilatenu shealah Aleha hakoret*, Tel Aviv, 1959, p. 336; also *Yad Vashem*, file SH-191-2131 (Luck); file R-240-3596 (Molczadz).
45 For example, Beresa Kartuska in *Pinkas mekhamesh kehilot khar evot*, Buenos Aires, 1958, p. 459. Also in *Sefer Mlynow-Merwic*, Haifa, 1970, p. 283; *Korzec*, p. 283; *Pinkas Ostrog*, Tel Aviv, 1960, p. 105; *Kolomyja*, p. 377.
46 For example *Sefer zikaron likdoshei Lanowce shenispu bashoat hanatsit*, Tel Aviv, 1970, p. 107; *Sefer zikaron Stolpce-Swerzana vhaaiarot hasmukhot*, Tel Aviv, 1964, p. 131; *Mlynow*, p. 377.

4 THE DISSOLUTION OF THE OLD ORDER AND EMERGENCE OF THE LONELY JEW

1 Information on Soviet policy towards the Jewish community in the USSR was drawn mainly from the following studies: S. W. Baron, *The Russian Jew under Tsars and Soviets*, New York, 1964; Z. Gitelman, *Jewish Nationality and Soviet Politics: The Jewish Sections of the CPSU, 1917–1930*, Princeton, 1972; B. Z. Goldberg, *The Jewish Problem in the Soviet Union*, New York, 1961; S. Schwartz, *The Jews in the Soviet Union*, Syracuse, 1951.
2 For a brief description of the history of the 1930s see 'The consolidation of Totalitarianism (1933–1941)', ch. 18, in D. W. Treadgold, *Twentieth-Century Russia*, Chicago, 1959. For an analysis of major features of totalitarianist society see C. J. Friedrich and Z. K. Brzezinski, *Totalitarian Dictatorship and Autocracy*, second edition, Praeger, 1965.
3 For Lenin's views on the subject see V. I. Lenin, *Polnoe Sobranie Sochinenii*, fifth edition, Moscow, 1967, vol. 7, pp. 95–101, 117–22, 245–6, 266–9. Lenin deals with the Jewish problem while defining his attitudes to the Jewish Bund. See also ibid., vol. 20, 'Kriticheskie zametki po natsionalnomu voprosu'.
4 See Gitelman, *Jewish Nationality and Soviet Politics*.
5 *Pinkas Byten*, Buenos Aires, 1954, p. 205.
6 *Yad Vashem Testimonial*, Jerusalem, file SH-191-2131 (Luck).
7 *Sefer edut vzikaron likhilat Pinsk-Karlin*, Tel Aviv, 1966, vol. 2, p. 76.
8 See also *Sefer izkor likhilat Sarny*, Tel Aviv, 1966, p. 78; *Shoat Yihudei Polin*, Jerusalem, 1940, p. 61 for eastern Galicia; *Yad Vashem*, file L-2-107 (Baranowicz); *Grodno-Entsiklopedia shel galuiot*, Jerusalem, 1973, no. 9, p. 505.
9 A. Zak, *Knecht zenen mir geven*, Buenos Aires 1956, vol. 1, p. 79. One of the board members described the situation in almost identical words in *Grodno*, p. 505.
10 B. Pinchuk, 'The Sovietization of the Jewish Community of Eastern Poland, 1939–1941', *The Slavonic and East European Review*, vol. 56, no. 3, 1978, p. 394.
11 *Shoat Yihudei Polin*, p. 61.
12 Ibid., p. 62.
13 B. Weinryb, 'Polish Jews Under Soviet Rule', in P. Meyer (ed.), *The Jews in the Soviet Satellites*, Syracuse, 1953, p. 338.
14 *Shoat Yihudei Polin*, pp. 24, 41, for Kolomea and other places in eastern Galicia.
15 See report of M. Kleinboim (Sne) in *Shoat Yihudei Polin*.
16 Ibid., pp. 35–6.
17 P. Shwarts, *Dos iz geven der onheib*, New York, 1943, p. 330; M. Tsanin, *Grenetsn biz tsum himl*, Tel Aviv 1970, p. 16.
18 K. Brodetski 'Di vanderungen fun Poilishn hekhaluts un zain arbet in lite un unter der sovetn okupatsie' in *Khalutsim in Poilin*, New York, 1961, pp. 48–52; *Shoat Yihudei Polin*, 36; *Yad Vashem*, file SH-191-2131, Weinryb, 'Polish Jews Under Soviet Rule', p. 365.
19 *Sefer Lida*, Tel Aviv, 1970, pp. 256–60; *Sefer hashomer hatsair*, Merkhaviah, 1969, vol. 2, p. 219. There were reports that as late as March 1940 underground conventions took place in Rowno and Lvov.

20 *Shoat Yihudei Polin*, pp. 23, 36. *Pinsk*, p. 187. The Soviet representatives tried to convince the Young pioneers to join the supporters of the new regime. Zionism, maintained the Soviet official, was 'needed' only in anti-Semitic Poland.

21 H. Smolar, 'Hakhaim hayehudiim bmaarav Belorussia hasovietit, 1939–1941: prikhah vshkiah', *Shvut*, 4, Tel Aviv, 1976, p. 131.

22 *Pinsk*, p. 318; *Lida*, p. 277.

23 *Sefer zikaron likhilat Augustow vhasviva*, Tel Aviv, 1966, p. 376; *Lida*, p. 266; *Pinsk*, p. 311; *Yad Vashem*, file SH-204-2275 (Lida); file B-60-789 (Siry); file L-28-313 (Mlynow).

24 On the Polish Communist Party, suspicions of Trotskyism, and its dissolution, see M. K. Dziewanowski, *The Communist Party of Poland*, Cambridge, Mass., 1959, pp. 149–54.

25 *Yad Vashem*, file SH-204-2275; file B-60-789; file K-175-1990; file S-109-3219; *Lida*, p. 266.

26 On the role of passports as a means of control, see L. Boim, 'Shitat hapasportim bibrit-hamoatsot vhashpaatah al matsavam shel hayihudim', *Shvut*, 3, Tel Aviv, 1975, pp. 7–16.

27 *Pinsk*, p. 319; *Yad Vashem*, file N-13-705 (Lvov); file F-114-1173 (Brzesc); file B-56-757 (Lvov); file K-175-1990 (Slonim).

28 *Janow al yad Pinsk, sefer zikaron*, Jerusalem, 1969, p. 225; *Sarny*, p. 79; *Pinsk*, p. 319; *Dubno*, p. 653; *Yad Vashem*, file N-13-705 (Lvov); file A-74-1205 (Lvov).

29 D. Lederman, *Fun iener zait forhang*, Buenos Aires, 1960, p. 127–8; Y. Bromberg, unpublished manuscript on Soviet rule in Pinsk, found in Gvat, p. 4.

30 *Oktiaber*, Minsk, 22 March 1940.

31 I. Fefer 'Soviet Passports', *Der Shtern*, Kiev, 4 June 1940.

32 *Pinsk*, p. 318. Also Lederman, *Fun iener zait forhang*, pp. 135–8. People who for one reason or another were not apprehended during the mass arrests that lasted several days were promised their freedom frequently. 'Yesterday there were arrests until 12. Whoever succeeded in remaining free – should remain so' was the response of a police official to a person who wanted to join his arrested family in Kovel, June 1940 – *Yad Vashem*, file L-91-1281; also *Yad Vashem*, file S-109-3219 (Hancewicze).

33 *Entsiklopedia Shel Galuiot Tarnopol*, no. 9, Jerusalem, 1965, p. 386; *Yad Vashem*, file F-206-2178 (Polesia); file M-85-1469 (Rawa-Ruska).

34 Tsanin, *Grenetsn biz tsum himl*, p. 9; Brodetski, 'Di vanderung', p. 48. Lederman, *Fun iener zait forhang*; Z. Segalowicz, *Gebrente trit*, Buenos Aires, 1947 and P. Shwarts *Dos iz geven der onheib*, quoted above, are actually their stories of evacuation from Warsaw and life in the Eastern provinces under Soviet rule.

35 For a detailed description of the arrest see his daughter's story in *Yad Vashem*, file T-82-3687.

36 Ibid.

37 *Jewish Chronicle*, 31 May 1940.

38 Ibid., 29 March 1940.

39 Ibid., 20 June 1941.

40 Tsanin, *Grenetsn biz tsum himl*, p. 16. See Schwartz, *The Jews in the Soviet Union*, pp. 330–1 on the arrest of the Bund's leaders in Vilno during the Soviet occupation of the city in September–October 1939.

41 Tsanin, *Grenetsn biz tsum himl*, pp. 29, 42; *Yad Vashem*, file L-2-107 (Baranowicz); file R-34-594 (Tarnopol); file SH-313-3522 (Lvov); file SH-191-2131 (Luck).

42 *Yad Vashem*, file R-71-1214 (Janow); file L-2-107 (Baranowicz); file SH-191-2131 (Luck); file CH-219-3404 (Pinsk); see also *Sefer Zikaron Likhilat Szczuczyn, Wasilishki, Ostryn, Nowydwur, Ruzanka*, Tel Aviv, 1966, p. 75; *Sefer zikaron Dubno*, Tel Aviv, 1966, p. 649.

43 *Pinsk*, p. 312.

44 *Shoat Yihudei Polin*, p. 23; Tsanin, *Grenetsn biz tsum himl*, p. 9; Brodetski, 'Di Vanderung', p. 48.

45 M. Kleinboim (Sne) 'Tazkir al matsava shel Yiahadut Mizrakh eiropa bereishit Milkhemet haolam hashnia', *Galed*, Tel Aviv, 1978, vols 4–5, p. 565.

46 *Shoat Yihudei Polin*, pp. 24–5; Brodetski, 'Di Vanderung', pp. 48–51; *Yad Vashem*, file SH-191-2131 (Luck); file R-219-3404 (Pinsk).

47 Kleinboim, 'Tazkir al matsavah', pp. 566–7.

48 *Jewish Chronicle*, London, 14 June 1940. See D. Porat's article 'Nsibot Vsibot Lmatan Vizot-Maavar Sovietiot Lplitei Polin Haihudiim Bvilna Bshanim 1940–1941', *Shvut*, 6, Tel Aviv, 1978, which deals specifically with the granting of Soviet visas to Jewish leaders who escaped to Vilno.

49 A British Foreign office report in Summer 1940 noted that Jews who actively supported the Soviet occupants were among the mass deportees FO 371-24472 and C-5744-116-55 in the Public Records Office, London. See also *The Sikorski Historical Institute*, London, file A-9-III-2a-21, Intelligence report presented to the Polish government on conditions in the occupied territories, dated 4 December 1940.

50 *Yad Vashem*, file V-195-3485 (Buczacz); *Tarnopol*, p. 383; *Szczuczyn*, p. 75; *Janow*, p. 225; *Pinsk*, p. 311.

51 *Augustow*, p. 377; *Tarnopol*, pp. 386–7; *Dubno*, pp. 652–4; *Pinsk*, p. 319; *Yad Vashem*, file F-206-2178 (Niesviesz); file K-175-1990 (Slonim); file N-13-705 (Lvov).

52 *Janow*, p. 225; *Pinsk*, p. 320; *Szczuczyn*, p. 75; *Yad Vashem*, file K-256-3112 (Lida); file K-175-1990 (Slonim).

53 *Pinsk*, p. 320.

54 The wave of June 1941 included tens of thousands of new deportees. On its first day we have testimonies to the effect of dozens of trains with 60–70 wagons each moving to the east, *Szczuczyn*, p. 78; *Pinsk*, p. 320. An episode typical of the behaviour of the NKVD in the annexed areas was the execution of political prisoners with the retreat of the Red Army, *Yad Vashem*, file R-49-3306; file SH-313-3522; file SH-204-2275.

55 S. M. Schwartz, *Evrei v Sovetskom Soiuze s nachala vtoroi mirovoi voiny (1939–1965)*, New York, 1966, p. 36.

56 Weinryb, 'Polish Jews Under Soviet Rule', p. 48.

57 *Polish Soviet Relations*, vol. 1, pp. 573–4.

5 LEARNING TO LIVE WITH THE SOVIET ECONOMIC SYSTEM

1 M. Kleinboim, (Sne), 'Tazkir al matsava shel Yiahadut Mizrakh eiropa bereishit milkhemet haolam hashnia', *Galed*, vols 4–5, Tel Aviv, 1978, p. 562.
2 Ibid. For similar descriptions see *Central Zionist Archive*, Jerusalem, file SS-642; *Shoat Yihudei Polin*, Jerusalem, 1940, pp. 57–59; FO 371-24471. All are reports from the Soviet-occupied territories.
3 *Yad Vashem Testimonial*, Jerusalem, file B-56-757 (Wolinia); file SH-313-3522 (Pomorzany); file L-242-3700 (Kozin); file K-247-2963 (Berezno); *Janow al yad Pinsk, sefer zikaron*, Jerusalem, 1969, p. 225; *Sefer izkor likhilat Sarny*, Tel Aviv, 1966, p. 79.
4 Also *Sefer Jezierzany vhasviva*, Jerusalem, 1959, p. 282. A. Zak, *Knecht zenen mir geven*, Buenos Aires, 1956, vol. 1, pp. 163–70; M. Grosman, *In Farkishuftn Land fun Legendern Dzugashvili*, Paris, 1950, vol. 1, p. 62.
5 *Pinkas Slonim*, Tel Aviv, 1962, vol. 2, p. 8; *Pinkas Kleck*, Tel Aviv, 1959, p. 85; *Sefer izkor Goniandz*, Tel Aviv, 1960, p. 584; *Pinkas Byten*, Buenos Aires, 1954, p. 202; *Shoat Yihudei Polin*, p. 58; *Yad Vashem*, file SH-191-2131 (Luck).
6 *Kleck*, p. 85. Similar instances were reported in *Sefer zikaron Dubno*, Tel Aviv, 1966, p. 646; *Sefer Stryj*, Tel Aviv, 1962, p. 161; *Shoat Yihudei Polin*, p. 58.
7 See *Central Zionist Archive*, SJ5-642; *Yad Vashem*, file A-238-3343 (Kosow); file B-41-1460 (Rubiel); file S-109-3219; file G-147-1908 (Radziwillow); *Sefer edut vzikaron likhilat Pinsk-Karlin*, Tel Aviv, 1966, p. 74. *Pinkas Slonim*, Tel Aviv, 1962, vol. 2, p. 8. *Yad Vashem*, file SH-191-2131 (Luck) has the story of a merchant who together with other businessmen formed a cooperative and invested in it all their resources. The merchants themselves served in minor subordinate jobs. It lasted for two months after which he was forced to leave town.
8 *Shoat Yihudei Polin*, pp. 43, 59; *Central Zionist Archive*, S-5-642; *Byten*, p. 204.
9 *Pinsk*, p. 79; Grosman, *In Farkishuftn Land*, p. 52; *Slonim*, p. 9; *Grodno-Entsiklopedia shel galuiot*, Jerusalem, 1973, pp. 139–40; *Shoat Yihudei Polin*, pp. 24, 43.
10 *Slonim*, vol. 2, p. 9; *Pinkas Kolomyja*, New York, 1957, p. 377; *Pinsk*, p. 79.
11 Kleinboim, 'Tazkir al matsava', p. 563; Grosman, *In Farkishuftn Land*, p. 53; *Pinsk*, p. 312; *Shoat Yihudei Polin*, p. 59.
12 Kleinboim, 'Tazkir al matsava', p. 563.
13 Grosman, *In Farkishuftn Land*, p. 53. The author maintained that the workers received their salaries in zloty, as he did. In spite of promises the money was not exchanged.
14 *Pinsk*, p. 312. See also *Yad Vashem*, file N-40-1447; file H-143-3525.
15 There were numerous reports of the operation of labour exchange offices in the new territories in the Soviet Yiddish newspapers the *Oktiaber* (Minsk) and *Der Shtern* (Kiev), during the months of October to December 1939: *Oktiaber*, 4, 29 November 1939; *Der Shtern*, 27 October, 26 December 1939. The information was confirmed by a non-Soviet source: *Jewish Chronicle*, London, 17 October 1939.
16 *Oktiaber*, 4, 29 November 1939, 4 January 1940.

17 *Oktiaber*, 12, 16, 20 January 1940.

18 *Oktiaber*, 10, 21 February, 16, 20 March, 1940; *Der Shtern*, 23 April 1940. 'Section 118 of Stalin's Constitution that promises work for all is being realised in the liberated territory', maintained the *Oktiaber* on 16 January 1940.

19 *Der Shtern*, 23 April 1940, reported the closing of labour exchange offices due to lack of demand for their services. Non-Soviet sources confirm, in general, the elimination of unemployment by the summer of 1940. See *Lubcza vdelticz, sefer zikaron*, Haifa 1971, p. 35–36; *Pinsk*, p. 290; *Kleck*, p. 90; *Janow*, p. 225.

20 *Pinsk*, p. 290.

21 The Hasidic Rabbi of Karlin was registered by his followers as a night watchman to prevent his deportation from Pinsk as a 'loiterer', ibid. Militia men checked passers-by for work permits in the streets of Bialystok, to apprehend loafers (*progulshchiki*), Grosman, *In Farkishuftn Land*, p. 70.

22 *Shoat Yihudei Polin*, pp. 24–5.

23 D. Grodner, 'In Soviet Poland and Lithuania,' *Contemporary Jewish Record*, vol. 4, April 1941, p. 140.

24 H. Smolar, 'Hakhaim hayehudiim bmaarav Belorussia hasovietit 1939–1941: prikhah vshkiah', *Shvut*, 4, Tel Aviv, 1976, p. 130.

25 *Sefer Dambrowica*, Tel Aviv, 1964, p. 682; *Sefer zikaron likhilat Augustow vhasviva*, Tel Aviv, 1966, p. 376; *Forverts*, 11, 13 March 1940; *Der Shtern* 12, 15 November 1939.

26 See Grodner, 'In Soviet Poland and Lithuania', p. 140; *Forverts*, 11 March 1940; Smolar, 'Hakhaim hayehudiim', p. 130. *Oktiaber* reported on 1,100 people who left before January and 11,000 from Bialystok. See *Oktiaber*, 12, 20 January 1940.

27 *Der Shtern*, 12, 21 November, 1939; *Forverts* 20 March 1940; *Oktiaber* 13, 20 January, 1940.

28 *Der Shtern*, 15 November 1939.

29 *Der Shtern*, 8 December 1939.

30 *Der Shtern*, 12, 21 November, 26 December 1940; *Oktiaber*, 12 February 1940.

31 *Forverts* on 17, 20, 23, and 27 March 1940 carried detailed reports of the episode.

32 Smolar, 'Hakhaim hayehudiim', p. 130. A report presented to the Polish Government in Exile also related the same incident: 'Almost one thousand of the registrants staged a demonstration in Minsk and forced the authorities to let them cross the old border', *The Sikorski Historical Institute*, London, file A-11-73/2.

33 *Sefer zikaron likhilat Augustow Vhasviva*, Tel Aviv, 1966, p. 376; *Sefer Dambrowica*, p. 683.

34 *Forverts*, 23 March 1940; Lederman, D., *Fun iener zait forhang*, Buenos Aires, 1960, pp. 126–7.

35 *Kleck*, p. 84; *Stryj*, p. 16; *Sarny*, p. 78; *Slonim*, vol. 2, p. 18.

36 *Sefer Mlynow-Merwic*, Haifa, 1970, p. 283. Identical stories were reported from many other shtetlach, see *Dambrowica*, p. 679; *Sarny*, p. 80; *Stryj*, p. 161; *Goniandz*, p. 584; *Yad Vashem*, file Z-36-1123 (Banira).

37 *Yad Vashem*, file A-74-1203 (Sarny); file I-24-883 (Bialystok); file S-118-3548 (Baranowicz); file K-247-2963 (Berezno).

38 *Shoat Yihudei Polin*, p. 56; *Central Zionist Archive*, S-5-642; R. Bertish, 'Pzurat Yihudei Polin bmilkhemet haolam hashniia', *Galed*, Tel Aviv, 1973, vol. 1, p. 268.

39 Smolar, p. 127, reports that F. K. Ponomarenko, the first party secretary of Belorussia and its Prime Minister, issued instructions to 'treat with the utmost suspicion "Westerners" and above all those who were formerly communists'. Smolar himself was previously the Communist Party secretary in Vilno. He emphasized that a majority of the local communists were Jews.

40 *Ibid.*, p. 128: Bertish, 'Pzurat Yihudei Polin', p. 268; *Shoat Polin*, p. 57; *Central Zionist Archive*, S-5-642.

41 S. M. Schwartz, *Evrei v Sovetskom Soiuze s nachala vtoroi mirovoi voiny (1939–1965)*, New York, 1966, p. 26; B. Weinryb, 'Polish Jews under Soviet Rule', P. Meyer (ed.), *The Jews in the Soviet Satellites*, Syracuse, 1953, p. 330. Also S. H. Redlich, 'Hayehudim bashtakhim shesupkhu librit-hamoatsot, 1939–1941', *Bekhinot*, 1, Tel Aviv, 1970, p. 74.

42 *Central Zionist Archive*, S-5-642; *Shoat Yihudei Polin*, p. 56.

43 *Forverts*, 24 February 1940.

44 *Sarny*, p. 80.

45 *Shoat Yihudei Polin*, p. 28.

46 *Yad Vashem*, files L-28-313, K-247-2963; *Mlynow*, p. 283. The Jewish council members in Mlynow were dismissed on the charge of being Zionists. Only one out of twelve council members was a Jew in the shtetl, which had 50 per cent Jews in its population.

47 *Shoat Yihudei Polin*, p. 56; *Central Zionist Archive*, S-5-642.

48 *Shoat Yihudei Polin*, p. 56. The *Oktiaber* on 17 February 1941 noted with satisfaction that on the railways of Belorussia one could now find Jews whereas during Polish rule they were molested even while travelling.

49 *Shoat Yihudei Polin*, p. 42.

50 FO 371-24471 (new C-2067-116-55).

51 *Kleck*, p. 85; *Sarny*, p. 78; *Stryj*, p. 171.

52 *Lubcza*, pp. 35–6.

53 *Dubno*, p. 235.

54 *Slonim*, p. 264. Jews filled the jobs vacated in the Slonim bank, ibid., p. 8.

55 *Sefer Budzanow*, Haifa, 1968, p. 159: 'Jews were found in all administrative offices in the shtetl'. *Goniandz*, p. 589: 'Life became easier within a short period ... Jews headed the cooperative stores that were organized. They were employed in the offices and institutions established in the shtetl.' See also *Jezierzany*, p. 283; *Sefer Chorostkow*, Tel Aviv, 1968, p. 383.

56 Fuks, *A Vanderung iber okupirte gebitn*, Buenos Aires, 1948, p. 44.

57 Weinryb, 'Polish Jews', p. 335.

58 *Yad Vashem*, file F-286-2967 (Doctor, western Ukraine); file F-70-1516 (Doctor); file L-105-1560 (Accountant, Lvov); file SH-313-3522 (Lawyer become teacher, Lvov); file K-316-3651 (Engineer, Bialystok); file L-65-890 (Music teacher, Rowno).

59 *Pinsk*, p. 312 (Pharmacists); *Sarny*, p. 78 (forest management); *Kleck*, p. 85, (all free technical professionals); *Shoat Yihudei Polin*, p. 58 (east Galicia, all professions).

60 *Sefer Zikaron likhilat Iwie*, Tel Aviv, 1968, p. 381.

61 *Lebn un umkum fun Holszany*, Tel Aviv, 1965, p. 170; *Grodno*, p. 503.

62 *Chorostkow*, p. 333; *Jezierzany*, p. 282; *Sefer zikaron shel khilat Lipniszki*, Tel Aviv, 1967, p. 252; *Yad Vashem*, file K-256-3112 (Nowogrodek); *Oktiaber*, 16th November, 1939; *Bialystoker Shtern*, 27 October 1940.

63 *Lipniszki*, p. 135; *Sefer zikaron likhilat Tuczyn-Krips*, Tel Aviv, 1967, p. 252; *Khilat Ilia*, Tel Aviv, 1962, p. 317; *Rishonim lamared, Lachwa*, Jerusalem, 1957, p. 36.

64 *Tuczyn*, p. 252.

65 *Lubcza*, p. 40.

66 *Pinsk*, p. 79; Lederman, *Fun iener zait forhang*, p. 109; Fuks, *A Vanderung*, p. 63.

67 *Yad Vashem*, file A-238-3343 (Kosow); file G-147-1908 (Radziwillow); file S-109-3219 (Hancewicze).

68 *Yad Vashem*, file H-143-3525 (Dawidgrodek); file K-147-1659 (Mizocz); file B-41-1460 (Rubiel). See also *Sefer Trubich* (Targowica), Haifa, 1967, p. 274.

69 *Sefer Zikaron Likhilat Kolno*, Tel Aviv, 1971, p. 413; *Stryj*, p. 161; *Kolomyja*, p. 377.

70 *Czortkow*, p. 224.

71 *Sarny*, p. 267; *Mlynow*, p. 285; *Dubno*, p. 235; *Sefer Kostopol: Khaieha umota shel khila*, Tel Aviv, 1967, p. 177; *Yad Vashem*, file SH-313-3522 (Pomorzany); file G-233-3130 (Nieswiez); file L-220-3459 (Sysztyn).

72 On the fast expanding commercial enterprises of different sizes and functions that numbered thousands of units, see *Der Shtern*, 14 January 1940.

73 *Kleck*, pp. 89–90: *Lachwa*, p. 37; *Lubcza*, p. 35; *Kolomyja*, p. 377; *Stryj*, p. 161; *Sefer zikaron likhilat Turka al nahar Stryj*, Haifa, 1966, p. 228; *Sefer zikaron likdoshei Szumsk*, Tel Aviv, 1968, p. 16.

74 P. Shwarts, *Dos iz geven der onheib*, New York, 1943, p. 285.

75 Ibid.

76 *Pinsk*, p. 290; *Lipniszki*, p. 138; *Kleck*, p. 89; *Sarny*, p. 79; *Lachwa*, p. 36; *Sefer Sokolka*, Jerusalem, 1968, p. 344.

77 *Sefer Dereczyn*, Tel Aviv, n.d., pp. 303–4; *Stryj*, 161; *Dubno*, p. 648; *Khilat Semiatycze*, Tel Aviv, 1965, p. 376.

78 *Stryj*, p. 161.

79 Unpublished manuscript of M. Bromberg. It relates to Pinsk during Soviet occupation. The manuscript is deposited in the Gvat library. Another Pinsk resident insisted that the taxes were 20 times higher than in the Polish period; *Pinsk*, p. 290.

80 *Semiatycze*, p. 377.

81 See detailed reports in *Oktiaber*, 30 November 1939, and *Der Shtern*, 9 December 1939.

82 *Lipniszki*, p. 139.

83 *Lachwa*, p. 36; *Semiatycze*, p. 377.
84 *Lachwa*, p. 37; *Yad Vashem*, file I-36-1299 (Nowogrodek); file G-233-3130 (Nieswiez); *Oktiaber*, 12 January 1940.
85 *Oktiaber*, 23 January, 4, 9, 22 February, 5 June, 25 December 1940. Reports from various parts of the annexed territories on the operation of the local producers' cooperatives.
86 *Oktiaber*, 22 February 1940. Report of N. P. Apiakin, member of the central cooperative committee of Belorussia.
87 *Oktiaber*, 4 March 1940.
88 *Oktiaber*, 8 August 1940.
89 *Oktiaber*, 18 January 1941.
90 *Grodno*, p. 512.
91 *Bialystoker Shtern*, 5 January 1941.
92 *Oktiaber*, 17 February 1941.
93 *Yad Vashem*, file L-220-3459 (Sysztyn); file I-36-1299 (Nowogrodek); file K-247-2963 (Berezno); file R-240-3597 (Molczadz). Also *Bransk: Sefer hazikaron*, New York, 1948, p. 249; *Dubno*, p. 235; *Slonim*, vol. 2, p. 265; *Sefer zikaron Stolpce-Swerzana vhaaiarot hasmukhot*, Tel Aviv, 1964, p. 457; *Kleck*, p. 90; *Kolomyja*, p. 377.
94 *Pinsk*, p. 291; *Forverts*, 25 May 1940; *Yad Vashem*, file N-13-705 (Lvov); file G-225-3046 (Szumsk).
95 *Yad Vashem*, file N-13-705; Jakshin, unpublished manuscript on Pinsk, p. 3 (in the Gvat library). The author maintains that there was a general decline of production because of low salaries. Also A. Zak, *Knecht zenen mir geven*, Buenos Aires, 1956, pp. 43–7. The author described life in Soviet Grodno. His major contention (for spring 1940) was that many found it difficult to survive on their official wages.
96 All headlines from the *Oktiaber*, 15th August 1940.
97 Headlines from *Oktiaber*, 16 August 1940.
98 See, for example, the news and detailed articles in the *Jewish Chronicle*, 1 December 1939; *Forverts*, 7, 9 March; 4 April 1940. The major themes in the papers were the hopes and disillusionment of the Jews in the Soviet-occupied territories of Poland.
99 *Stolpce*, p. 457.
100 *Janow*, p. 225.
101 *Sarny*, p. 79.
102 *Kleck*, p. 90.
103 *Kolomyja*, p. 377; *Yad Vashem*, file L-242-3700 (Kozin); *Turka*, p. 228 – 'Only a few wealthy Jews suffered, their fortune being confiscated', summarized the author. The many poor found a living under the new regime.
104 *Yad Vashem*, file K-247-2963.
105 *Szumsk*, p. 16.
106 *Stryj*, p. 161.
107 *Wolozyn, Sefer shel hair vshel Eshivat ets khaiim*, Tel Aviv, 1970, p. 530.
108 *Sikorski*, file A-11-73/2, A-9-III-2c/35; Reports from Poland on the economy in the Soviet-occupied territories.

109 *Yad Vashem*, file G-225-3046 (Szumsk); file R-240-3597 (Molczadz); file K-247-2963 (Berezno); *Sefer Lida*, Tel Aviv, 1970, p. 277.
110 Zak, *Knecht zenen mir geven*, p. 89.
111 *Jezierzany*, p. 282. 'Speculation' as the illegal trading was called in official jargon, was punishable by 5–15 years of imprisonment.
112 Grodner, 'In Soviet Poland and Lithuania', p. 140.
113 Shwarts, *Dos iz geven*, p. 314.
114 Zak, *Knecht zenen mir geven*, pp. 40–1.
115 *Yad Vashem*, file K-247-2963 (Berezno).
116 *Yad Vashem*, file G-261-3581 (Podkamien); file L-28-313 (Mlynow); M. Smoler, *Neevakti al Khaiai*, Tel Aviv, 1978, p. 40.
117 Zak, *Knecht zenen mir geven*, p. 36.
118 *Yad Vashem*, file CH-21-1592; file SH-21-762 (Lvov); file K-33-410 (Bialystok); Smoler, *Neevakti al Khaiai*, p. 40: Smolar, 'Hakhaim hayehudiim', p. 130.
119 *Kostopol*, p. 117; Smoler, *Neevakti al Khaiai*, p. 40; *Dambrowica*, p. 678.
120 *Bransk*, p. 249; *Dambrowica*, p. 678.
121 *Yad Vashem*, file K-33-410 (Bialystok); file K-247-2963 (Berezno); *Bransk*, p. 249.
122 Smolar, 'Hakhaim hayehudiim', p. 130. Smolar relates an interesting story about the visit of I. Kupala, the famous Belorussian poet of the time. 'When the official tour ended Kupala said "And now let us get acquainted with the folklore." I looked at him with amazement: what kind of folklore had the great Belorussian poet in mind in a city that had almost no Belorussians (Bialystok)? He noticed my surprise and explained: "Now let us go to the market to acquire goods that there in the East belong to ancient folklore".'
123 *Yad Vashem*, file K-247-2963.
124 *Kostopol*, p. 117.
125 On the corruption among Soviet officials in the territories see also Grosman, *In Farkishuftn Land*, p. 76; *Bransk*, p. 249.
126 On the origin of the term see A. Nove, *The Soviet Economic System*, London, 1977, p. 100.
127 *Forverts*, 8 March 1940.
128 Shwarts, *Dos iz geven*, p. 362; M. Tsanin, *Grenetsn biz tsum himl*, Tel Aviv, 1970, p. 34.
129 Zak, *Knecht zenen mir geven*, p. 35.
130 Tsanin, *Grenetsn biz tsum himl*, p. 41.
131 *Kleck*, p. 317.
132 *Kostopol*, p. 181.
133 Zak, *Knecht zenen mir geven*, pp. 36–9. The author, like other people who lived in the territories at the time, relates numerous anecdotes on the strange behaviour, and naivety of the Soviet men in regard to Western products.
134 *Yad Vashem*, file N-40-1447; file N-13-705; file K-33-410.
135 *Forverts*, 21 February 1941. In the article, 'Life of the Jews in the Countries Occupied by Stalin', the European correspondent reported that while the official exchange rate was 1 dollar to 5 roubles, in the Black market it was 1:360.

136 Zak, *Knecht zenen mir geven*, p. 91.

137 FO 371-24471 (C2946-116-55). Mr Russel, Third Secretary of the British Embassy in Moscow, visited the Soviet-occupied territories in January and February 1940, for the purpose of supervising the evacuation of British subjects from Soviet Poland. The quotation is from his memorandum presented at the end of his tour.

138 *Forverts*, 25 May 1940; *The Bialystoker Shtern* on 6 April 1941 reported from the court on a 35-year-old Jew from Semiatycze who was apprehended with 25 pairs of galoshes, 10 kilos of sugar, 6 pairs of socks and 590 roubles in cash. The defendant claimed that he had bought the goods for the shtetl people. It turned out that the galoshes were stolen from a factory with the connivance of the manager and some of the personnel. All were Jews. They were sentenced to between one and seven years in prison!

139 B. Weinryb, 'Antisemitism in Soviet Russia', L. Kochan (ed.), *The Jews in Soviet Russia Since 1917*, Oxford, 1970, pp. 34–5; S. M. Schwartz, *The Jews in the Soviet Union*, Syracuse, NY, 1951, p. 22. Both provide an unbalanced picture of the economic situation of the Jews in the Soviet-occupied territories, mainly because they use information made available during the period of Soviet rule.

140 *Bialystoker Shtern*, 30 March 1941. In its 13 April 1941 issue the paper described the difficulties encountered by Sokolka Jews who tried to form a kolkhoz of their own, in spite of the fact that they were ready to work on *Shabat*. Yet another failure of productivization.

6 EMERGENCE OF A NEW CULTURE

1 *Sefer izkor likhilat Sarny*, Tel Aviv, 1966, p. 268; *Sefer Kostopol: Sefer zikaron likhilatenu shealah aleha hakoret*, Tel Aviv, 1959, p. 179; *Shoat Yihudei Polin*, Jerusalem, 1940, p. 41; *Sefer Stryj*, Tel Aviv, 1962, p. 163.

2 *Sarny*, p. 268; *Kostopol*, p. 179; *Forverts* 3 February 1941 reports in detail the fines on rabbis in the Soviet-occupied territories. The advice to publish announcements on the cessation of religious services by the rabbis was received from the Soviet area proper. See also *Jewish Chronicle*, 9 May 1941.

3 *Sefer Mir; Entsiklopedia shel galuiot*, Jerusalem, 1962, p. 585.

4 *Sefer zikaron likdoshei Lanowce shenispu bashoah hanatsit*, Tel Aviv, 1970, p. 113; *Sefer izkor likhilat Luboml*, Tel Aviv, 1973, p. 243; *Tysmienica: A matseve oif di khurvot fun a Farnichteter Yiddisher Khilah*, Tel Aviv, 1974, p. 219; *Forverts*, 3 January, 1941, reported the intense anti-religious propaganda, mainly against ritual slaughtering.

5 *Wolozyhn Sefer shel hair vshel yishivat ets khayim*, Tel Aviv, 1970, p. 530; *Mir*, p. 585. The entire yeshiva of Mir was smuggled through to Vilno after several months of Soviet rule. See *Sefer Iwnic-Kamihn vhasviva*, Tel Aviv, 1973, p. 314.

6 *Sefer Dereczyn*, Tel Aviv, n.d., p. 385; *Wolozyn*, p. 532.

7 Title of article in *Bialystoker Shtern*, 13 April 1941.

8 *Bialystoker Shtern*, 6 April 1941.

9 Ibid, 6 October 1940; see also 16 February, 30 March 1940; *Oktiaber*, 21

August 1940, 11 May 1941.

10 *Bialystoker Shtern*, 27 October 1940.

11 *Oktiaber*, 10 March 1941.

12 *Bialystoker Shtern*, 23 March 1941.

13 *Sefer edut zikaron likhilat Pinsk-Karlin*, Tel Aviv, 1966, p. 320. The workers were forced on that occasion to sign a petition to convert several synagogues into workers' clubs.

14 *Pinkas Ostrog*, Tel Aviv, 1960, p. 105; *Sarny*, p. 267; *Pinsk*, p. 291.

15 *Yad Vashem Testimonial*, Jerusalem, file K-295-3460 (Smorgon).

16 'The Rabbi's Influence is on the Decline', *Oktiaber*, 21 August 1940.

17 *Sefer Dambrowica*, Tel Aviv, 1964, p. 690. See also on *Pesakh*, M. Grosman, *In Farkishuftn Land fun Legendern Dzugashvili*, Paris, 1950, pp. 75–6.

18 *Pinsk*, p. 128. Indicative of the attitude of the authorities is the fact that on the eve of *Pesakh*, 'All stores stocked white *khallot*. They were an extremely rare commodity during the winter, and now you could buy any quantity, you did not even have to stand in line. They were even cheap. Our Christian neighbour remarked wryly: it is the first time we benefit from your *Pesakh*', Grosman, *In Farkishuftn Land*, p. 75.

19 *Bialystoker Shtern*, 6 October 1940.

20 On the role of the synagogue in shtetl life, see M. Zborowski and E. Herzog, *Life is with People: The culture of the Shtetl*, New York, 1962, part 1, ch. 2.

21 *Sefer zikaron Stolpce: Swerzana vhaaiarot hasmukhot*, Tel Aviv, 1964, p. 131.

22 *Sefer zikaron Dubno*, Tel Aviv, 1966, p. 236.

23 *Sefer zikaron likhilat Lipniszki*, Tel Aviv, 1968, p. 135.

24 *Sefer zikaron likhilat Iwie*, Tel Aviv, 1968, p. 295.

25 *Forverts*, 3 February 1941, has reports on the closing down of synagogues in many towns and shtetlach in western Ukraine.

26 *Sefer Nisvizh*, Tel Aviv, 1976, p. 122.

27 *Janow al yad Pinsk, sefer zikaron*, Jerusalem, 1969, p. 313.

28 *Lubcza Vdelticz sefer zikaron*, Haifa, 1971, p. 38.

29 *Nisvizh*, p. 122; *Yad Vashem*, file B-314-3467 (Zoludek). In Semiatycz a delegation of the local community succeeded in persuading the shtetl Soviet not to confiscate the central synagogue. Such behaviour was an exception. See *Khilat Semiatycz*, Tel Aviv, 1965, p. 377.

30 *Pinsk*, p. 291; Y. Bromberg, *Pinsk Under Soviet Rule*, unpublished, p. 3.

31 *Janow*, p. 312.

32 *Kostopol*, p. 178; *Sefer Mlynow-Merwic*, Haifa, 1970, p. 286; *Dambrowica*, p. 681; *Khilat Lanin Sefer zikaron*, Tel Aviv, 1957, p. 48; *Tysmienica*, p. 219.

33 *Pinkas Kolomyja*, New York, 1957, p. 270; *Rishonim lamered Lachwa*, Jerusalem, 1957, p. 37; *Yad Vashem*, file SH-191-2131 (Luck).

34 A. Zak, *Knecht zenen mir geven*, Buenos Aires, 1956, p. 32.

35 *Central Zionist Archive*, Jerusalem, file S5-642; *Shoat Yihudei Polin*, Jerusalem, 1940, p. 60; N. Vakar, *Byelorussia*, Cambridge, Mass., 1956, p. 60.

36 On the attitude to the Hebrew language in the USSR and the reasons behind it see Gitelman, *Jewish Nationality and Soviet Politics: The Jewish Sections of the CPSU 1917–1930*, Princeton, 1972, pp. 276–7.

37 *Pinsk*, p. 311; *Sefer zikaron likhilat Kolno*, Tel Aviv, 1971, p. 347.
38 H. Smolar, 'Hakhaim hayehudiim bmaarav Belorussia hasovietit 1939–1941: prikhah vshkiah', *Shvut*, 4, Tel Aviv, 1976, p. 133.
39 Ibid, p. 136.
40 Ibid, pp. 134–6.
41 E. Markish, *Lakhazor miderekh aruka*, Tel Aviv, 1977, p. 89. The episode is related also by Smolar, 'Hakhaim hayehudiim', p. 134. On Markish and the Jewish cultural elite in the territories, see pp. 138–9.
42 There are numerous records of the fate of this group in the Soviet-occupied area. See for example Zak, *Knecht zenen mir geven*, pp. 18–25; Grosman, *In Farkishuftn Land*, p. 19. Sh. Broderzon, *Main Laidns Veg Mit Moshe Broderzon*, Buenos Aires, 1960, pp. 19–29.
43 T. Fuks, *A Vanderung iber okupirte gebitn*, Buenos Aires, 1948, p. 71; Grosman, *In Farkishuftn Land*, pp. 40–1.
44 Grosman, *In Farkishuftn Land*, p. 58; Broderzon, *Main Laidns*, p. 30.
45 On the life and internal relations within the writers community in Lvov and A. Katsizna's central role in it, see A. Weiss, 'Teatron vsifrut yiddish begalitsia hamizrakhit bashanim, 1939–1941', *Bekhinot*, 8–9, Jerusalem, 1980, pp. 113–26. Also Katsizna's daughter's testimony in *Yad Vashem*, file K-2-174. On Bialystok's centre see among others the Grosman and Broderzon memoirs.
46 See Broderzon, *Main Laidns*, p. 25. The poet stopped writing since he could not find a way to express his feelings on the destruction of Polish Jewry. On the entire subject see pp. 133–9.
47 Fuks, *A Vanderung*, pp. 104–6. The founding journalists came from Kiev in the spring of 1941.
48 Smolar, *Hakhaim hayehudiim*, pp. 128–9. According to Smolar, he himself and Z. Akselrod, the poet from Minsk, Belorussia, were the main founders of the *Bialystoker Shtern*.
49 Ibid.
50 *Bialystoker Shtern*, 10 February 1940.
51 Weiss, '*Teatron vsifrut*', p. 125.
52 Zak, *Knecht zenen mir geven*, pp. 79–80; *Grodno-Entsiklopedia shel galuiot*, Jerusalem, 1973, p. 506.
53 Grosman, *In Farkishuftn Land*, pp. 56–7; *Yad Vashem*, file R-170-2808 (Bialystok). The witness who took part in the purge of the Bialystok central Jewish library relates that the inspectors who came from Minsk, the capital of Soviet Belorussia, brought a detailed list of books forbidden to be read.
54 Weiss, '*Teatron vsifrut*', pp. 125–6; *Yad Vashem*, file L-28-313 (Mlynow).
55 *Ofboi* No. 3, Riga, January 1941. The *Ofboi* was a Soviet monthly in Yiddish dedicated mainly to cultural affairs, published in Riga, Latvia, after its annexation by the USSR.
56 *Oktiaber*, 19 February 1940.
57 *Der Shtern*, 18 September 1939.
58 *Der Shtern*, 30 September 1939.
59 *Oktiaber*, 6 October 1939.
60 See *Oktiaber*, 10, 20, October; 3 November 1939.

61 *Der Shtern*, 7 May 1941.
62 Bromberg, *Pinsk Under Soviet Rule*, p. 3.
63 Fuks, *A Vanderung*, p. 105.
64 *Lanin*, p. 48.
65 *Dubno*, p. 651.
66 *Bransk: Sefer Hazikaron*, New York, 1948, p. 249.
67 Smolar, 'Hakhaim hayehudiim', p. 133.
68 Weiss, 'Teatron vsifrut', p. 114. Ida Kaminska organized and directed the theatre after fleeing Warsaw with her husband (Melman) another famous Jewish actor.
69 *Yad Vashem*, file K-326-3736 (Testimony of Ida Kaminska). According to Kaminska, actors from the disbanded Yiddish theater of Dniepropetrovsk, Soviet Ukraine, joined her theatre in spring 1940, forcing the dismissal of some of the performers. According to *Oktiaber*, 17 January 1940, the Yiddish theatre of Baku was to be transferred to Brest-Litovsk and together with the participation of local actors would form the local city theatre.
70 Broderzon, *Main Laidns*, p. 24.
71 Weiss, 'Teatron vsifrut', p. 117; Zak, *Knecht zenen mir geven*, p. 71; *Oktiaber*, 15 January 1941; *Yad Vashem*, file R-170-2808 (Pinsk).
72 *Oktiaber*, 6 March 1941; *Bialystoker Shtern*, 23 March 1941.
73 Fuks, *A Vanderung*, p. 61.
74 Smolar, 'Hakhaim hayehudiim', p. 133. 'The House of People's Art' served as a centre for many Yiddish amateur performers in Bialystok.
75 *Oktiaber*, 15 March 1940, 15 January 1941; reports on the 'Olympic Artistic Competitions' in the western provinces, with the participation of Yiddish, Belorussian, Polish, Russian and Ukrainian performers.
76 In an article in *Der Shtern*, 1 March 1940.
77 Lederman, *Fun iener zait forhang*, Buenos Aires, 1960, pp. 101, 117. Lederman, like others who came from 'free enterprise' theatres, was amazed at the great differences in salary of the performers. Also *Yad Vashem*, file K-326-3736.
78 Eleven of the 17 plays of the Lvov theatre were pre-war works and could be found on any Yiddish language stage in the West. See Weiss, 'Teatron vsifrut', p. 116; also *Bialystoker Shtern*, 1 January 1940, where are enumerated the 175 performances of the Bialystok theatre.
79 On the extensive tours of the Jewish theatres, see Zak, *Knecht zenen mir geven*, p. 144; Broderzon, *Main Laidns*, p. 24. The Yiddish press covered the tours, interviewing the directors and performers. See *Der Shtern*, 20 May 1940; *Oktiaber*, 3 August 1940.
80 *Oktiaber*, 23 May 1941.
81 *Der Shtern*, 22 October; 18 November 1939; *Oktiaber*, 12, 20 January; 3, 8 February; 11, 15 August, 1940; 31 May 1941.

7 EDUCATING THE NEW SOVIET CITIZEN

1 On the goals of Soviet education see G. Bereday and J. Pennar (eds), *The*

Politics of Soviet Education, New York, 1960, pp. 3–27.

2 On eastern Galicia see A. Weiss, 'Tmurot bakhinukh shel yehudei galitsiah hamizrakhit bitkufat hashilton hasovieti, 1939–1941', *Galed*, 4–5, Tel Aviv, 1978, pp. 428–9. On Poland in general see Ts. Sharfshtein, *Toldot hakhinukh beisrael badorot haakharonim*, New York, 1949.

3 There was a wide variety of Jewish, mostly public, schools of every religious, national, and social section of the Jewish community. See Sharfshtein, *Toldot hakhinukh*, pp. 129–91.

4 *Shoat Yihudei Polin*, Jerusalem, 1940, p. 41; *Pinkas Kleck*, Tel Aviv, 1959, p. 86.

5 *Sefer edut vzikaron likhilat Pinsk-Karlin*, Tel Aviv, 1966, p. 133; *Kleck*, p. 86; *Pinkas Ludmir* (Wladzimierz), Tel Aviv, 1962, pp. 337–42.

6 In Ludmir instruction in Hebrew lasted until 15 November 1939 with explicit agreement of the local Soviet officials. The principal resigned when ordered to change to Yiddish. See *Ludmir*, pp. 339–41.

7 T. Fuks, *A Vanderung iber okupirte gebitn*, Buenos Aires, 1948, p. 81 (Polish high school in Lvov); *Oktiaber* 19 March 1940 (Pinsk); *Tarnopol: Entsiklopedia shel Galuiot*, Jerusalem, 1965, p. 185.

8 *Tarnopol*, p. 381.

9 H. Smolar, 'Hakhaim hayehudiim bmaarav Belorussia hasovietit 1939–1941: prikhah vshkiah', *Shvut*, 4, Tel Aviv, 1976, p. 132.

10 A. Zak, *Knecht zenen mir geven*, Buenos Aires, 1956, pp. 80–8; *Grodno-Entsiklopedia shel galuiot*, Jerusalem, 1973, p. 506.

11 *Oktiaber*, 27 January 1940. For a similar attitude see in *Oktiaber*, 9 February 1940, on Volkovisk.

12 *Oktiaber*, 14 February, 5 May, 13 December 1940.

13 E. Schulman, *A History of Jewish Education in the Soviet Union*, New York, 1973, ch. 10.

14 *Tarnopol*, pp. 382–3.

15 Zak, *Knecht zenen mir geven*, p. 83.

16 *Sefer zikaron Dubno*, Tel Aviv, 1966, p. 650.

17 *Yad Vashem Testimonial*, Jerusalem, file K-256-3112 (Nowogrodek).

18 *Forverts*, 25 April 1940.

19 M. Smoler, *Neevakti al Khaiai*, Tel Aviv, 1978, p. 41.

20 Fuks, *A Vanderung*, pp. 92–3; *Yad Vashem*, file T-30-1640 (Lvov).

21 *Yad Vashem*, file SH-191-2131 (Luck); *Sefer Dambrowica*, Tel Aviv, 1964 p. 681; *Sefer zikaron likhiat Iwie*, Tel Aviv, 1968, p. 384; *Khurban Glebokie, Szarkowszczyzna*, Buenos Aires, 1956, pp. 295–6.

22 *Oktiaber*, 27 January 1940; *Lubcza vdelticz sefer zikaron*, Haifa, 1971, p. 26.

23 *Lubcza*, pp. 33–4.

24 *Kleck*, p. 87.

25 Arguments put forward by parents in discussion of the language of instruction: *Iwie*, p. 384; *Kleck*, p. 87.

26 *Pinsk*, p. 133; *Dubno*, pp. 649–50; *Kleck*, p. 87; *Iwie*, p. 383.

27 *Kleck*, p. 87; *Iwie*, p. 384; *Oktiaber*, 9 February 1941.

28 *Oktiaber*, 3, 23 January 1940.

29 *Oktiaber*, 11 February 1941, 'On Communist Education in the Jewish School System'. See also *Oktiaber*, 23 July 1940; *Yad Vashem*, file Z-11-3599.
30 Schulman, *A History of Jewish Education*, p. 106.
31 *Chrestomatie far dem zekstn klass*, Kiev, 1938.
32 *Iwie*, p. 352; *Pinsk*, p. 133; *Rokitno vhasviva sefer edut vzikaron*, Tel Aviv, 1967, p. 107.
33 *Pinsk*, p. 128.
34 *Oktiaber*, 3 April, 30 May, 18 June 1940; *Der Shtern*, 14 February 1940.
35 Smolar, 'Hakhaim hayehudiim', p. 133; Weiss, 'Tmurot bakhinukh', pp. 438–9.
36 *Oktiaber*, 22, 28 July 1940, 13 May 1941; *Der Shtern*, 7 May 1941.
37 *Der Shtern*, 5 October 1940.
38 Towards the end of the school year 1940–41 the Yiddish papers again carried reports on shortages of school books and on plans for the future: *Der Shtern*, 14 May, 14 June 1941; *Oktiaber*, 29 May 1941.
39 *Oktiaber*, 4 May 1941.
40 *Iwie*, p. 384.
41 Weiss, 'Tmurot bakhinukh', p. 437; *Kleck*, p. 92; *Yad Vashem*, file SH-191-2131 (Luck).
42 *Oktiaber*, 3 November 1939 reports on courses for teachers in western Belorussia. A three-month course in Russian and Belorussian and a six-month course for teachers for grades five to seven.
43 *Iwie*, p. 381.
44 *Oktiaber*, 1 February, 5 July 1940; *Der Shtern*, 14 January 1940; *Bialystoker Shtern*, 21 January 1941.
45 *Baranowicz*, p. 211; *Pinsk*, p. 128; Fuks, *A Vanderung*, p. 91 (Lvov); *Stolin*, Tel Aviv, 1952, p. 110; *Kleck*, p. 92.
46 G. Bereday and J. Pennar (eds.), *The Politics of Soviet Education*, New York, 1960, pp. 132–143.
47 *Sefer Kostopol: Khaieha umota shel khila*, Tel Aviv, 1967, p. 179.
48 Weiss, 'Tmurot bakhinukh', p. 436.
49 *Dambrowica*, p. 382; Fuks, *A Vanderung*, pp. 90–1; *Oktiaber*, 7 October 1939; 6 March 1941.
50 *Iwie*, p. 381; Fuks, *A Vanderung*, pp. 59–65; *Oktiaber*, 7 October 1939; *Der Shtern*, 1 March, 11 June 1940.
51 *Kostopol*, p. 185.
52 See Heller, *On the Edge of Destruction: Jews in Poland Between the Two World Wars*, New York, 1977, p. 244.
53 *Sefer Lida*, Tel Aviv, 1970, p. 257.
54 *Sefer Busk, lzecher hakhila shekharva*, Haifa, 1968, p. 265; *Rishonim lamared Lachwa*, Jerusalem, 1957, p. 36; *Lubcza*, p. 39; *Pinkas Kolomyja*, New York, 1957, p. 270.
55 *Yad Vashem*, file K-247-2963 (Berezno); see also *Yad Vashem*, file A-7-119 (Szcuczyn); *Telechany*, Los Angeles, 1963, p. 93.
56 *Kolomyja*, p. 270; *Telechany*, p. 119; *Kleck*, p. 325; *Bialystoker Shtern*, 20 April 1941.
57 *Sefer zikaron likdoshei Szumsk*, Tel Aviv, 1968, p. 118.

58 Smoler, *Neevakti al Khaiai*, pp. 47–8. The author complains about close friends who refused to acknowledge even formal acquaintance with him after the occupation.
59 *Grodno*, p. 511.
60 *Nieswizs*, pp. 123–6; *Korzec: Sefer zikaron likhilatenu shealah aleha hakoret*, Tel Aviv, 1959, p. 333.
61 *Kleck*, p. 324; See also *Nieswizs*, p. 126; *Lubcza*, p. 39.

8 THE SHTETL CHANGES ITS FACE

1 A. Zak, *Knecht zenen mir geven*, Buenos Aires, 1956, p. 315; *Der Shtern*, 22 February 1940. In an article 'When the New is Born', the paper's correspondent described the changes that occurred in Dubno, for example in the names of the streets and their outward appearance.
2 Grosman, *In Farkishufin Land fun Legendern Dzugashvili*, Paris, 1950, p. 19.
3 *Oktiaber* 30 November 1939; 4 January, 16 August 1940; 21, 22 June 1941; *Der Shtern*, 10 September 1940.
4 *Oktiaber*, 12 March 1940; 10, 24 May 1941; *Der Shtern*, 14 May 1940; *Bialystoker Shtern*, 27 October 1940; 1 January 1941.
5 *Sefer Dambrowica*, Tel Aviv, 1964, p. 680; *Sefer edut vzikaron likhilat Pinsk-Karlin*, Tel Aviv, 1966, p. 291; *Sefer zikaron likhilat Kolno*, Tel Aviv, 1971, p. 344; *Sefer Mir: Entsiklopedia shel galuiot*, Jerusalem, 1962, p. 586; *Pinkas mekhamesh khilat kharevot Pruzana*, Buenos Aires, 1958, p. 460.
6 *Bialystoker Shtern*, 1 January 1941.
7 *Kolno*, p. 344.
8 Bromberg, *Pinsk Under Soviet Rule*, unpublished, p. 1; *Mir*, p. 587; *Pruzana*, p. 460; *Oktiaber*, 10 May 1941; *Bialystoker Shtern*, 27 October 1940.
9 *Pinkas Kleck*, Tel Aviv, 1959, p. 321.
10 Y. Bromberg, *Pinsk Under Soviet Rule*, p. 3.
11 *Sefer izkor lehantsakhat kdoshei khilat Czortkow*, Tel Aviv, 1961, p. 224.
12 Ibid.
13 *Dambrowica*, pp. 688–90.
14 *Sefer izkor likhilat Luboml*, Tel Aviv, 1973, p. 237; *Sefer Nisvizh*, Tel Aviv, 1976, p. 364.
15 *Mir*, p. 588; *Pruzana*, p. 461.
16 *Wolozyn, Sefer shel hair vshel yishivat ets khaiim*, Tel Aviv, 1970, p. 530; *Sefer Kostopol: Khaieha umota shel khila*, Tel Aviv, 1967, p. 184.
17 *Yad Vashem Testimonial* file SH-258-2987 (Krasno).
18 P. Shwarts, *Dos iz geven der onheib*, New York, 1943, p. 288.
19 *Pinkas Krynki*, Tel Aviv, 1970, p. 229; *Entsiklopedia shel galuiot Tarnopol*, Jerusalem, 1965, p. 380.
20 Shwarts, *Dos iz geven*, p. 285.
21 *Tarnopol*, p. 380; *Bransk: Sefer Hazikaron*, New York, 1948, p. 247.
22 *Czortkow*, p. 224.
23 Isroel Emiat, 'Andere Tsaitn' (Different Times), *Oktiaber*, 6 February 1940.

24 *Bialystoker Shtern*, 30 March 1941.

25 *Kostopol*, p. 181.

26 *Nieswizs*, p. 121; 'Shmuel Josef a poor artisan, a militia man now, decided to pay a visit to the former employer of his sisters, a rich store owner. He knocked on the door. From inside one could hear the frightened voice of the store owner: who is it? Shmuel Josef! Which Shmuel Josef? Shmuel Josef the government! was the short confident answer.' This short episode demonstrates the changed social relations in the shtetl under the Soviet regime.

27 *Bialystoker Shtern*, 30 March 1940, from an article in a series on the annexed territories, 'Banaite Shtet Un Shtetlach' (Renewed towns and Shtetlach).

28 *Oktiaber*, 30 July 1940; *Bialystoker Shtern*, 6 April, 5th May 1941.

29 *Sefer Borszczow*, Tel Aviv, 1960, p. 173.

30 *Sefer Zulkiew*, Jerusalem, 1969, p. 551.

31 *Sefer zikaron likhilat Lomza*, Tel Aviv, 1952, p. 287.

32 *Sefer Jezierna*, Haifa, 1974, p. 186. Also *Sefer Targowica*, Haifa, 1967, p. 274; *Yad Vashem*, file K-247-2963 (Berezno); file L-2-107 (Baranowicz).

33 *Oktiaber*, 23 January 1940.

34 *Oktiaber*, 14 October 1939; 3, 23 January, 5 July 1940.

35 *Bialystoker Shtern*, 6 April 1940. 'Why do you hide your identity?' asked the peasant when he discovered that I was a Jew. 'It is easier to be a Jew than a Christian under Soviet rule', the peasant maintained angrily. The Jews had caught the government was his unreserved opinion; M. Tsanin, *Grenetsn biz tsum himl*, Tel Aviv, 1970, p. 50.

36 *The Sikorski Historical Institute*, London, files A9III2a30b, A9III2a18.

37 *Targowica*, p. 274.

38 *Yad Vashem*, file L-2-107 (Baranowicz); *Borszczow*, p. 173; *Zulkiew*, p. 551.

39 *Kleck*, p. 84.

40 *Shoat Yihudei Polin*, Jerusalem, 1940, p. 25; *Sefer zikaron Stolpce-Swerzana vhaaiarot hasmukhot*, Tel Aviv, 1964, p. 132; *Yad Vashem*, file 1-36-1299 (Nowogrodek); *Sefer izkor likhilat Sarny*, Tel Aviv, 1966, p. 79; *Kostopol*, p. 181.

41 See reports on suppression of anti-Semitic gangs in eastern Galicia in the *Jewish Chronicle*, 29 December 1939; 1 March, 14 June 1940. Also report by Arnold J. Toynbee from the 11 February 1940 entitled *Notes on Jews in Poland* in FO 371-24471 (new designation C-2393-N6-55).

42 *Stolpce*, p. 132. The same sentiment is reported in *Sefer zikaron Dubno*, Tel Aviv, 1966, p. 238; *Sarny*, p. 79.

43 *Sikorski*, A9III2A-30, report from June 1940.

44 *Sikorski* A-9III2a-19.

45 *Mir*, p. 583.

46 *Pinsk*, p. 317.

47 From conversations of Ukrainian peasants, *Dambrowica*, p. 690.

48 Even educated Ukrainians expressed strong primitive anti-Semitic ideas about the 'Jewish world power'. A Ukrainian student in Lvov University found it difficult to believe that there were only 16 million Jews in the world. 'There are 40 million Ukrainians in the world and nobody knows about them, and 16

million Jews and the entire world does not cease talking about them', he remarked, *Yad Vashem*, file K-247-2963 (Lvov).

49 *Kostopol*, pp. 181–4; *Jezierna*, p. 185.

50 'Your redeemers are bound to leave and ours are not far away', warned the Poles of Semiatycz, *khilat Semiatycz*, Tel Aviv, 1965, p. 202. Also *Dambrowica*, pp. 683–4.

51 *Sefer zikaron likhilat Iwie*, Tel Aviv, 1968, pp. 184, 383; *Sefer zikaron likhilat Lipniszki*, Tel Aviv, 1968, p. 138; *Korzec: Sefer zikaron likhilatenu shealah aleha hakoret*, Tel Aviv, 1959, p. 336; *Bialystoker Shtern*, 12 January 1941.

52 *Yad Vashem*, file K-295-3460 (Smorgon).

53 *Kleck*, p. 324.

54 *Sefer zikaron likdoshei Lanowce shenispy bashoat hanatsit*, Tel Aviv, 1970, p. 109.

55 *Lubcza*, p. 39.

56 *Sefer Dereczyn*, Tel Aviv, n.d., pp. 384–5.

57 On 9 March 1940 a detailed report appeared in the *Forverts* (New York) about Lvov under Soviet rule:

> It is impossible to recognize the town, even though there is gas and electricity, and the streets are lighted and the trams operate. The shops are closed, the hotels occupied by Soviet officers and Bolshevik commissars. Lvov's famous cafés were converted into soldiers' clubs. The smaller cafés are open, but have nothing to offer. The streets are filled with thousands of barefoot refugees who wander aimlessly, etc.

About two months later, on 14 May 1940, quite a different description appeared in *Der Shtern*, Kiev, by the famous Soviet Yiddish writer, I. Fefer. The article is one long ode to Soviet Lvov. The town is blooming and its inhabitants full of joy.

> The city is all in red, the colour of the revolution. Everywhere one can sense the great love of the new Lvov, Soviet Lvov. It is vital, bustling, full of activity. Even its original residents do not recognize their town. They have never seen such active life in the city. Songs in all languages, including Yiddish, are heard all over.

There is no doubt that the impression one gets from each reports is quite different.

58 *Yad Vashem*, file L-2-107; also *Luboml*, p. 248; *Lanowce*, p. 108.

59 Zak, *Knecht zenen mir geven*, pp. 108–9.

60 Ibid, p. 144; also *Rishonim lamered Lachwa*, Jerusalem, 1957, p. 37.

61 Zerubavel, *Na vanad*, Buenos Aires, 1947, pp. 88–97; *Forverts*, 30 April 1940.

62 *Yad Vashem*, file L-2-107 (Baranowicz).

63 Zak, *Knecht zenen mir geven*, p. 76.

64 *Pinsk*, p. 318.

9 REFUGEES

* First published as an article in *Jewish Social Studies* vol. 40, 1978.

1 G. Stoessinger, *The Refugee and the World Community*, Minneapolis, 1956, pp. 35–41.
2 Ibid, p. 38.
3 See H. Feingold, *The Politics of Rescue*, New Brunswick, 1970.
4 J. Vernant, *The Refugee in the Post War World*, Geneva 1951, p. 60.
5 A. Tartakower and K. R. Grosman, *The Jewish Refugee*, New York, 1944, p. 343.
6 The following devote more space to the subject: Y. Litvak, 'Hashilton hasovieti vehatshalat yehudim polanim umaaraviim', *Bekhinot*, 2–3, Tel Aviv, 1972, pp. 47–80; S. M. Schwartz, *Evrei v Sovetskom Soiuze s nachala vtoroi mirovoi voiny*, New York, 1966; and B. D. Weinryb, 'Polish Jews under Soviet Rule', P. Meyer. (ed.) *The Jews in the Soviet Satellites*, Syracuse, NY 1953.
7 L. B. Schapiro, *The Government and Politics of the Soviet Union*, New York, 1967, p. 92.
8 N. Bentwich, *Wanderer Between Two Worlds*, London, 1941, p. 268.
9 Feingold, *The Politics of Rescue*, p. 27. The Soviet Union joined the intergovernmental Committee for Refugees only in 1943. See Vernant, *The Refugee in the Post War World.*
10 M. Prager, *Yiven metsulah hekhadash*, Tel Aviv, 1941, pp. 28–9.
11 Z. Segalowicz, *Gebrente trit*, Buenos Aires, 1947, pp. 40–57.
12 *Shoat Yihudei Polin*, Jerusalem, 1940.
13 N. Vakar, *Byelorussia*, Cambridge, 1956, pp. 157–8.
14 S. Broderzon, *Main Laidns Veg Mit Moshe Broderzon*, Buenos Aires, 1960, p. 17; *Sefer Radzin*, Tel Aviv, 1957, pp. 218–19. These are detailed descriptions of the friendly attitudes shown by Soviet soldiers on the border.
15 *Sefer Sokal-Tartakow vhasvivah*, Tel Aviv, 1967, pp. 278–9.
16 *Sefer kehilat Ostroleka*, Tel Aviv, 1963, p. 358.
17 *Shoat Yihudei Polin*, p. 63.
18 See D. Grodner, 'In Soviet Poland and Lithuania', *Contemporary Jewish Record*, vol. 4, April 1941, pp. 137–8; D. Lederman, *Fun iener zait forhang*, Buenos Aires, 1960, pp. 68–74; *Sokal*, pp. 278–9; all carried numerous reports on the sufferings of those who tried to cross the Soviet border at the time.
19 *Izvestia*, 20 November 1939.
20 Prager, *Yiven metsulah*, pp. 35–6.
21 The protest note was handed to Count von Schulenburg, the German ambassador to Moscow. See. G. Reitlinger, *The Final Solution*, London, 1953, p. 49.
22 R. J. Sontag and J. S. Beddie, (eds) *Nazi–Soviet Relations, 1939–1941: Documents from the Archives of the German Foreign Office*, Washington D.C., 1948, p. 128.
23 See *Yad Vashem Testimonial*, file K-116-1324; A. Pinsker, *Ud Mutsal*, Tel Aviv, 1957, pp. 18–20; and Prager, *Yiven metsulah*, p. 32.
24 *Jewish Telegraphic Agency News*, 6, no. 122.
25 A. Peteshnik, *Yidn un Yidishkeit in Sovet-Rusland*, New York, 1943, pp. 59–60.
26 *Jewish Affairs*, New York, August 1941.
27 Weinryb, 'Polish Jews', p. 342.
28 See Schwartz, *Evrei v Sovetskom Soiuze*, p. 33. Litvak, 'Hashilton', p. 56, estimates the number of refugees to have been between 300,000 and 400,000.

29 *Sokal*, p. 278.
30 *Sefer Dereczyn*, Tel Aviv, n.d., p. 248.
31 *Janow al Yad Pinsk, sefer zikaron*, Jerusalem, 1969, p. 264.
32 *Yad Vashem*, file SH-191-2131.
33 In Lubcza, according to a census taken in September 1940, there were 35 Jewish refugees in the different professions; see *Lubcza vdelticz sefer zikaron*, Haifa, 1971, pp. 33–5. Similar data come from such places as Kletsk; see *Ostroleka*, pp. 358–9; and Dubno, see *Sefer zikaron Dubno*, Tel Aviv, 1966, pp. 648–52 and Prager, *Yeven metsulah*, pp. 33–5.
34 The *Oktiaber* of 4 January 1940 reported that the population of Bialystok had increased from 105,000 to 200,000 since its annexation. Lvov, too, had almost doubled its Jewish population. See *Shoat Yihudei Polin*, p. 43.
35 On the acute housing problem, see T. Fuks, *A Vanderung iber okupirte gebitn*, Buenos Aires, 1948, p. 49; F. Zerubavel, *Na vanad*, Buenos Aires, 1947, p. 65 and Lederman, *Fun iener zait*, pp. 74–99. These three represent a small sample of memoirs published by Jewish journalists, authors and artists who fled to the Soviet part of Poland. They describe in detail the fate of the Jewish refugees between 1939 and 1941, and served, with others, as an important source for this survey.
36 Grodner, 'In Soviet Poland', p. 138.
37 Ibid.
38 *Shoat Yihudei Polin*, p. 43.
39 Ibid.
40 Ibid., p. 63.
41 See Broderzon, *Main Laidns*, pp. 18–20, and also M. Grosman, *In Farkishufin Land fun Legendern Dzugashvili*, Paris, 1950, vol. 1.
42 Grosman, *In Farkishufin Land*, vol. 1 p. 27.
43 Ibid., pp. 35–6. The author recalls the refusal of the *Bialystoker Shtern* to publish anything about the fate of the Jews in Nazi Poland. See also Broderzon, *Main Laidns*, p. 31.
44 Thirty-four of the 170 members of the Writers' Union were Jews. See *Bialystoker Shtern*, 6 February 1940.
45 *Ofboi*, 3, January 1941, 98.
46 Ibid.
47 *Ofboi*, 9 May 1941, 12–13.
48 *Bialystoker Shtern*, 2 February 1940.
49 See Appendix.
50 *Vilner Emes*, 12 November 1940.
51 Ibid.
52 *Vilner Emes*, 8 December 1940, carried Moshe Broderzon's article 'On Our Trip Through the Soviet Union'. After describing the 'enthusiastic' receptions, the author admits that 'the press drew to our attention that we have to adopt a Soviet repertoire.' The author promises to do so. But several months later *Der Shtern*, on 15 February 1941, reported that the theatre collective had promised to prepare two performances which would 'reflect its absorption in their country; and adapt it to Soviet reality'.

53 Grodner, 'In Soviet Poland', p. 140.
54 Weinryb, 'Polish Jews', p. 344, maintains that 'in the last month of 1939 registration for work in Russia commenced.' Yet a report from a Mr Helman, the *Hekhaluts* representative in eastern Galicia, describes registration for work occurring as early as the end of September. See *Shoat Yihudei Polin*, pp. 24–5.
55 Ibid., p. 63.
56 A witness from Radzin recalls his departure from Brisk in *Radzin*, p. 219.
57 Grosman, *In Farkishuftn Land*, p. 30.
58 Grodner, 'In Soviet Poland', p. 140.
59 The *Oktiaber* of 20 January reported that seven trains carrying over 11,000 people left Bialystok recently for work in Soviet enterprises. The *Bialystoker Shtern* of 2 February 1940 in a polemical exchange with the *Forverts*, maintained that 30,000 refugees left for the interior in the last month.
60 The *Bialystoker Shtern* carried an article on 13 February 1940 reporting the arrival of a representative from Magnitogorsk to register 1,500 refugees for work in its building industry.
61 A representative article, entitled 'The Found Homeland', containing letters of refugee registrants from the Urals, appeared in the 28 January 1940 *Bialystoker Shtern*.
62 Lederman, *Fun iener zait*, pp. 119–20.
63 *Yad Vashem* file SH-71-262; Lederman, *Fun iener zait*, pp. 126–7.
64 Grosman, *In Farkishuftn Land*, p. 84.
65 *Documents on Polish–Soviet Relations, 1939–1945*, London, 1961, I, 92.
66 Ibid., p. 541. Article 3 of the Soviet Citizenship and Naturalization Laws of 19 August 1938 stated that: 'Aliens of any nationality or race could become Soviet citizens by their own request and the decision of the Presidium of the Supreme Soviet of the USSR or the Presidium of the Supreme Soviet of the Republic where they reside.'
67 *Yad Vashem*, file A-74-1203; file G-13-705 and file SH-71-762.
68 Grosman, *In Farkishuftn Land*, p. 84.
69 Lederman, *Fun iener zait*, pp. 126–30; Grosman, *In Farkishuftn Land*, pp. 94–6; *Dubno*, p. 654; and *Izkor bukh fun Pulawy*, New York, 1964, p. 345. This is just a small selection of testimonials coming from different parts of eastern Poland. Basically they all repeat the same story.
70 At Pinsk attempts were made to persuade the refugees to register to return, see *Sefer edut vzikaron likhilat Pinsk-Karlin*, Tel Aviv, 1966, p. 313.
71 Weinryb, 'Polish Jews', p. 346. Grodner, 'In Soviet Poland', p. 141, served as Weinryb's source for these assertions.
72 Schwartz, *Evrei v Sovetskom Soiuze*, pp. 36–7.
73 Litvak, 'Hashilton', pp. 64–5.
74 Lederman, *Fun iener zait*, pp. 121–6. *Shoat Yihudei Polin*, p. 38, contains a report of Jews from eastern Galicia crossing the border to the Nazi area.
75 See, *Sefer Strizov vehasvivah*, Tel Aviv, 1969, p. 330; *Khurban Glebokie Szarkowszczyzna*, Buenos Aires, 1956, p. 38 and Lederman, *Fun iener zait*, p. 130.
76 N. Khrushchev, *Khrushchev Remembers*, Boston, 1970, p. 141.
77 Grosman, *In Farkishuftn Land*, p. 93.

78 Lederman, *Fun iener zait*, pp. 130–31.
79 Fuks, *A Vanderung*, pp. 79–80.
80 *Khrushchev Remembers*, p. 141.
81 Grosman, *In Farkishuftn Land*, p. 94. Fuks, who personally witnessed the registration in Lvov, relates in *A Vanderung*, on p. 80, that the Soviet officials questioned 'is our regime that distasteful to the Jews that they want to return to Hitler? If that is the case then certainly they should be regarded as hostile elements, and we had better get rid of them.'
82 Grosman, *In Farkishuftn Land*, p. 94. The author heard the story from the actor Schumacher's wife, who was among the refugees coming from the Nazi side.
83 Schwartz, *Evrei v Sovetskom Soiuze*, p. 35.
84 *Janow*, p. 313.
85 *Yad Vashem*, file B-56-756.
86 *Janow*, p. 369.
87 *Yad Vashem*, file SH-71-762.
88 Grosman, *In Farkishuftn Land*, p. 76.
89 Fuks, *A Vanderung*, p. 50.
90 Grosman, *In Farkishuftn Land*, p. 50.
91 Lederman, *Fun iener zait*, pp. 135–42; Grosman, *In Farkishuftn Land*, pp. 99–101.
92 For the text of Serov's detailed instructions on 'the procedure for carrying out the deportation of anti-Soviet elements', see B. J. Kaslas (ed.), *The USSR-German Aggression Against Lithuania*, New York, 1973, pp. 327–34.
93 *Pinsk*, p. 320. (See note 70.)
94 *Sefer Lida*, Tel Aviv, 1970, p. 278.

10 WHY DID THEY STAY?

1 B. Pinchuk, 'Soviet Media on the Fate of Jews in Nazi Occupied Territory (1939–1941)', *Yad Vashem Studies*, vol. 11, Jerusalem, 1976.
2 Y. Gilboa, *The Black Years of Soviet Jewry*, Boston, Mass., 1971, pp. 18–19.
3 S. Broderzon, *Main Laidns Veg Mit Moshe Broderzon*, Buenos Aires, 1960, p. 31.
4 M. Grosman, *In Farkishuftn Land fun Legendern Dzugashvili*, Paris, 1950, pp. 35–6.
5 Gilboa, *The Black Years*, pp. 27–8.
6 Quoted from a German Intelligence report, 4 August 1941, in R. Hilberg, *The Destruction of the European Jews*, Chicago, 1967, p. 207.
7 F. Soloman-Luts, *Naara mul gardom*, Ramat Gan, 1971, p. 55.
8 Ibid.
9 *Sefer Zulkiew*, Jerusalem, 1969, p. 552; *Yad Vashem Testimonial*, file M-165-2876 (Mielnica-Podolska); file T-30-1640 (Lvov).
10 *Korzec: Sefer zikaron likhilatenu shealah aleha hakoret*, Tel Aviv, 1959, p. 337; also *Yad Vashem*, file T-36-2022 (Bogdanowka); file Z-36-1123 (A refugee from the German occupied territory); file B-21-39 (Sarny).

11 *Yad Vashem*, file Z-36-1123.
12 *Wolozyn, Sefer shel hair vshel yishivat ets khaiim*, Tel Aviv, 1970, p. 531.
13 *Sefer Kostopol: Khaieha umota shel khila*, Tel Aviv, 1967, p. 191; *Sefer Stryj*, Tel Aviv, 1962, p. 164; *Rokitno vhasviva sefer edut vzikaron*, Tel Aviv, 1967, p. 247; *Lebn un umkum fun Holszany*, Tel Aviv, 1965, p. 171; *Sefer zikaron Dubno*, Tel Aviv, 1966, pp. 241–242; *Yad Vashem*, file K-174-1988 (Lanin).
14 *Yad Vashem*, file SH-191-2131.
15 *Kostopol*, p. 192.
16 *Stryj*, p. 164; *Rishonim lamered Lachwa*, Jerusalem, 1957, p. 43.
17 See B. Pinchuk, *Yehudei Brit-Hamoatsot Mul Pnei Hashoa (Soviet Jews in Face of the Holocaust)*, Tel Aviv, 1980, pp. 85–96.
18 Ibid.
19 A. Seaton, *The Russo-German War, 1941–1945*, New York, 1970, p. 95.
20 *Istoria Velikoi Otechestvennoi Voiny Sovetskogo Soiuza: 1941–1945*, vol. 2, Moscow, 1963, p. 147.
21 *Sefer zikaron likdoshei Lanowce shenispu bashoat hanatsit*, Tel Aviv, 1970, p. 109.
22 *Dubno*, p. 242.
23 *Kostopol*, p. 191.
24 Ibid. Also *Yad Vashem*, file N-39-1441 (Lvov); file F-320-3332 (Nowogrodek); file F-182-1907 (Radziwilkow); file K-147-1659 (Mizocz); file A-88-1342 (Maniewicz); file K-175-1990 (Slonim); file CH-51-3450 (Ratno); file A-74-1203 (Sarny).
25 *Yad Vashem*, file KH-49-3306; file T-30-1643; file A-131-1937; file N-55-2089; file J-65-890; file H-950-2963.
26 *Sefer Lida*, Tel Aviv, 1970, pp. 280–281.
27 *Yad Vashem*, file SH-174-1746 (Sarny).
28 *Yad Vashem*, file K-247-2963.
29 *Yad Vashem*, file H-145-3570; file SH-191-2131.
30 *Yad Vashem*, file R-49-3306; file N-39-1441; file T-30-1640; file H-95-2065; file M-170-3042; file A-131-1937.
31 The numbers are from S. Schwartz, *Antisemitism v Sovetskom Soiuze*, New York, 1952, p. 243.
32 *Yad Vashem*, file Y-24-883, a military employee relates that the Soviet officials and families fled during the second night of the war, leaving behind a bewildered civilian population. Also *Yad Vashem*, file K-316-3651; file A-181-2572; file B-64-813; file K-1-173; file KH-41-761; file K-2-174; file M-210-3652.
33 Broderzon, *Main Laidns*, p. 32.
34 *Yad Vashem*, file B-303-3347; file M-210-3652.
35 *Rokitno*, p. 251.
36 *Yad Vashem*, file CH-51-3450.
37 *Sefer Dereczyn*, Tel Aviv, n.d., pp. 386–387.
38 *Yad Vashem*, file F-196-2060 (Druj); file A-88-1342 (Maniewicz); file G-233-3130 (Nieswiez); file SH-236-2653 (Luboml).
39 On the problem of Soviet evacuation policy, see B. Pinchuk, 'Was there a Soviet Policy for Evacuating the Jews?: The Case of the Annexed Territories', *Slavic Review*, vol. 39, March 1980.

40 *Yad Vashem*, file K-175-1990 (Slonim); file A-8-9 (Brisk); file K-147-1659 (Mizocz); file KH-27-2009 (Rogotin); file A-74-1203 (Sarny); file K-2-174 (Tarnopol).

41 *Yad Vashem*, file KH-27-2009 (Rogotin); file K-147-1659 (Mizocz); file L-2-107 (Baranowicz); file F-320-3332 (Nowogrodek).

42 *Yad Vashem*, file SH-174-1946; file K-169-1939; *Rowno*, Tel Aviv, 1956, pp. 520–9.

43 *Yad Vashem*, file A-228-3118; file F-320-3332; file Y-36-1299. 'It was like a nightmare. People fled without knowing where to go. Some arrived from neighbouring shtetlach seeking refuge in Nowogrodek, others went back and forth, aimless and forlorn', describes a survivor from the shtetl the days following the outbreak of hostilities, file A-228-3118.

44 *Yad Vashem*, file L-2-107; file K-111-1292; file S-118-3548.

45 *Lida*, pp. 278–80.

46 *Yad Vashem*, file SH-258-2987; also file L-141-2650 (Stolpce); file K-285-3315; file G-225-3046 (Szumsk); *Lida*, p. 280.

47 *Holszany*, p. 293. Also *Khilat Lanin Sefer zikaron*, Tel Aviv, 1957, p. 13; *Janow al yad Pinsk, Sefer zikaron*, Jerusalem, 1969, p. 313.

48 *Yad Vashem*, file B-192-2053; file F-182-1907; file B-41-1460; file G-226-3047.

49 *Lachwa*, p. 48.

50 *Yad Vashem*, file G-226-3947; file SH-2-107; file K-147-1659.

APPENDIX: ENCOUNTERS WITH SOVIET JEWS

1 On the impact of the renewed contacts with Soviet Jewry see Y. Gilboa, *The Black Years of Soviet Jewry*, Boston, 1971, pp. 22–4. The author stresses the eagerness of Soviet Jews for information about the Jewish people abroad. He also shows that there was a significant increase in Jewish cultural activity in the Soviet Union as a result of the addition of many new consumers of that culture.

2 *Sefer Lida*, Tel Aviv, 1970, p. 257.

3 *Sefer Zulkiew*, Jerusalem, 1969, p. 548.

4 T. Fuks, *A Vanderung iber okupirte gebitn*, Buenos Aires, 1948, pp. 91–6; P. Schwarts, *Dos iz geven der onheib*, New York, 1943, pp. 275–9; *Sefer zikaron lesrim vshalosh khilot shenekhrevu bezor Swieciany*, Tel Aviv, 1965, p. 519.

5 *Rishonim Lamered Lachwa*, Jerusalem, 1957, p. 39; *Pinkas Kleck*, Tel Aviv, 1959, p. 319.

6 *Kleck*, p. 326.

7 *Yad Vashem Testimonial*, file 1-36-1299 (Nowogrodek); *Sefer Nisvizh*, Tel Aviv, 1976, p. 123; *Wolozyn, Sefer shel hair vshel yishivat ets khaiim*, Tel Aviv, 1970, p. 523.

8 *Sefer zikaron Dubno*, Tel Aviv, 1966, p. 234.

9 *Lachwa*, p. 38; *Wolozyn*, pp. 530–2.

10 A. Zak, *Knecht zenen mir geven*, Buenos Aires, 1956, p. 14; M. Grosman, *In Farkishuftn Land fun Legendern Dzugashvili*, Paris, 1950, pp. 71–3.

11 Grosman, *In Farkishuftn Land.*

12 Lederman, *Fun iener zait forhang*, Buenos Aires, 1960, p. 80.

13 There were even instances of Soviet Jews who tried to cross into the German area while on visits to the annexed territories. See Grosman, *In Farkishuftn Land*, pp. 66–8.

14 *Der Shtern*, 20 June 1940; *Oktiaber*, 10 August 1940; Lederman, *Fun iener zait*, p. 134.

15 *Der Shtern*, 20 June 1940. While on tour to the Soviet interior, Jewish troupes from the territories were exposed to the eagerness for Jewish culture among Soviet citizens, *Oktiaber*, 10 May, 3 August 1940.

16 *Oktiaber*, 26 November 1939; *Der Shtern*, 27 December 1939, reports on huge crowds that greeted the visiting writers. Also H. Smolar, 'Hakhaiim hayehudiim bmaarav Belorussia hasovietit 1939–1941: prikhah vshkiah', *Shvut*, 4, Tel Aviv, 1976, p. 133.

17 *Der Shtern*, 24 February 1940, on the visit to Lvov of the 'writers' brigade' led by I. Fefer. On the visit to Bialystok, see *Oktiaber*, 21 February 1940. Among the visitors were P. Markish, I. Fefer, L. Kvitko, Sh. Halkin, I. Nusinov and others.

18 S. Broderzon, *Main Laidns Veg Mit Moshe Broderzon*, Buenos Aires, 1960, p. 26; Grodner, 'In Soviet Poland and Lithuania', *Contemporary Jewish Record*, vol. 4, April 1941, p. 143; Lederman, *Fun iener zait*, pp. 103–4.

19 Grosman, *In Farkishuftn Land*, p. 42. Grodner reported that I. Fefer, in a speech before local writers in Bialystok exclaimed 'Back to the past! We are celebrating at present the eight hundredth anniversary of Judah Halevi: Judah the Maccabee and the Hashmonaeans are national heroes and revolutionaries.' There was no reference to such a speech in the press, Grodner, 'In Soviet Poland', p. 143.

20 Gilboa, *The Black Years*, p. 19.

21 Fuks, *A Vanderung*, p. 94. Grosman relates a similar story of how the Jewish poets R. Boimvol and M. Lifshits on a visit to Bialystok justified the recent purges of Jewish poets. They did not cease to praise Stalin: Grosman, *In Farkishuftn Land*, pp. 23–4.

22 Ibid. p. 31.

23 Lederman, *Fun iener zait*, p. 103, on his secret conversations with P. Markish. Also Grosman, *In Farkishuftn Land*, pp. 31–9.

24 Interview with R. Koren in *Maariv*, Tel Aviv, 27 March, 1959. On her visit to Moscow with A. Katsizna, B. Shnapir, H. Veber, see also the official reports in *Der Shtern*, 25 February 1941; *Oktiaber*, 25 February 1941.

25 Fuks, *A Vanderung*, p. 98.

26 Lederman, *Fun iener zait*, pp. 106–8. Markish referred to M. Nadir's article 'We have Raised a Snake Around Our Necks'. The article expressed the disillusionment of a Jewish Communist with the USSR in the wake of the Stalin-Hitler agreement. Markish expressed his fear that the snake (Stalin's USSR), would strangle the Jews and their culture.

27 Fuks, *A Vanderung*, pp. 97–8; Gilboa, *The Black Years*, p. 26.

28 E. Markish, *Lakhazor miderech aruka*, Tel Aviv, 1977, pp. 88–9.

29 See M. Tsanin, *Grenetsn biz tsum himl*, Tel Aviv, 1970, p. 46. The author fails

to see any sarcasm, only a plain, brutal statement.

30 A. Zak, *Knecht zenen mir geven*, Buenos Aires, 1956, pp. 25–7.

31 Grosman, *In Farkishuftn Land*, p. 30.

32 Zak, *Knecht zenen mir geven*, p. 27.

33 Broderzon, *Main Laidns*, p. 28; Gilboa, *The Black Years*, pp. 26, 356–7.

Bibliography

The following list includes only sources actually consulted in the preparation of this study.

ARCHIVAL MATERIAL

British Public Record, London.
Central Zionist Archive, Jerusalem.
The Sikorski Historical Institute, London.
Yad Vashem Testimonial, Jerusalem.

NEWSPAPERS

Bialystoker Shtern, Bialystok.
Emes, Vilno.
Forverts, New York.
Isvestia, Moscow.
Jewish Chronicle, London.
Oktiaber, Minsk.
Der Shtern, Kiev.

MEMORIAL BOOKS

Augustow – *Sefer zikaron likhilat Augustow vhasviva*, Tel Aviv, 1966.
Borszczow – *Sefer Borszczow*, Tel Aviv, 1960.
Bransk – *Bransk: Sefer Hazikaron*, New York, 1948.

Buczacz – *Sefer Buczacz, matsevet zikaron likhila kdosha*, Tel Aviv, 1956.
Budzanow – *Sefer Budzanow*, Haifa, 1968.
Busk – *Sefer Busk, lzecher hakhila shekharva*, Haifa, 1968.
Byten – *Pinkas Byten*, Buenos Aires, 1954.
Chorostkow – *Sefer Chorostkow*, Tel Aviv, 1968.
Czortkow – *Sefer izkor lehantsakhat kdoshei khilat Czortkow*, Tel Aviv, 1961.
Dambrowica – *Sefer Dambrowica*, Tel Aviv, 1964.
Dereczyn – *Sefer Dereczyn*, Tel Aviv, n.d.
Dubno – *Sefer zikaron Dubno*, Tel Aviv, 1966.
Glebokie – *Khurban Glebokie Szarkowszczyzna*, Buenos Aires, 1956.
Goniandz – *Sefer izkor Goniandz*, Tel Aviv, 1960.
Grodno – *Grodno-Entsiklopedia shel galuiot*, Jerusalem, 1973.
Holszany – *Lebn un umkum fun Holszany*, Tel Aviv, 1965.
Ilia – *Khilat Ilia*, Tel Aviv, 1962.
Iwie – *Sefer zikaron likhilat Iwie*, Tel Aviv, 1968.
Iwnic-Kamin – *Sefer Iwnic-Kamin vhasviva*, Tel Aviv, 1973.
Janow – *Janow al yad Pinsk, sefer zikaron*, Jerusalem, 1969.
Jezierna – *Sefer Jezierna*, Haifa, 1974.
Jezierzany – *Sefer Jezierzany vhasviva*, Jerusalem, 1959.
Kleck – *Pinkas Kleck*, Tel Aviv, 1959.
Kolno – *Sefer zikaron likhilat Kolno*, Tel Aviv, 1971.
Kolomyja – *Pinkas Kolomyja*, New York, 1957.
Korzec – *Korzec: Sefer zikaron likhilatenu shealah aleha hakoret*, Tel Aviv, 1959.
Kostopol – *Sefer Kostopol: Khaieha umota shel khila*, Tel Aviv, 1967.
Krynki – *Pinkas Krynki*, Tel Aviv, 1970.
Lachwa – *Rishonim lamered, Lachwa*, Jerusalem, 1957.
Lanin – *Khilat Lanin sefer zikaron*, Tel Aviv, 1957.
Lanowce – *Sefer zikaron likdoshei Lanowce shenispu bashoah hanatsit*, Tel Aviv, 1970.
Lida – *Sefer Lida*, Tel Aviv, 1970.
Lipniszki – *Sefer zikaron shel khilat Lipniszki*, Tel Aviv, 1968.
Lomza – *Sefer zikaron likhilat Lomza*, Tel Aviv, 1952.
Lubcza – *Lubcza vdelticz, sefer zikaron*, Haifa, 1971.
Luboml – *Sefer izkor likhilat Luboml*, Tel Aviv, 1973.
Luck – *Sefer Luck*, Tel Aviv, 1961.
Ludmir – *Pinkas Ludmir*, Tel Aviv, 1962.
Mir – *Sefer Mir: Entsiklopedia shel galuiot*, Jerusalem, 1962.
Mlynow – *Sefer Mlynow-Merwic*, Haifa, 1970.
Nisvizh – *Sefer Nisvizh*, Tel Aviv, 1976.
Pinsk – *Sefer edut zikaron likhilat Pinsk-Karlin*, Tel Aviv, 1966.
Pruzana – *Pinkas mekhamesh kehilat kharevot Pruzana*, Buenos Aires, 1958.
Przemsyl – *Sefer Przemysl*, Tel Aviv, 1964.
Pulawy – *Izkor bukh fun Pulawy*, New York, 1964.
Ostrog – *Pinkas Ostrog*, Tel Aviv, 1960.
Ostroleka – *Sefer Ostroleka*, Tel Aviv, 1963.

Radzin – *Sefer Radzin*, Tel Aviv, 1957.
Rokitno – *Rokitno vhasviva sefer edut vzikaron*, Tel Aviv, 1967.
Rowno – *Rowno*, Tel Aviv, 1956.
Sarny – *Sefer izkor likhilat Sarny*, Tel Aviv, 1966.
Semiatycz – *Khilat Semiatycz*, Tel Aviv, 1965.
Slonim – *Pinkas Slonim*, Tel Aviv, 1962.
Sokal – *Sefer Sokal-Tartakow vhasvivah*, Tel Aviv, 1967.
Sokolka – *Sefer Sokolka*, Jerusalem, 1968.
Sopotkin – *Korot aiara akhat, Sopotkin*, Tel Aviv, 1960.
Stolin – *Stolin*, Tel Aviv, 1952.
Stolpce – *Sefer zikaron Stolpce-Swerzana vhaaiarot hasmukhot*, Tel Aviv, 1964.
Strizow – *Sefer Strizow vehasviva*, Tel Aviv, 1969.
Stryj – *Sefer Stryj*, Tel Aviv, 1962.
Swieciany – *Sefer zikaron lesrim vshalosh khilot shenekhrevu bezor Swieciany*, Tel Aviv, 1965.
Szcuczyn – *Sefer zikaron likhilat Szcuczyn Wasiliscki, Ostryn, Nowyzbor, Rozanka*, Tel Aviv, 1966.
Szumsk – *Sefer zikaron likdoshei Szumsk*, Tel Aviv, 1968.
Targowica – *Sefer Targowica*, Haifa, 1967.
Tarnopol – *Tarnopol-Entsiklopedia shel galuiot*, Jerusalem, 1965.
Telechany – *Telechany*, Los Angeles, 1963.
Tuczyn – *Sefer zikaron likhilat Tuczyn-Krips*, Tel Aviv, 1967.
Turka – *Sefer zikaron likhilat Turka al nahar Stryj*, Haifa, 1966.
Tysmienica – *Tysmienica: A matseve oif di khurvot fun a Farnichteter Yiddisher Khila*, Tel Aviv, 1974.
Ulika – *Pinkas hakhila Ulika sefer izkor*, Tel Aviv, 1972.
Wlodzimierz – *Pinkas Wlodzimierz*, Tel Aviv, 1962.
Wolozyn – *Wolozyn, Sefer shel hair vshel yishivat ets khaiim*, Tel Aviv, 1970.
Wysniowiec – *Sefer zikaron likdoshei Wysniowiec*, Tel Aviv, n.d.
Zulkiew – *Sefer Zulkiew*, Jerusalem, 1969.

MEMOIRS AND DOCUMENTS

Aviram, Ts., 'Epizodn un Refleksn', *Grodner Opklangen*, Buenos Aires, 1975.
Broderzon, Sh., *Main Laidns Veg Mit Moshe Broderzon*, Buenos Aires, 1960.
Brodetski, K., 'Di vanderungen fun Poilishn hekhaluts un zain arbet in lite un unter der sovetn okupatsie', *Khalutsim in Poilin*, New York, 1961.
Bromberg, Y., *Pinsk under Soviet Rule*, unpublished.
Degras, J. (ed.), *Soviet Documents on Foreign Policy, 1933–1941*, London and New York, 1953.
Documents on Polish Soviet Relations, 1939–1945, London, 1961.
Druk, Sh., *Yudenshtat Yavorov*, New York, 1950.
Dvorzecki, M., *Yrushalaim Dlita Bmeri Ubshoah*, Tel Aviv, 1951.
Fuks, T., *A Vanderung iber okupirte gebitn*, Buenos Aires, 1948.
Gar, Y., *Viderklangen*, Tel Aviv, 1961.

Grodner, D., 'In Soviet Poland and Lithuania', *Contemporary Jewish Record*, vol. 4, April 1941.
Grosman, M., *In Farkishufin Land fun Legendern Dzugashvili*, Paris, 1950.
Katsherginski, Sh., *Tsvishn Hamer un Serp*, Paris, 1949.
Khrushchev, N., *Khrushchev Remembers*, Boston, 1970.
Kleinboim (later Sne), M., 'Tazkir al matsava shel Yiahadut Mizrakh eiropa bereishit milkhemet haolam hashnia', *Galed*, vols 4–5, Tel Aviv, 1978.
Korchak, R., *Lehavot Baefer*, Tel Aviv, 1965.
Lederman, D., *Fun iener zait forhang*, Buenos Aires, 1960.
Markish, E., *Lakhazor miderekh aruka*, Tel Aviv, 1977.
Markish, E., *Mul haoiev hanatsi*, Tel Aviv, 1961.
Pinsker, A., *Ud Mutsal*, Tel Aviv, 1957.
Prager, M., *Yiven metsulah hekhadash*, Tel Aviv, 1941.
Sefer Hashomer hatsair, Merkhaviah, 1969.
Segalowicz, Z., *Gebrente trit*, Buenos Aires, 1947.
Shoat Yihudei Polin, Jerusalem, 1940.
Shwarts, P., *Dos iz geven der onheib*, New York, 1943.
Smolar, H., *Fun Minsker geto*, Moscow, 1946.
Smolar, H., 'Hakhaim hayehudiim bmaarav Belorussia hasovietit 1939–1941: prikhah vshkiah', *Shvut*, 4, Tel Aviv, 1976.
Smoler, M., *Neevakti al Khaiai*, Tel Aviv, 1978.
Solomon-Luts, F., *Naara mul gardom*, Ramat Gan, 1971.
Sontag, R. J., and Beddie, J. S. (eds), *Nazi–Soviet Relations, 1939–1941: Documents from the Archives of the German Foreign Office*, Washington, 1948.
Special Report No. 1 of the Select Committee on Communist Aggression, House of Representatives, 83rd Congress, Second Session, Washington, 1954.
Tsanin, M., *Grenetsn biz tsum himl*, Tel Aviv, 1970.
Vest, B., *Naftulei dor*, Tel Aviv, 1955.
Vest, B., *Bkhevlei Chlaia*, Tel Aviv, 1963.
Yanosevich, Y., *Mit Yidishe shraiber in rusland*, New York, 1956.
Zak, A., *Knecht zenen mir geven*, Buenos Aires, 1956.
Zerubavel, F., *Na vanad*, Buenos Aires, 1947.

SECONDARY WORKS

Armstrong, J., *Ukrainian Nationalism, 1939–1945*, New York, 1955.
Baron, S., *The Russian Jew Under Tsars and Soviets*, New York, 1964.
Beloff, M., *The Foreign Policy of Soviet Russia*, Oxford, 1966.
Belonosov, I., 'Evakuatsia naseleniia iz prifrontovoi polosy v 1941–1942 g.g.', from A. Poliakov (ed.), *Eshelony idut na vostok*, Moscow, 1966.
Bereday, G. and Pennar, J. (eds), *The Politics of Soviet Education*, New York, 1960.
Bertish, R., 'Pzurat Yihudei polin bmilkhemet haolam hashniia', *Galed*, vol. 1, Tel Aviv, 1973.
Boim, L., 'Shitat hapasportim bibrit-hamoatsot vhashpaatah al matsavam shel hayihudim', *Shvut*, 3, Tel Aviv, 1975.

Bronsztein, S., 'The Jewish Population of Poland in 1931', *The Jewish Journal of Sociology*, no. 6, 1964.

Cardwell, A., *Poland and Russia*, New York, 1944.

Chrestomatie far dem zekstn klass, Kiev, 1938.

Conquest, R., *The Nation Killers: The Soviet Destruction of Nationalities*, London, 1970.

Conquest, R., *The Soviet Deportation of Nationalities*, London, 1960.

Davies, N., *God's Playground: A History of Poland*, Oxford, 1981.

Dmitryshyn, B., *Moscow and the Ukraine, 1918–1953*, New York, 1956.

Dombrowska, O., A. Vain, A. Weis (eds), *Pinkas Khilot Polin, Galitsia hamizrakhit*, Jerusalem, 1980.

Dubina, K. (ed.), *Istoriia Ukrainskoi SSR*, Kiev, 1962.

Dziewanowski, M. K., *The Communist Party of Poland*, Cambridge, Mass., 1959.

Eck, N., 'The Educational Institutions of Polish Jewry, 1921–1939', *Jewish Social Studies*, vol. 9, 1947.

Eisenstein, M., *Jewish Schools in Poland, 1919–1939: The Philosophy and Development*, New York, 1950.

Erickson, J., *The Soviet High Command*, New York, 1962.

Etinger, S., *History of the Jewish People, Vol. III, Modern Times* (Hebrew).

Etinger, S., 'Shorshei haantishemiut ha-sovietit umaavaka bayihudim', *Molad*, 18, Tel Aviv, 1971.

Evreiskii Narod V Borbe Protiv Fashizma, Moscow, 1945.

Feingold, H., *The Politics of Rescue*, New Brunswick, 1970.

Fischer, L., *Stalin and Hitler*, London, 1940.

Fridman, F., *Hashmadat Yihudei Polin bashanim 1939–1945*, Tel Aviv, n.d.

Friedrich, C. J., and Brzezinski, Z. K., *Totalitarian Dictatorship and Autocracy*, Praeger, 1965.

Gilboa, Y., *The Black Years of Soviet Jewry*, Boston, 1971.

Gitelman, Z., *Jewish Nationality and Soviet Politics: The Jewish Sections of the CPSU, 1917–1930*, Princeton, 1972.

Gnatowski, M. (ed.), *Bialostockie*, Warsaw, 1969.

Goldberg, B. Z., *The Jewish Problem in the Soviet Union*, New York, 1961.

Gorbunov, T. S., et al., *Istoriia Belorusskoi SSR*, Minsk, 1962.

Guillaume, A., *The German Russian War*, London, 1956.

Halecki, V., 'Poland and Europe: Geographic Position', in B. Schmidt (ed.), *Poland*, 1945.

Heller, C., *On the Edge of Destruction: Jews in Poland Between the Two World Wars*, New York, 1977.

Hilberg, R., *The Destruction of the European Jews*, Chicago, 1967.

Istoriia Velikoi Otechestvennoi Voiny Sovetskoyo Soiuza, 1941–1945, vol. 2, Moscow, 1963.

Kaganovich, M., *Der Yidisher onteil in der partizaner bavegung fun Sovet rusland*, Rome, 1948.

Karmish, S. J., Krakowski, *Polish Jewish Relations during Second World War*, New York, Jerusalem, 1974.

Kaslas, B. J. (ed.), *The USSR-German Aggression Against Lithuania*, New York, 1974.

Kochan, L. (ed.), *The Jews in Soviet Russia since 1917*, Oxford, 1970.

Korzen, M., 'Problems Arising out of Research into the history of Jewish Refugees in the USSR during the Second World War', *Yad Vashem Studies*, vol. 3, Jerusalem, 1959.

Kot, S., *Conversations with the Kremlin and Dispatches from Russia*, New York, 1963.

Kulisher, E., *Europe on the Move: War and Population Changes 1917–1947*, New York, 1948.

Lamont, C., *The Peoples of the Soviet Union*, New York, 1946.

Landau, Z., Tomaszewski, J., *Gospodarka Polski Miedzywojennej*, Warsaw, 1971.

Lebed, A., 'Destruction of National Groups through Compulsory Migration and Resettlement', in A. Lebed (ed.), *Genocide in the USSR*, Munich, 1958.

Lestchinsky, Y., *Di Yidn in Soviet Rusland*, New York, 1943.

Levin, D., 'Brit Hamoatsot Vhatsalat Yihudim', *Davar*, Tel Aviv, 18 April 1974.

Litvak, Y., 'Hashilton hasovieti vehatsalat yehudim polanim umaaraviim', *Bekhinot*, 2–3, Tel Aviv, 1972.

Loth, J., Petrazycka, Z., *Geografia Gospodarcza Polski*, Warsaw, 1960.

Lubachko, I., *Belorussia under Soviet Rule, 1917–1957*, Lexington, 1972.

Mahler, R., *Yihudei Polin bein shtei milkhamot olam*, Tel Aviv, 1968.

Mendelsohn, E., 'Yihudei mizrakh – merkaz eiropa bein shtei milkhamot haolam', in Y. Tsur (ed.), *Hatfutsa: Mizrakh Eiropa*.

Meyer, P. (ed.), *The Jews in the Soviet Satellites*, Syracuse, NY, 1953.

Michaelis, M., 'Stalin Ribentrop and the Jews', *Bulletin on Soviet and East European Jewish Affairs*, 5, London, 1970.

Mints, M., 'Mistifikatsia Sovietit shel hayihudi', *Shvut*, 1, Tel Aviv, 1973.

Morse, A., *While Six Million Died*, London, 1968.

Nalkowski, W., *Poland as a Geographical Entity*, London, 1917.

Nove, A., *The Soviet Economic System*, London, 1977.

Olekhanovich, G., 'Ot pripiati Za Volgu', A. Poliakov (ed.), *Eshelony idut na vostok*, Moscow, 1966.

Parkas, J., *The Emergence of the Jewish Problem*, Oxford, 1946.

Peteshnik, A., *Yidn un Yidishkeit in Sovet-Rusland*, New York, 1943.

Pinchuk, B. C., 'Jewish Refugees in Soviet Poland 1939–1941', in *Jewish Social Studies*, vol. 40, New York, 1978.

Pinchuk, B. C., *Yehudei Brit-Hamoatsot Mul Pnei Hashoa (Soviet Jews in Face of the Holocaust)*, Tel Aviv, 1980.

Poliakov, A. (ed.), *Eshelony idut na vostok*, Moscow, 1966.

Polish Research Center, Eastern Poland, London, 1949.

Polonsky, A., *Politics in Independent Poland, 1921–1939*, Oxford, 1972.

Proudfoot, M., *European Refugees 1939–1953*, Evanston, 1956.

Rabinovich, Sh., *Yidn in Sovetn farband*, Moscow, 1965.

Rabinowicz, H., *The Legacy of Polish Jewry*, New York, 1965.

Redlich, Sh., 'Hayehudim bashtakhim shesupkhu librit-hamoatsot, 1939–1941', *Bekhinot*, 6, Tel Aviv, 1970.

Reitlinger, G., *The Final Solution*, London, 1953.
Rozental, N., *Yidish lebn in ratnfarband*, Tel Aviv, 1971.
Schapiro, L. B., *The Government and Politics of the Soviet Union*, New York, 1967.
Schechtman, J., *European Population Transfers*, New York, 1946.
Schulman, E., *A History of Jewish Education in the Soviet Union*, New York, 1973.
Schwartz, S. M., *The Jews in the Soviet Union*, Syracuse, NY, 1951.
Schwartz, S. M., *Antisemitism v Sovetskom Soiuze*, New York, 1952.
Schwartz, S. M., *Evrei v Sovetskom Soiuze s nachala vtoroi mirovoi voiny 1939–1965*, New York, 1966.
Seaton, A., *The Russo-German War 1941–1945*, New York, 1970.
Seton-Watson, H., *Eastern Europe Between the Wars, 1918–1941*, New York, 1967.
Sharfshtein, Ts., *Toldot hakhinukh beisrael badorot haakharonim*, New York, 1949.
Sontag, R. J. and Beddie, J. S. (eds), *Nazi–Soviet Relations, 1939–1941*, Washington, 1948.
Stoessinger, J., *The Refugee and the World Community*, Minneapolis, 1956.
Sullivant, R. S., *Soviet Politics and the Ukraine, 1917–1957*, New York, 1962.
Tartakower, A. and Grosman K., *The Jewish Refugee*, New York, 1944.
Taylor, J., *The Economic Development of Poland, 1919–1950*, New York, 1952.
Tomaszewski, J., *Z Dziejow Polesia, 1921–1939*, Warsaw, 1963.
Treadgold, D. W., *Twentieth-Century Russia*, Chicago, 1959.
Ulam, A., *Expansion and Coexistence*, New York, 1968.
Vakar, N., *Byelorussia*, Cambridge, Mass., 1956.
V Velikoi otechestvennoi voine 1941–1945, Kratkaia Khronika, Moscow, 1970.
Vernant, J., *The Refugee in the Post War World*, Geneva, 1951.
Wanklyn, H., *The Eastern Marchlands of Europe*, London, 1941.
Weinryb, B. D., 'Polish Jews Under Soviet Rule', P. Meyer (ed.), *The Jews in the Soviet Satellites*, Syracuse, NY, 1953.
Weinryb, B. D., 'Antisemitism in Soviet Russia', L. Kochan (ed.), *The Jews in Soviet Russia Since 1917*, Oxford, 1970.
Weiss, A., 'Teatron vsifrut yiddish begalitsia hamizrakhit bashanim 1939–1941', *Bekhinot*, 8–9, Jerusalem, 1980.
Weiss, A., 'Tmurot bakhinukh shel yehudei galitsiah hamizrakhit bitkufat hashilton hasovieti, 1939–1941', *Galed*, 4–5, Tel Aviv, 1978.
Werth, A., *Russia at War*, New York, 1974.
Young, P., *World War 1939–1945*, London, 1966.
Zborowski, M. and Herzog, E., *Life is with People: The culture of the Shtetl*, New York, 1952.
Zoltowski, A., *Border of Europe. A study of the Polish Eastern Provinces*, London, 1950.

Index